FOUNDATIONS OF
AMERICAN DIPLOMACY,
1775-1872

FOUNDATIONS OF AMERICAN DIPLOMACY,

1775-1872

Edited by

ROBERT H. FERRELL

Cartography by
Norman J. G. Pounds

HARPER TORCHBOOKS
Harper & Row, Publishers
New York and Evanston

For Lila and Carolyn

FOUNDATIONS OF AMERICAN DIPLOMACY,
1775–1872

Introduction, editorial notes, and compilation
copyright © 1968 by Robert H. Ferrell.

Printed in the United States of America.

All rights reserved.

First edition: HARPER TORCHBOOKS, 1968
Harper & Row, Publishers, Incorporated,
49 East 33rd Street, New York, N.Y. 10016.

A clothbound edition of this title is published by
the University of South Carolina Press.

Library of Congress Catalog Card Number: 68–65041.

Contents

XIV: THE REPUBLIC AT PEACE

Maps

Foreword

The following volume represents the first of a three-volume documentary history of American diplomacy from its beginning in 1775 to the present day. *Foundations of American Diplomacy* covers the period from the opening of the American Revolution through the year of the Geneva arbitration, 1872. The second volume, *America as a World Power,* will treat the diplomatic record to the end of World War II. The third, *America in a Divided World,* will consider the era from 1945 to the present.

RICHARD B. MORRIS,
GENERAL EDITOR

Acknowledgments

All books need an expression of thanks to individuals who have helped, and this volume not least. I do wish to thank John Garry Clifford who searched out documents in the National Archives and had them copied, and discovered in the Library of Congress some vituperative letters written in 1808 to President Thomas Jefferson. David M. Pletcher carefully criticized Parts X and XI on the Mexican War and the Northeast and Northwest Boundaries. Thomas H. Etzold ensured the authenticity of the documentary texts. Norman J. G. Pounds drew the maps, without which this volume would make little sense in many places; it is difficult to overstate my indebtedness to a distinguished scholar for his extraordinary kindness in this regard. Richard B. Morris, prince of editors, prevented errors and suggested many topics for inclusion or emphasis. And may I also thank Hugh Van Dusen and his hardworking staff at Harper and Row.

R. H. F.

I

Introduction

I

The first requisite of Americans once they had declared their independence was to maintain it—and so over the next fifty years, until the time of the Monroe Doctrine, the diplomacy of the United States dealt with independence. Such a subject of policy might seem odd today when the United States is the most powerful nation in the world. In the late eighteenth and early nineteenth centuries, when the American republic was a small if growing power, well below the stature of France, Russia, Austria, and Prussia on the Continent, not to mention the former mother country, Great Britain, independence was no achievement to take for granted.

The vigilance with which the early diplomats sought to ensure independence has rightfully become a source of pride to later generations. The customs of the eighteenth and early nineteenth centuries were conducive neither to the birth nor growth of new nations conceived in liberty and dedicated to absurd propositions such as that all men are created equal and endowed by their Creator with certain unalienable rights. In his account of European diplomacy of the time, the opening section of his great work on *L'Europe et la révolution française* (8 vols., 1885–1904), Albert Sorel set out the merciless customs of nations during the classic era of balance of power. The Spanish statesman Alberoni, Sorel remarked, cut and gnawed at states and kingdoms as if they were Dutch cheese. The maxims of the day were straight from the writings of French diplomatic philosophers such as François de Callières, who in his *On the Manner of Negotiating with Princes* (1716) brought together all the conceits and deceits he could think of. The American Revolution occurred in the time of Frederick the Great, who as a young man had composed a long dissertation refuting Machiavelli and who spent the rest of his life refuting the refutation. In the eighteenth and early nineteenth centuries there was no United Nations to which small powers might go to denounce a great power. It was the genius of America's first diplomats in this unemotional age that they realized the nature of their international opposition—which included all the powers of the day, not excepting France—and adroitly maneuvered their country's case through the snares and traps of Europe until they irrevocably had achieved national independence.

America's ally in Europe until the year 1800, and presumed friend thereafter, France, was not least in the roster of diplomatic opponents. American diplomats well understood that the French monarchy intervened in the Revolution in 1778 for the major purpose of humbling its ancient enemy, Great Britain. They needed no documents from the French archives to prove it, such as Henri Doniol provided a century later in his *Histoire de la participation de la France à l'établissement des Etats-Unis d'Amérique* (5 vols., 1884–92). The problem of the early diplomats during and after the Revolution was to watch the changing power balance in Europe so as to discern, before events passed beyond recall, when France's interests no longer corresponded with those of the United States. In a dark moment the French, whether under the monarchy, Convention, Directory, Consulate, or the régime of Napoleon I, would not have hesitated to abandon the Americans.

The initial occasion when the Americans came to distrust the French arose toward the end of the American Revolution. That conflict the Americans never could have won without the help of French munitions and arms; Saratoga in 1777 was a victory achieved with French gunpowder, and at Yorktown in 1781 more Frenchmen were present than Americans. Withal the French during the war indirectly pledged American independence to the achievement of an aim of the Spanish monarchy, the capture of Gibraltar by Franco-Spanish forces. In the secret Treaty of Aranjuez of 1779 the two European nations had pledged themselves to take Gibraltar from the British. Meanwhile in the alliance of 1778 the Americans had promised the French to make no separate peace. Apparently they would have to wait until the great "pile of rocks" passed to Spain. Other examples of the different purposes of France and the United States were not wanting. Just before Yorktown the French foreign minister, Charles Gravier Comte de Vergennes, contemplated peace on the basis of the war map of the moment which would have excluded the Americans from New York, Charleston, and Savannah, not to mention Maine and much of the Great Lakes country. The French minister to the United States, the Chevalier de la Luzerne, was managing (so he claimed in a letter to Vergennes) the election of Robert R. Livingston as secretary for foreign affairs to the Congress, and Livingston was concerting with La Luzerne the instructions to the American negotiators then in Paris; surely with the approval of the French minister, possibly under his direction, Congress through Livingston instructed the American peace commissioners appointed in June 1781 to do nothing without the advice and consent of the French court. It seemed in 1781 as if the French government, having done some good things for the Americans, if for a purpose European in nature, was at last ready to employ with the new American nation the techniques of the Spaniard Alberoni.

In retrospect, with the advantage of the now-open French archives, it appears to us that it may not have been necessary at this juncture for John Jay, John Adams, and Benjamin Franklin to negotiate behind Vergennes's back, contrary to their instructions and to the letter of the alliance of 1778, signing with a British representative on November 30, 1782, a "preliminary treaty" which in everything but name was a final treaty. After the Franco-American victory at Yorktown, Vergennes appears to have ceased contemplating an American peace on the basis of uti possidetis. It may be that Jay and Adams became unnecessarily alarmed in their belief that Vergennes was about to take advantage of the United States. The Americans could not be sure. They knew the habits of the French monarchy, the continuingly dissolute and unpredictable nature of court life at Versailles, the backstairs tradition of European diplomacy. If Franklin later claimed that Adams had become unduly suspicious, and wrote in 1784 to Livingston that his fellow commissioner was "always an honest man, often a wise one, but sometimes in some things, absolutely out of his senses," the sage of Passy carefully allowed himself to be drawn into the separate negotiation with the Britisher Richard Oswald, and may even have initiated it.

Whatever the misinterpretation of French motives, if there was such, the commissioners' independent diplomacy proved a stroke of genius. If they miscalculated Vergennes in 1781–82, the figuring was all on the side of the independence which was their first diplomatic purpose. Vergennes seems not to have been too saddened by the result. In a perfunctory way the foreign minister protested a breach of faith by the commissioners. But he had obtained for France the humbling of Great Britain, his own primary purpose. He gave Franklin another loan, which that insouciant philosopher asked for in the same breath as he explained his own and his countrymen's lack of *bienséance*. Vergennes immediately set about disentangling himself from the now-inconvenient Spanish, who clearly were not going to obtain Gibraltar; the British a short time before had repulsed a combined Franco-Spanish fleet and lifted the siege of the fortress.

In this first and totally successful confrontation between American diplomats and the Old World, one may conclude with Richard B. Morris in his masterful *The Peacemakers* (1965) that: "The peacemaking began as an encounter between innocence and guile, but the Americans rapidly acquired a measure of sophistication sufficient for the task at hand. Neophytes in the arts of secret diplomacy at the start, they were the peers of their Old World counterparts at the finish."

In later years the problem of French interests versus American arose again, and it is instructive how each time the statesmen of the New World repulsed any possible French challenge to independence. It was a curious situation when after 1789 the second new nation appeared as a threat to the first. The changes of régime in France seemed only to make the French more willing to abridge the rights of Americans. Threats took different forms. In the 1790's it was a case of a succession of French ministers to the United States seeking to enlist part of the American populace against the other, all in the interest of France in Europe or—as was the case in the late 1790's—France in the New World. Genet, Fauchet, Adet, all thought they could subvert the American government as easily as France was subverting Holland, that they could turn the United States into a client nation as easily as the Grand Nation acquired Naples. Adet had analyzed the object of much French attention, Thomas Jefferson, secretary of state in 1790 to 1793 and the leader of a gathering and supposedly pro-French political party, in a way which the French government might better have remembered: "Jefferson, I say, is American and, by that title, cannot be sincerely our friend. An American is the born enemy of all European peoples." Least of all did Adet follow his own analysis, and like the great majority of his countrymen he continued to think that the Jeffersonians essentially were democrats of the French persuasion. Only after the three errant ministers had departed, and France and the United States had come into open hostilities during the quasi war of 1797–98, did French diplomats begin to sense that even if their country had numerous vocal supporters in the United States they would not be able to pursue with the Americans the techniques which worked in Europe.

At the time of the "XYZ affair" the French minister, Talleyrand, was conceiving a scheme to recreate the empire lost with the Treaty of Paris of 1763. He wished to obtain Louisiana by negotiation with Spain, and Canada by conquest from Britain, both territories to support the sugar islands of Guadeloupe and Santo Domingo. Talleyrand had been an unwilling resident of the United States in 1795–96 as a result of the reign of terror, and had sensed the vitality of the American republic. He knew that if France were to recreate the New World empire of Louis XIV he would have to move quickly before the Americans themselves took up the western territories. The only result of this scheme—wonderful result for Americans—was the Louisiana Purchase, caused by the accession of Louisiana to France just at a time when the young first consul, Napoleon, thirty-four years old, was bursting with his own plans for Europe and could not restrain himself long enough to create an empire across the Atlantic. The purchase of 1803 was no mark of French friendship for the United States but the fortuitous result of a train of events which, but for the Old World ambitions of Napoleon, would have drastically constricted American territorial expansion and might have extinguished American independence.

The government of the United States was well aware of the enmity of Napoleon during the long years of European war from 1803 to 1815 which ended in the emperor's final defeat and banishment to St. Helena. Both the Jefferson and Madison administrations knew that the French, with or without an alliance with the United States (the Americans had ended the alliance in the Treaty of Mortefontaine in 1800), would look after their own interests. The Federalists tried to make out a case against Jefferson, claiming the President to be "the lackey" of the emperor. They contended that the embargo of 1807–09 reinforced the continental system at the moment of its greatest extension. The Federalists sent Jefferson innumerable accusatory letters, among which was a missive dated from Boston, March 4, 1808:

> To His Excellents & Supreme French Majesty
>   Thomas the First
>   Slave of Napoleon
>   Cowardly Emperour
> Enclosed receive as true statement of the feelings
>   of your Subjects and after due reflection if
>   you have not remorse of conscience Thou hast none.
>   Thy Friend
>   Anti-Bonaparte

The President endorsed this letter "Anon. Blackguard." Another communication (endorsed "ribaldry") came from New York on August 25, 1808:

> Thomas Jefferson
> You are the damdest
> dog that God put life into
> God dam you.

But no one found the slightest trace of evidence supporting the canard of a secret alliance between Jefferson and "his master." When Jefferson put into effect the embargo it was not because the measure aided Napoleon; it was because the opposing belligerent systems of France and Britain had so entrapped American neutral commerce that common sense advised a stop to that commerce. An alliance with France was about as plausible as the latter-day notion that President Franklin D. Roosevelt sank the Pacific fleet at Pearl Harbor in 1941. The Emperor Napoleon in 1810 may have told the Duc de Cadore what that statesman put into a communication to the American minister in Paris, General John Armstrong:

> His Majesty loves the Americans. Their prosperity and their commerce are within the scope of his policy. The independence of America is one of the principal titles of glory to France. Since that epoch, the Emperor is pleased in aggrandizing the United States, and, under all circumstances, that which can contribute to the independence, to the prosperity, and the liberty of the Americans, the Emperor will consider as conformable with the interests of his empire.

President James Madison did not believe this pleasantry for a moment. When Congress in 1812 was debating the declaration of war against Great Britain, much sentiment emerged for a double war, against both Britain and France.

What of Britain, as compared to France? Was there not more of a threat to independence from the British? Such was the case, except that the threat differed from that presented by France. The truth was that once the American colonies had been lost, the British accepted them for lost. No one much wished them back in the British Empire. In a famous phrase uttered upon receipt of news of Saratoga, William Pitt the elder lamented that America "was, indeed, the fountain of our wealth, the nerve of our strength, the nursery and basis of our naval power." To modern-day students an easy solution to this complaint would have been reconquest. The idea enjoyed little support in London in the years after the end of the Revolution. The threat of Great Britain to American independence was less obvious. Before the imperialism of the latter nineteenth century, colonies had as their chief justification the advantage of trade. Their duty was to take manufactures of the mother country and send back raw materials and specie. After Yorktown the British government decided that the American Revolution was a fairly minor political convulsion and that independence could not change the facts of economic life which bound the United States to the trade of England. The scornful British attitude toward American independence in the years at least until the end of the Napoleonic wars came from this belief, which commerce of those years amply supported. The country cousins of the New World otherwise would have had to garb themselves in bark and skins. The credit of the federal government inaugurated in 1789 rested upon the trade with England. It was only a passing fear that problems of Europe might engage American attention against British interests which persuaded the British government in 1791, long after the end of the Revolution, to send a minister to New York. They sent a young man of twenty-seven, George Hammond, who almost at once secured the treasonous assistance of Secretary of the Treasury Alexander Hamilton. Hamilton already had been talking with Major George Beckwith, who in cipher messages to the governor general of Canada, Lord Dorchester, had denominated the secretary as "Number 7"—as Julian P. Boyd has so ably shown in a recent book (1964) of that name. With the secretary of the treasury in their pocket, and trade likewise, the British doubtless reasoned that the Revolution had wrought only a surface change.

Britain's supercilious belief in the economic dependence of the United States eventually produced the War of 1812, the conflict which Americans fought ostensibly over neutral rights and impressment but actually for the assertion of independence. The British government had refused to respect American nationality. Henry Clay in a famous declamation on the last day of the year 1811 inquired of his fellow members of the war hawk Congress:

> What are we to gain by war . . . ? In reply, he would ask, what are we not to lose by peace?—commerce, character, a nation's best treasure, honor! . . . He had no disposition to swell, or dwell upon the catalogue of injuries from England. . . . What nation, what individual was ever taught in the schools of ignominious submission, the patriotic lessons of freedom and independence? . . . Let us come home to our own history. It was not by submission that our fathers achieved our independence. The patriotic wisdom that placed you, Mr. Chairman, said Mr. C., under that canopy, penetrated the designs of a corrupt Ministry, and nobly fronted encroachment on its first appearance. It saw beyond the petty taxes, with which it commenced, a long train of oppressive measures terminating in the total annihilation of liberty; and, contemptible as they were, did not hesitate to resist them.

Historians have remarked the foolhardiness of the War of 1812, and how the British might have turned the United States into a kind of self-supporting colony if Prevost, Ross, and Pakenham had won in 1814–15, if Napoleon had not escaped from Elba and placed the politics of the Continent in jeopardy until his final defeat at Waterloo. The diplomacy leading to the War of 1812 showed something less than the care which earlier had marked American foreign relations. Madison the sometime theorist and James Monroe the sometime zealot succumbed to the occasion of British high seas authoritarianism, but the purpose of the War of 1812—a sideshow compared to the grand theater in Europe—was to assert, if in a foolishly strident way, American independence. The Jefferson chapter of accidents then worked out to the good of the United States. Upon sending the Treaty of Ghent to the Senate, President Madison said that it was "highly honorable to the nation, and terminates, with peculiar felicity, a campaign signalized by the most brilliant successes." The war was a series of almost unmitigated military disasters. But Americans forgot the spectacle of the burning of their capital city, of President Madison fleeing across the Potomac in a small boat, of the incomparable Dolley scurrying out of the Executive Mansion carrying the portrait of George Washington, of General Ross helping his soldiers pile furniture outside the mansion preparatory to setting the place on fire. They remembered "The Star-Spangled Banner," composed shortly thereafter.

The success of American independence over the long span of years by careful diplomacy, if during one short span by sheer luck, received its ultimate testimony in President Monroe's message of 1823.

2

The second theme of the foreign policy of the United States in the years covered by the present volume, from 1775 to the Geneva arbitration of 1872, was freedom of commerce. Protection and increase of commerce was an end of American diplomacy second only to independence.

One might think freedom of commerce a prosaic subject. It was a vital one, in the truest sense of that overworked adjective. The growth of the American nation, its rise to the position of most formidable of all world powers, would have been impossible without the commerce of the early years. Americans of the latter twentieth century sometimes like to recall that exports now take only a small portion of the gross national product, four per cent, and the assumption behind such remarks often is that the United States could turn in upon itself. Whatever the truth of any such belief today, it was untrue of the initial years of American independence when the country had few industries and depended on export of foodstuffs and naval stores. American vessels also earned specie by carrying much of Europe's colonial and coastal trade.

The perils of the sea made commerce no prosaic business, either. The typical sailing vessel of the first half century of independence carried a freight of about 250 tons, and required a large crew to shorten and lengthen the great spread of sails. To be a sailor meant a life of long, buffeting days in vessels a fraction the size of, say, today's destroyers with their notorious pitches and rolls. A gale was a frightening experience, and vessels often went down with all hands. The ship that took the text of the Declaration of Independence to Europe left Philadelphia in July 1776 and disappeared without trace. The vessel that transported Franklin to Europe next year, the good ship *Reprisal*, shortly thereafter went down with her commander, Captain Wickes, off the banks of Newfoundland. Commodore Stephen Decatur in 1815 sent the sloop *Epervier* back to the United States from the Mediterranean bearing the treaty he had negotiated with the Algerine pirates. The sloop was seen on July 12, 1815, sailing through the Straits of Gibraltar, after which it passed inexplicably into the dark corridors of history.

Because of the essential importance of trade, also in recognition that merchants and sea captains and crews suffered from enough natural dangers to deserve assistance against human restrictions, the American government zealously moved to protect its citizens' commerce in peace and war. Peace held problems, to be sure. The nations of Europe disliked having American vessels "horning in" on their own trade, whether between ports on the Continent or between European and colonial ports. But the largest troubles came in wartime. And war was the common condition of Europe during the early years of independence. The wars of the French Revolution and Napoleon began in 1793 and continued until 1815, with the exception of an interlude in 1802–3. In two treaty plans, ideal articles for treaties of commerce, those of 1776 and 1784, Congress therefore carefully set out provisions for neutral, that is, American, trading rights in wartime. The hope was that incorporation of such articles in a series of bilateral commercial treaties (if the United States signed enough of them, with the important maritime powers) would establish rights in advance of a war.

The campaign to establish the American view of neutral trading rights in wartime proved extremely difficult. The American government signed up some of the lesser nations to the idea that free (neutral) ships make free goods, the right to trade between two or more ports of a belligerent (to pick up either the coastal carrying trade or the trade between colonies and mother country), a tight definition of contraband excluding foodstuffs and naval stores, and —this was the peculiar contribution of the treaty plan of 1784—a definition of blockaded ports as those at which vessels seeking to enter would find themselves in imminent danger. France had agreed to American neutral rights in 1778, and treaties followed with the Netherlands (1782), Sweden (1783), Prussia (1785), and

Spain (1795). All that was necessary was for the British government to adhere to American ideas of neutrality, but the British refused. In Jay's Treaty of 1794, the first treaty of commerce between the United States and Great Britain, the London ministry refused to do anything more than admit that the royal navy's captures might be subject to compensation. Discouraged, the Americans toward the end of the century proved willing to negotiate similarly restricted treaties with other countries, including France. The youthful diplomat John Quincy Adams renegotiated the commercial treaty with Prussia in 1799. Then Napoleon in the Treaty of Mortefontaine of September 1800, decided to reaffirm America's neutral rights according to the plans of 1776 and 1784 in hope of support in raising a league of armed neutrals against his enemy Britain. French recognition, though, was one thing, and respect for those rights another. During the wars of the French Revolution and Napoleon, not merely the British government but also the French government was glad to find excuses to confiscate American ships. The British restricted American commerce partly to prevent aid to the French but often to hurt a commercial rival (the American merchant marine was second in size in the world only to the merchant marine of Great Britain). The French seized American ships and goods so as to sell them and obtain money to prosecute the European war. Not until the peace of Vienna beginning in 1815 was the problem of neutral rights solved by the elimination of major war from Europe. The World War of 1914–18 reopened the whole issue, and the British government in 1915 reprinted the publicist James Stephen's pamphlet of 1805, *War in Disguise; Or, the Frauds of the Neutral Flags.*

In the republic's early years trade—and its protection and increase—was a continuing concern. During the first decades of independence, Americans tried to establish a large commerce with a country other than Great Britain. There was some hope that the French might prove interested in filling the trade gap left by the exclusion of the United States from the British imperial system. The French were not interested in this American problem, except during wartime—and then the British invoked their own Rule of the War of 1756, that trade not open in time of peace should not be open in time of war. The Spanish colonies might have been another place where Americans could trade, but the Bourbons of Spain tried as long as possible to continue the mercantilist restrictions which had made Spain great in the sixteenth century and contributed to her decline ever since; and when the Spanish colonial trade did open up in the course of the revolt in Spain against French domination which began on May 2, 1808—the famous *Dos de Mayo*, Spain's Fourth of July—the British government managed to get most of the trade. To use Foreign Secretary Canning's later braggadocio, Britain called the New World into existence to redress the balance of the Old. The Americans meanwhile sought a trade with China. It was no accident that the year after the end of the Revolution the *Empress of China*, a merchantman in which Robert Morris of Philadelphia possessed an interest, went out to Canton and became the first vessel of the United States to trade to a Chinese port. The China trade was a modest success, sometimes a huge success in terms of an individual voyage. In addition to the tea, cotton goods, and silks brought by the returning vessels the merchants of the era graced the drawing rooms of their houses with scrolls and vases and bric-a-brac. As a substitute for trade with Britain the China business was a failure.

This discussion of commerce has said nothing of trade on the Mississippi and its tributaries. The Mississippi question constituted an issue in diplomacy which if not as long-lasting as neutral rights or entrance into other powers' commercial empires was certainly as productive of instructions, dispatches, memoranda, conversations, even—for a moment in 1802–3—talk of alliance. Had it not ended abruptly and with full success for the United States in 1803, it might have produced a war.

It would be difficult to conceive of a water system more important than the Mississippi. Other river systems of the world were small by comparison: the Elbe, the Rhine, the Danube, the rivers of India, and China. The diplomacy of the United States in the Mississippi question was the more contentious because, coupled with an almost instinctive understanding of the need of access to the great waterway, went a diplomatic position in regard to the issue that was extremely weak. The Spanish controlled the river by virtue of possession of Louisiana. Before the end of the Revolution the only argument the United States could raise in support of unrestricted navigation was that the colonial land grants had reached to the Mississippi as a result of the Treaty of Paris between Britain and Spain in 1763, and that this same treaty had given Britain and the colonists the right of navigation. The Spanish properly remarked that the war between Spain and Britain beginning in 1779 had cancelled the servitude on the Mississippi and even the boundaries of 1763. Moreover, throughout the American Revolution the Spanish did not recognize American independence. Congress accredited John Jay to Spain with the hope that he could obtain recognition, a loan, and confirmation of American rights on the Mississippi. It is worth noting that his belief in the importance of the Mississippi question proved stronger than that of Congress, which body in 1781, perhaps under French influence, instructed Jay that if necessary he might offer a forebearance of navigation from the thirty-first parallel south to the Gulf of Mexico in return for recognition of independence and an alliance. Jay wisely made his offer to the Spanish court conditional upon immediate acceptance, and when the Spanish did not take up this proposition he withdrew it.

The treaty of peace between the United States and Britain granted navigation of the Mississippi. The Americans noticed uneasily that the British said nothing about rights on the Mississippi in their separate treaty of peace with Spain.

Jay as secretary for foreign affairs from 1784 to 1789 almost made a mistake over the Mississippi question. In 1786 he proposed an amendment to his instructions by Congress, to permit him to offer the Spanish minister, Diego de Gardoqui, a forebearance of navigation for twenty-five or thirty years. In a closely argued speech before Congress the secretary sought to show that the advantages of trade with Spain to be derived under the treaty he proposed to sign—not to mention the prestige to the United States from a treaty with so great a power as Spain—would compensate for the forebearance of a right which, if looked at closely, was no right at all but a hope. This hope, he believed, could not be realized in the foreseeable future, given the huge territory which Americans would have to settle before the navigation of the Mississippi could become a subject of pressing importance. What Jay overlooked, easterner that he was, was that fifty thousand American settlers had passed over the mountains during the first year after the Treaty of Paris of 1783, turning a theoretical question into an economic necessity. These settlers had produced their first small crops of grain and tobacco in 1785 and wished to send this produce down the river to New Orleans. It was far easier to send goods downriver from Pittsburgh and thence by ocean vessel to Philadelphia than to use the

axle-breaking trails across Pennsylvania from Pittsburgh to Philadelphia. The vote on Jay's request for congressional authorization
was seven states for and five against, Delaware abstaining. The
margin was too close, and Jay abandoned his ill-considered project.
As a result the constitutional convention in 1787 wrote the two
thirds rule for treaties into the federal constitution.

At last the United States achieved an agreement with Spain in
Pinckney's Treaty of 1795, signed after a negotiation which has
been a subject of scholarly disagreement between the two leading
twentieth-century authorities, Samuel Flagg Bemis and Arthur P.
Whitaker. Bemis's *Pinckney's Treaty* (1926) bears in its subtitle a
thesis which this scholar of American foreign policy claims has
marked almost all the diplomacy of the early years: "America's Advantage from Europe's Distress." Bemis believes that Spain's withdrawal from the first coalition against revolutionary France in 1795 so
concerned the Spanish foreign minister, Manuel de Godoy, that the
latter was willing to give the Americans the navigation of the
Mississippi in order to prevent the United States from siding with
Britain against Spain (and incidentally taking all Spain's North
American possessions). Godoy considered that Jay's Treaty of
1794 might be an alliance with Britain, openly in the treaty text or
in a secret article. Whitaker in *The Spanish-American Frontier*
(1927) maintains that the pressure of frontiersmen upon Spanish
possessions had made the Madrid government so nervous that it
conceded to the Americans what it could not prevent. Westward
from the Mississippi lay New Mexico and California; to the south
below the thirty-first parallel (Pinckney's Treaty established the
Spanish-American boundary at that parallel) the Floridas,[1] Texas,
Mexico, South America. As Godoy said at one juncture, "You
cannot lock up an open field."

The truth of the argument between Bemis and Whitaker is
difficult to ascertain, except to say that Bemis can demonstrate
Spanish diplomatic fears by citing instructions and dispatches,
whereas Whitaker has a much more difficult problem illustrating
the effect of frontier pressure.

The end of the Mississippi question proved unexpected and illus-
trated Bemis's thesis of America's advantage from Europe's distress

---

[1] See below, p. 133.

rather than any pressure from that other diplomatic force, the frontier. No sooner had United States representatives signed the Treaty of Mortefontaine on September 30, 1800, than Napoleon the next day, October 1, concluded a secret treaty with Spain for the "retrocession" of Louisiana—France had given the territory to Spain in 1763. Rumor of this cession reached America in subsequent months. President Jefferson was alarmed, and early in 1802 took the liberty of writing a letter to his minister in Paris, the same Livingston who earlier had been secretary for foreign affairs, that if a strong power such as France occupied Louisiana the United States would be forced to "marry the British fleet and nation." When in the autumn of 1802 the Spanish intendant at New Orleans closed the port to American commerce, it seemed like a plot to clean up the title of Louisiana, in advance of French possession, by erasing the article of Pinckney's Treaty which had promised that American goods coming down the river on flatboats might have a place of deposit from whence to reload on ocean-going vessels. It turned out that the intendant had taken this decision on his own, without advice from Madrid or Paris. Jefferson did not understand this and could only proceed from appearances. As is well known, he commissioned Livingston to buy the "island," that is, the vicinity, of New Orleans, and also the Floridas. Instead Livingston was offered and took the whole of Louisiana.

It is not so well known that while Livingston was concluding his bargain in Paris with the help of Monroe, who had gone over on special mission, Jefferson and the cabinet debated in the solitude of the little village of Washington, and decided in April 1803 that if the French did not sell New Orleans, the United States should make an immediate alliance with Britain. The Mississippi question meant that much to the President and the American people.

3

The third principle of policy set out in the documents to follow in the present volume is continental expansion.

With the purchase of 1803 a spirit of expansion took hold of almost the entire nation. The Louisiana Purchase ensured a feeling of what the Democratic Party journalist John L. O'Sullivan in 1845 denominated "manifest destiny." The Floridas, Texas, New Mexico, and California; Canada to the north; Mexico, Cuba and the other Caribbean islands, the Isthmus, South America to Tierra del Fuego: a wild view opened to imaginative diplomacy! Manifest destiny dominated American diplomacy until almost the terminal year of the present volume, 1872.

The full sweep of American ambition was not visible to the statesmen who presided over the affairs of the republic into the latter 1820's. Monroe and John Quincy Adams were both men who had grown up on the eastern seaboard in a fairly static society, who had known the Europe of the French Revolution and Napoleon and felt that turmoil was not good for the western hemisphere. Monroe had been a more exuberant young man than John Quincy Adams; the latter somehow was old even in youth. Oddly, Adams with his tradition of Federalism—he had become a Republican only in 1808—saw more boldly than Monroe who, living so close to Monticello, should have caught some of the view from that noble edifice. Perhaps (one might add, glumly) it all was because the Monroe house near Monticello was rather down in the valley. It was Secretary Adams instead of the President who in the summer of 1818, for reasons not yet divined and to which he did not at the time testify in his diary, talked the Spanish minister, Luis de Onís y Gonzales, into running the border between Spanish and American western possessions on out to the Pacific coast along the forty-second parallel. This act of vision on the part of Adams, at the time he was negotiating the cession of the Floridas from Spain, is difficult to explain. The historian of the Adams-Onís Treaty of 1819, Philip C. Brooks, believes that John Jacob Astor may have persuaded Adams into this extension of the Spanish-American border. Astor at that time was inquiring at the state department about some of his commercial concerns. Adams proposed the border during the year of the convention that set the boundary with British Canada along the forty-ninth parallel out to the "Stony Mountains." Perhaps the idea of Pacific boundaries was in the air. He later took full credit for the suggestion, as a testimony to his anticipation of western expansion. But one fact was certain about those first years after the War of 1812, namely, that the Monroe administration had little interest in Texas. Adams talked about Texas in the negotiation with Onís. Adams again saw farther than Monroe and would have pressed for a boundary west of the

Sabine River (the present-day boundary between the states of Louisiana and Texas) if the President and cabinet would have supported him. Not merely did they refuse to do so, but cabinet members communicated their refusal to the French minister, Baron Guillaume-Jean Hyde de Neuville, and to Onís. Adams, in February 1819, carefully asked the opinion of General Andrew Jackson about getting Texas from Onís, and even that champion of the West said that what Adams was getting, the Floridas and a continental boundary with Spain, was worth much more than Texas.

Within a few years the fat was in the fire, and Adams for the rest of his life would have to defend his "failure" to obtain Texas in 1819. The national will to empire had moved that rapidly. One of the most interesting documents in the sections that follow concerns Adams and President James K. Polk and the Texas question. The President of 1845 had written a letter the year before claiming that Adams had been remiss in failing to get Texas. Polk had forgotten this piece of electioneering, and one day asked his friend Secretary of the Navy George Bancroft, the historian, to sound old Adams on the subject of coming to dinner at the Executive Mansion. Adams raised the issue of Polk's pronouncement on Texas, and said he wouldn't come until Polk took it back. Polk angrily withdrew the projected invitation, saying to Bancroft that he didn't need to dine with Adams anyway. "I told Mr. Bancroft that it was a matter of no consequence whether he was invited to dinner or not, and that certainly I had no explanations to make." A little more than two years thereafter Adams died, and Polk was mildly sorry.

Adams, like Monroe, had not anticipated what was going to happen in Texas. Beginning in 1821 with the colonization projects of Stephen A. Austin, Texas filled with American settlers. Manifest destiny was plainly visible by the middle of the 1820's, when American secretaries of state began to propose the purchase of the territory from Mexico with arguments which were as sincere as they were ingenious. Henry Clay, ever a master of western logic, contended in an instruction to the American minister to Mexico City, Joel Poinsett (who gave his name to the genus *Poinsettia*), that if Mexico ceded Texas it would make Mexico City more central to the rest of the national territory. The most extraordinary negotiator for Texas was the representative of President Jackson, Colonel Anthony Butler, whose correspondence with the President became so exuberantly importunate that Jackson in exasperation endorsed one Butler letter: "A. Butler: What a scamp." What seems to have exercised Jackson more than Butler's barefaced proposal to bribe the statesmen of Mexico was that the colonel had neglected to put some of his most intimate propositions in cipher.

A lull followed in the Texas agitation while the Lone Star Republic maintained its independence, until President John Tyler in 1844 placed annexation before Congress as an issue suitable for passage by a joint resolution of both houses rather than a two-thirds vote of the Senate. Tyler signed the resolution on March 1, 1845.

A little more than a year later the Mexican government obliged President Polk by engaging the troops of General Zachary ("Old Zack") Taylor along the Rio Grande, and the war was on. Polk chronicled the events of the war in his extraordinary diary, and one almost can see the somber President, with his black hair and piercing eyes, moving from room to room of the Executive Mansion, receiving a delegation of Sunday School children in one room, perhaps the secretary of war in another, taking time out to attend church which if in company of his wife was the Presbyterian Church and if by himself was his own preference, the Methodist Church. The minister once preached on vanity and death, and Polk set down in his diary his ruminations thereon. He beheld countless plots against himself and the war, and found it difficult to disentangle personal issues from public. At last he got the nation out of the war in a way which struck some of his supporters as irregular but which he had the good judgment to see was sensible and even appropriate.

Was the Mexican War a war of aggression? Not technically, for the Mexican troops attacked first. As Polk put it in his war message, it was war "by the act of Mexico herself." Perhaps the President provoked the high-spirited Mexicans by annexing Texas and sending Taylor's troops down into a disputed area between the Nueces River and the Rio Grande. Readers of Polk's quite personal diary must draw their own conclusion.

The late Robert F. Kennedy, visiting in Indonesia in 1962, said concerning the Mexican War that "Some from Texas might disagree, but I think we were unjustified. I do not think we can be proud of that episode." He did not offer to give Texas back to Mexico, which may not have been what he had in mind, although he soon received a volume of critical correspondence on this subject. Governor Price Daniel of Texas spoke of Kennedy's "glaring ignorance of history." The Republican Party's national publication, *Battle Line*, said that Kennedy perhaps would like to tear down the Alamo for the purpose of urban renewal.

The result of the war—of President Polk's war, said many people including Congressman Abraham Lincoln of Illinois—was an imperial domain similar to that of the Louisiana Purchase. This domain together with the Gadsden Purchase of 1853 and the Alaska Purchase of 1867 rounded off the continental territory of the United States as we know it today.

In the 1840's and 1850's manifest destiny was not merely continental but turned outward in a series of expansive projects. The Clayton-Bulwer Treaty arranged for a future isthmian canal. Commodore Matthew C. Perry opened Japan, and the subsequent diplomacy of Townsend Harris converted Perry's shipwreck convention into a regular treaty of commerce. Meanwhile the United States had begun a diplomacy with China. In the course of negotiating the first Sino-American treaty, the Cushing Treaty of 1844, President Tyler signed a letter to the emperor of China which read almost like a child's composition, detailing by name the states of the Union over which Tyler presided and expressing the President's felicitation, "I hope your health is good." A far cry from the unpleasantness of Sino-American relations in the latter twentieth century.

The Civil War and its diplomatic aftermath brought American territorial expansion to a close. On the field of battle the Union armies preserved rather than advanced American nationality and manifest destiny. In the foreign ministries of Europe, especially London and Paris, ministers of the United States pursued the essentially negative task of reminding Europeans that the South under Jefferson Davis had not made a nation. A postscript to the Civil War was the expulsion of French troops from Mexico, in which the diplomacy of Secretary of State William H. Seward received reinforcement through the presence of American troops on the Mexican border.

The era closed with the Alaska Purchase and the Geneva arbitration. The purchase of 1867 was as fortuitous as the purchase of 1803, and its critics as strenuous ("Walrussia," "Seward's Folly," "Andy Johnson's polar bear garden"). After he left the state department Seward made a triumphal tour of his purchase and listened to some brave talk, and indulged in a little himself. Even he did not altogether understand what he had done, though like Jefferson he knew that he had made a noble bargain. The full value of the purchase would not become evident until well into the twentieth century. Alaska marked the end of American territorial ambitions for at least a generation, and when President Ulysses S. Grant shortly afterward sought to acquire Santo Domingo he was treated to the condemnations of his bitter political enemy, Senator Charles Sumner, who likened Grant's desire for Santo Domingo to the desire of King Ahab for Naboth's vineyard (1 Kings 21). The United States government turned to the consolidation of its international position in the Washington Treaty of 1871 and the ensuing Geneva arbitration of 1872, wherein Great Britain admitted culpability for escape of the Alabama and other Confederate cruisers.

The award of 1872 was a fitting end to the era. The American judge in 1872, Charles Francis Adams, the son of John Quincy Adams, realized that in accepting an arbitral award the British were making a formal apology in which the Alabama was only the nominal issue. The British were apologizing for a century of miscalculation and mistake and at last welcoming the United States as a full-fledged member of the family of nations—indeed, the small circle of great powers. With his fellow arbitrators Adams listened to the arguments in a little room in a building almost in the shadow of John Calvin's old church, and the setting may well have reminded him of his country's predestination.

II

Independence

Eight years passed between the opening skirmishes of the American Revolution and the Treaty of Paris of 1783, and in this long and wearisome struggle independence often seemed a likely casualty. Obstacles raised themselves one after the other. The military course of the war gradually became evident with the surrender of General John Burgoyne in 1777 and the capture of Lord Cornwallis's troops in 1781. Diplomacy with the monarchies of Europe continued, and Americans easily could have lost in the peace what they gained in war—the possibility, quaintly enough, loomed long before people were to begin to argue about always winning wars and losing the peace.

1. The committee of secret correspondence

At the outset of the Revolution most Americans did not like the idea of seeking foreign aid for their rebellion, but the need for munitions and other supplies of war, not to mention the advantage of trying to press concessions from the British by threat of alliance with the French, forced the Congress to appoint a secret committee. This committee, after April 17, 1777, became known as the committee for foreign affairs. A secretary for foreign affairs, acting under direct control of Congress, supplanted the committee in 1781, and his office gave way to the Department of State in 1789. For the following resolution of Congress appointing the committee of secret correspondence, November 29, 1775, see Francis Wharton (ed.), The Revolutionary Diplomatic Correspondence of the United States (6 vols., Washington, D.C., 1889), II, 61–62.

Resolved, That a committee of five be appointed for the sole purpose of corresponding with our friends in Great Britain, Ireland, and other parts of the world, and that they lay their correspondence before Congress when directed.

Resolved, That this Congress will make provision to defray all such expenses as may arise by carrying on such a correspondence, and for the payment of such agents as they may send on this service.

The members chosen, Mr. [Benjamin] Harrison, Dr. [Benjamin] Franklin, Mr. [Thomas] Johnson, Mr. [John] Dickinson, and Mr. [John] Jay.

Arthur Lee, of the Lee family of Virginia, had been the colonial agent for Massachusetts in London, and the committee wrote him on December 12, 1775, while he still was in the British capital. Source: ibid., 63–64. Lee was a suspicious, intriguing individual and was to cause Franklin much trouble in Paris.

By this conveyance we have the pleasure of transmitting to you sundry printed papers, that such of them as you think proper may be immediately published in England.

We have written on the subject of American affairs to Monsieur C. G. F. Dumas, who resides at The Hague. We recommend to you to correspond with him, and to send through his hands any letters to us which you can not send more directly. He will transmit them via St. Eustatia. When you write to him direct your letter thus: "A. Mons. C. G. F. Dumas, chez Mad^le. V. Loder, a la Hague," and put it under cover directed to Mr. A. Stuchy, merchant, at Rotterdam.

Mr. Story may be trusted with any dispatches you think proper to send us. You will be so kind as to aid and advise him.

It would be agreeable to Congress *to know the disposition of foreign powers towards us,* and we hope this object will engage your attention. We need not hint that *great circumspection and impenetrable secrecy* are necessary. The Congress rely on your zeal and abilities to serve them, and will readily compensate you for whatever trouble and expense a compliance with their desire may occasion. We remit you for the present £200.

Whenever you think the importance of your dispatches may require it, we desire you to send an express boat with them from England, for which service your agreement with the owner there shall be fulfilled by us here.

We can now only add that we continue firm in our resolutions to defend ourselves, notwithstanding the *big threats* of the ministry. We have just taken one of their ordnance storeships, in which an abundance of carcasses and bombs, intended for burning our towns, were found.

The committee of secret correspondence advised another agent, Silas Deane, in a letter of March 3, 1776. Source: ibid., 78–80. Deane was an early diplomat whose career, like that of Lee, caused a good deal of controversy. While in France during the Revolution he did some private trading and laid himself open to the accusation that he had benefited from an inside knowledge of events. He also incurred the hatred of Lee. After the Revolution he went to England—a mistake for an individual who had to argue his patriotism—where he died in 1789 at the moment of setting out to return to the New World. Toward the end of the present letter the reader will notice the advice that Deane should get in touch with "Mr. Bancroft"—Edward Bancroft, later secretary to Franklin in Paris. Not until more than a century later was it discovered that Bancroft was a double agent.

On your arrival in France you will, for some time, be engaged in the business of providing goods for the Indian trade. This will give good countenance to your appearing in the character of a merchant, which we wish you continually to retain among the French in general, it being probable that the court of France may not like it should be known publicly that any agent from the Colonies is in that country. When you come to Paris, by delivering Dr. Franklin's letter to Monsieur Le Roy, at the Louvre, and M. Dubourg, you will be introduced to a set of acquaintance, all friends to the Americans. By conversing with them you will have a good opportunity of acquiring Parisian French, and you will find in M. Dubourg a man prudent, faithful, secret, intelligent in affairs, and capable of giving you very sage advice.

It is scarce necessary to pretend any other business at Paris than the gratifying of that curiosity, which draws numbers thither yearly, merely to see so famous a city. With the assistance of Monsieur Dubourg, who understands English, you will be able to make immediate application to Monsieur de Vergennes, *ministre des affaires etrangères*, either personally or by letter, if M. Dubourg adopts that method, acquainting him that you are in France upon business of the American Congress, in the character of a merchant, having something to communicate to him that may be mutually beneficial to France and the North American Colonies; that you request an audience of him, and that he would be pleased to appoint the time and place. At this audience, if agreed to, it may be well to show him first your letter of credence, and then acquaint him that the Congress, finding that in the common course of commerce, it was not practicable to furnish the continent of America with the quantity of arms and ammunition necessary for its defense (the ministry of Great Britain having been extremely industrious to prevent it), you have been dispatched by their authority to apply to some European power for a supply. That France had been pitched on for the first application, from an opinion that if we should, as there is a great appearance we shall, come to a total separation from Great Britain, France would be looked upon as the power whose friendship it would be fittest for us to obtain and cultivate. That the commercial advantages Britain had enjoyed with the Colonies had contributed greatly to her late wealth and importance. That it is likely great part of our commerce will naturally fall to the share of France, especially if she favors us in this application, as that will be a means of gaining and securing the friendship of the Colonies; and that as our trade was rapidly increasing with our increase of people, and, in a greater proportion, her part of it will be extremely valuable. That the supply we at present want is clothing and arms for twenty-five thousand men, with a suitable quantity of ammunition, and one hundred field pieces. That we mean to pay for the same by remittances to France, or through Spain, Portugal, or the French Islands, as soon as our navigation can be protected by ourselves or friends; and that we, besides, want great quantities of linens and woolens, with other articles for the Indian trade, which you are now actually purchasing, and for which you ask no credit, and that the whole, if France should grant the other supplies, would make a cargo which it might be well to secure by a convoy of two or three ships of war.

If you should find M. de Vergennes reserved, and not inclined to enter into free conversation with you, it may be well to shorten your visit, request him to consider what you have proposed, acquaint him with your place of lodging, that you may yet stay sometime at Paris, and that, knowing how precious his time is, you do not presume to ask another audience; but that, if he should have any commands for you, you will, upon the least notice, immediately wait upon him. If, at a future conference, he should be more free, and you find a disposition to favor the Colonies, it may be proper to acquaint him that they must necessarily be anxious to know the disposition of France on certain points, which, with his permission, you would mention, such as whether, if the Colonies should be forced to form themselves into an independent State, France would probably acknowledge them as such, receive their embassadors, enter into any treaty or alliance with them, for commerce or defense, or both? If so, on what principal conditions? Intimating that you shall speedily have an opportunity of sending to America, if you do not immediately return, and that he may be assured of your fidelity and secrecy in transmitting carefully anything he would wish to convey to the Congress on that subject. In subsequent conversations you may as you find it convenient, enlarge on those topics that have been the subjects of our conferences with you, to which you may occasionally add the well-known substantial answers we usually give to the several calumnies thrown out against us. If these supplies on the credit of the Congress should be refused, you are to endeavor the obtaining a permission of purchasing those articles, or so much of them as you can find credit for. You will keep a daily journal of all your material transactions, and particularly of what passes in your conversation with great personages; and you will, by every safe opportunity, furnish us with such information as may be important. When your business in France admits of it, it may be well to go into Holland, and visit our agent there, M. Dumas, conferring with him on subjects that may promote our interest, and on the means of communication.

You will endeavor to procure a meeting with Mr. Bancroft by writing a letter to him, under cover to Mr. Griffiths, at Turnham Green, near London, and desiring him to come over to you in France or Holland, on the score of old acquaintance. From him you may obtain a good deal of information of what is now going forward in England, and settle a mode of continuing a correspondence. It may be well to remit a small bill to defray his expenses in coming to you, and avoid all political matters in your letter to him. You will also endeavor to correspond with Mr. Arthur Lee, agent of the Colonies in London. You will endeavor to obtain acquaintance with M. Garnier, late *chargé des affaires de France en Angleterre*, if now in France, or, if returned to England, a correspondence with him, as a person extremely intelligent and friendly to our cause. From him you may learn many particulars occasionally, that will be useful to us.

.

2. The French alliance

More than a half century ago the distinguished political scientist Edward S. Corwin discovered an unsigned document in the French archives, dated January 13, 1778, bearing the title "Considerations upon the Necessity of France declaring at once for the American Colonies, even without the Concurrence of Spain." Corwin noticed that this "omnium gatherum of all the arguments for French intervention" contained expressions from earlier papers by the French foreign minister, Charles Gravier Comte de Vergennes. He first printed this memorandum in his French Policy and the American Alliance of 1778 (Princeton University Press: Princeton, N.J., 1916), pp. 389–403.

The quarrel which exists between England and the Colonies of North America is as important to France as to Great Britain, and its issue will have equal influence on the reputation and power of those two Crowns. It is, therefore, essential that France should decide upon and fix the policy it is advisable she should adopt in such a conjuncture.

The Americans have been struggling for the last three years against the efforts of Great Britain, and they have up to the present maintained a sort of superiority; but the war which they wage fatigues and exhausts them, and must necessarily weary the people and awaken in them a desire for repose.

England, for her part, crushed by the expenditure occasioned by this same war, and convinced of the impossibility of reducing the Colonies, is occupied with the means of re-establishing peace. With this view she is taking the most urgent and animated steps with the Deputies from Congress, and it is natural that the United States should at last decide to listen to their proposals.

In this state of affairs it is desirable to examine what course it is proper for France to take.

There exist two courses only,—that of abandoning the Colonies, and that of supporting them.

If we abandon them, England will take advantage of it by making a reconciliation, and in that case she will either preserve her supremacy wholly or partially, or she will gain an ally. Now it is known that she is disposed to sacrifice that supremacy and to propose simply a sort of family compact, that is to say, a league against the House of Bourbon.

The result of this will be that the Americans will become our perpetual enemies, and we must expect to see them turn all their efforts against our possessions, and against those of Spain. This is all the more probable as the Colonies require a direct trade with the sugar islands. England will offer them that of our islands after having conquered them, which will be easy for her.

Thus the coalition of the English and the Americans will draw after it our expulsion, and probably that of the Spaniards, from the whole of America; it will limit our shipping and our commerce to the European seas only, and even this trade will be at the mercy of English insolence and greed.

It would be a mistake to suppose that the United States will not lend themselves to the proposals of the Court of St. James's. Those States took up arms only in order to establish and defend their independence and the freedom of their commerce; if, therefore, England offers them both, what reason will they have for refusing? Their treaty with that Power will give them more safety than the engagements which they might make with other Powers, or than all the guarantees which we might offer them. Indeed, what opinion can they have of our means, and even of our good-will, since we have not dared to co-operate in securing an independence of which we would afterwards propose the empty guarantee? Their surest guarantee will be in the community of interests and views which will be established between them and their former mother-country; we have nothing to offer which can counterbalance that.

Such will be the effects of the independence of the United States of America, if it is established without our concurrence.

It follows from this that the glory, the dignity and the essential interest of France demand that she should stretch out her hand to those States, and that their independence should be her work.

The advantages which will result are innumerable; we shall humiliate our natural enemy, a perfidious enemy who never knows how to respect either treaties or the right of nations; we shall divert to our profit one of the principal sources of her opulence; we shall shake her power, and reduce her to her real value; we shall extend our commerce, our shipping, our fisheries; we shall ensure the possession of our islands, and finally, we shall re-establish our reputation, and shall resume amongst the Powers of Europe the place which belongs to us. There would be no end if we wished to detail all these points; it is sufficient to indicate them in order to make their importance felt.

In presupposing that the independence of the Americans is to be the work of France, it is necessary to examine what line of conduct it is desirable for us to observe in order to attain that end; there is but one,—to assist the Colonies.

But in order to determine the sort of assistance to be given, it is essential not to deviate from the two following truths: 1st, that whatever sort of assistance we give the Americans, it will be equivalent to a declaration of war against Great Britain: 2nd that when war is inevitable, it is better to be beforehand with one's enemy than to be anticipated by him.

Starting with these two principles, it appears that France cannot be too quick in making with the Americans a treaty of which recognised independence will be the basis, and that she should take her measures for acting before England can anticipate her.

It is all the more urgent to hasten the arrangements to be made with the Americans, as the Deputies are hard pressed by emissaries of the English Ministry, and as, if we are not the first to bind them, they will give the Court of London a foundation for proposing a plan of reconciliation at the re-assembly of Parliament, which will take place on the 20th instant, and then all will be over with us, and it will only remain for us to prepare to undertake war against the English and against the insurgents, whereas we could and ought to have begun it in concert with the latter.

In all that has just been said, the co-operation of Spain has been presupposed.

But in the event of that Power not adopting the principles and plan of France, or of her judging the moment of putting it into execution not yet arrived, what course will France, thus isolated, have to follow?

The independence of the Colonies is so important a matter for France, that no other should weaken it, and France must do her utmost to establish it, even if it should cost her some sacrifices; I mean that France must undertake the war for the maintenance of American independence, even if that war should be in other respects disadvantageous. In order to be convinced of this truth, it is only necessary to picture to ourselves what England will be, when she no longer has America.

Thus France must espouse the American cause, and use for that purpose all her power, even if Spain should refuse to join her. From this one of two things will happen; either that Power will still remain neutral, or she will decide to join France. In the first case, although she will be passive, she will nevertheless favour our operations, because she will be armed, and England will see her constantly placed behind us, and ready, if need be, to assist us: but in order to maintain this opinion, we must also maintain that of a good understanding between the two Courts. The second case has no need of development.

But Spain is awaiting a rich fleet from Vera Cruz, and that fleet will not arrive until about next spring. Its arrival must unquestionably be ensured, and that may be done in two ways; 1st by prolonging the period of our operations, or else, 2nd, by sending a squadron to meet the fleet. Spain has vessels at Cadiz and Ferrol; they are armed and ready to put to sea. A cruise might be given as a pretext in order to mask their real destination.

If the King adopts the course of going forward without the participation of Spain, he will take away from that Power all just reason for complaint, by stipulating for her eventually all the advantages which she would have claimed, had she been a contracting party. These advantages will be the same as those which His Majesty will ask for himself.

Franklin, Lee, and Deane signed the treaty of alliance on February 6, 1778. Source: Hunter Miller (ed.), Treaties and Other International Acts of the United States of America (8 vols., Washington, D.C., 1931–48), II, 35–40. For the treaty of amity and commerce concluded the same day, see below, Part III, pp. 48–53.

The most Christian King and the United States of North America, to wit, Newhampshire, Massachusetts Bay, Rhodes island, Connecticut, Newyork, New Jersey, Pennsylvania, Delaware, Maryland, Virginia, North Carolina, South Carolina, and Georgia, having this Day concluded a Treaty of amity and Commerce, for the reciprocal advantage of their Subjects and Citizens have thought it necessary to take into consideration the means of strongthening those engagements and of rondring them useful to the safety and tranquility of the two parties, particularly in case Great Britain in Resentment of that connection and of the good correspondence which is the object of the said Treaty, should break the Peace with france, either by direct hostilities, or by hindring her commerce and navigation, in a manner contrary to the Rights of Nations, and the Peace subsisting between the two Crowns; and his Majesty and the said united States having resolved in that Case to join their Councils and efforts against the Enterprises of their common Enemy, the respective Plenipotentiaries, impower'd to concert the Clauses & conditions proper to fulfil the said Intentions, have, after the most mature Deliberation, concluded and determined on the following Articles.

Art. 1

If War should break out betwan france and Great Britain, during the continuance of the present War betwan the United States and England, his Majesty and the said united States, shall make it a common cause, and aid each other mutually with their good Offices, their Counsels, and their forces, according to the exigence of Conjunctures as becomes good & faithful Allies.

Art. 2

The essential and direct End of the present defensive alliance is to maintain effectually the liberty, Sovereignty, and independance absolute and unlimited of the said united States, as well in Matters of Gouvernement as of commerce.

Art. 3

The two contracting Parties shall each on its own Part, and in the manner it may judge most proper, make all the efforts in its Power, against their common Ennemy, in order to attain the end proposed. . . .

Art. 5

If the united States should think fit to attempt the Reduction of the British Power remaining in the Northern Parts of America, or the Islands of Bermudas, those Contries or Islands in case of Success, shall be confederated with or dependant upon the said united States.

Art. 6

The Most Christian King renounces for ever the possession of the Islands of Bermudas as well as of any part of the continent of North america which before the treaty of Paris in 1763 or in virtue of that Treaty, were acknowledged to belong to the Crown of Great Britain, or to the united States heretofore called British Colonies, or which are at this Time or have lately been under the Power of The King and Crown of Great Britain.

Art. 7

If his Most Christian Majesty shall think proper to attack any of the Islands situated in the Gulph of Mexico, or near that Gulph, which are at present under the Power of Great Britain, all the said Isles, in case of success, shall appertain to the Crown of france.

Art. 8

Neither of the two Parties shall conclude either Truce or Peace with Great Britain, without the formal consent of the other first obtain'd; and they mutually engage not to lay down their arms, until the Independence of the united states shall have been formally or tacitly assured by the Treaty or Treaties that shall terminate the War. . . .

Art. 11

The two Parties guarantee mutually from the present time and forever, against all other powers, to wit, the united states to his most Christian Majesty the present Possessions of the Crown of france in America as well as those which it may acquire by the future Treaty of peace: and his most Christian Majesty guarantees on his part to the united states, their liberty, Sovereignty, and Independence absolute, and unlimited, as well in Matters of Government as commerce and also thair Possessions, and the additions or conquests that their Confederation may obtain during the war, from any of the Dominions now or heretofore possessed by Great Britain in North America, conformable to the 5th & 6th articles above written, the whole as their Possessions shall be fixed and assured to the said States at the moment of the cessation of their present War with England. . . .

3. A little impropriety

After signing "the preliminaries" of a peace treaty with the British representative Richard Oswald, the peace commissioners—Franklin, John Adams, John Jay, and Henry Laurens—explained their action in a letter of December 14, 1782, to the secretary for foreign affairs, Robert R. Livingston. After all, Article 8 of the treaty of alliance now was in ques-

tion. Livingston also had instructed the commissioners to concert their diplomacy with the French court. Source: Charles Francis Adams (ed.), The Works of John Adams (10 vols., Boston, 1850–56), VIII, 18–20. The preliminary articles negotiated with Oswald received incorporation in the definitive Anglo-American treaty signed on September 3, 1783, the same day the British concluded peace treaties with France and Spain. The separate article mentioned in the letter to Livingston related to the boundary of the United States with Florida, should the British manage to reconquer that territory from Spain; the British failed to do so, and the article lapsed. For maps showing the boundaries achieved in the negotiation with Oswald, see below, pp. 38–39.

We have the honor to congratulate congress on the signature of the preliminaries of a peace between the Crown of Great Britain and the United States of America, to be inserted in a definitive treaty so soon as the terms between the Crowns of France and Great Britain shall be agreed on. A copy of the articles is here inclosed, and we cannot but flatter ourselves that they will appear to congress, as they do to all of us, to be consistent with the honor and interest of the United States, and we are persuaded congress would be more fully of that opinion, if they were apprised of all the circumstances and reasons which have influenced the negotiation. Although it is impossible for us to go into that detail, we think it necessary, nevertheless, to make a few remarks on such of the articles as appear most to require elucidation.

Remarks on Article 2d, relative to Boundaries

The Court of Great Britain insisted on retaining all the territories comprehended within the Province of Quebec, by the act of parliament respecting it. They contended that Nova Scotia should extend to the River Kennebec; and they claimed not only all the lands in the western country and on the Mississippi, which were not expressly included in our charters and governments, but also such lands within them as remained ungranted by the King of Great Britain. It would be endless to enumerate all the discussions and arguments on the subject.

We knew this Court and Spain to be against our claims to the western country, and having no reason to think that lines more favorable could ever have been obtained, we finally agreed to those described in this article; indeed, they appear to leave us little to complain of, and not much to desire. Congress will observe, that although our northern line is in a certain part below the latitude of forty-five, yet in others it extends above it, divides the Lake Superior, and gives us access to its western and southern waters, from which a line in that latitude would have excluded us.

Remarks on Article 4th, respecting Creditors

We had been informed that some of the States had confiscated British debts; but although each State has a right to bind its own citizens, yet, in our opinion, it appertains solely to congress, in whom exclusively are vested the rights of making war and peace, to pass acts against the subjects of a power with which the confederacy may be at war. It therefore only remained for us to consider, whether this article is founded in justice and good policy.

In our opinion, no acts of government could dissolve the obligations of good faith resulting from lawful contracts between individuals of the two countries, prior to the war. We knew that some of the British creditors were making common cause with the refugees and other adversaries of our independence; besides, sacrificing private justice to reasons of state and political convenience, is always an odious measure; and the purity of our reputation in this respect, in all foreign commercial countries, is of infinitely more importance to us than all the sums in question. It may also be remarked, that American and British creditors are placed on an equal footing.

Remarks on Articles 5th and 6th, respecting Refugees

These articles were among the first discussed and the last agreed to. And had not the conclusion of this business at the time of its date been particularly important to the British administration, the respect, which both in London and Versailles, is supposed to be due to the honor, dignity, and interest of royalty, would probably have forever prevented our bringing this article so near to the views of congress and the sovereign rights of the States as it now stands. When it is considered that it was utterly impossible to render this article perfectly consistent, both with American and British ideas of honor, we presume that the middle line adopted by this article, is as little unfavorable to the former as any that could in reason be expected.

As to the separate article, we beg leave to observe, that it was our policy to render the navigation of the River Mississippi so important to Britain as that their views might correspond with ours on that subject. Their possessing the country on the river north of the line from the Lake of the Woods affords a foundation for their claiming such navigation. And as the importance of West Florida to Britain was for the same reason rather to be strengthened than otherwise, we thought it advisable to allow them the extent contained in the separate article, especially as before the war it had been annexed by Britain to West Florida, and would operate as an additional inducement to their joining with us in agreeing that the navigation of the river should forever remain open to both. The map used in the course of our negotiations was Mitchell's.

As we had reason to imagine that the articles respecting the boundaries, the refugees, and fisheries, did not correspond with the policy of this Court, we did not communicate the preliminaries to the minister until after they were signed; (and not even then the *separate article*). We hope that these considerations will excuse our having so far deviated from the spirit of our instructions. The Count de Vergennes, on perusing the articles appeared surprised, (but not displeased), at their being so favorable to us.

We beg leave to add our advice, that copies be sent us of the accounts directed to be taken by the different States, of the unnecessary devastations and sufferings sustained by them from the enemy in the course of the war. Should they arrive before the signature of the definitive treaty, they might possibly answer very good purposes.

Shocked at the liberal concessions the British had made to the Americans, the Comte de Vergennes urged the peace commissioners not to send the text of the preliminary treaty to Congress. The commissioners nonetheless applied to the British government for a passport for protection of the dispatch ship Washington, and received it. In a cheeky note, Franklin apprised the foreign minister of the passport and said that the Washington afforded a safe conveyance for any part of the loan that the United States lately had requested of France. There followed Vergennes's letter of December 15, 1782. Source: Albert H. Smyth (ed.), The Writings of Benjamin Franklin (10 vols., New York, 1905–7), VIII, 641.

I cannot but be surprised, that, after the explanation I have had with you, and the promise you gave, that you would not press the application for an English passport for the sailing of the packet

Washington, you now inform me, that you have received the passport, and that at ten o'clock to-morrow morning your courier will set out to carry your despatches. I am at a loss, Sir, to explain your conduct, and that of your colleagues on this occasion. You have concluded your preliminary articles without any communication between us, although the instructions from Congress prescribe, that nothing shall be done without the participation of the King. You arc about to hold out a certain hope of peace to America, without even informing yourself on the state of the negotiation on our part.

You are wise and discreet, Sir; you perfectly understand what is due to propriety; you have all your life performed your duties. I pray you to consider how you propose to fulfil those, which are due to the King? I am not desirous of enlarging these reflections; I commit them to your own integrity. When you shall be pleased to relieve my uncertainty, I will entreat the King to enable me to answer your demands.

Franklin responded two days later. Source: ibid., 642–643.

I received the letter your Excellency did me the honour of writing to me on the 15th instant. The proposal of having a passport from England was agreed to by me the more willingly, as I at that time had hopes of obtaining some money to send in the Washington, and the passport would have made its transportation safer, with that of our despatches, and of yours also, if you had thought fit to make use of the occasion. Your Excellency objected, as I understood it, that the English ministers, by their letters sent in the same ship, might convey inconvenient expectations into America. It was therefore I proposed not to press for the passport till your preliminaries were also agreed to. They have sent the passport without being pressed to do it, and they have sent no letters to go under it, and ours will prevent the inconvenience apprehended. In a subsequent conversation, your Excellency mentioned your intention of sending some of the King's cutters, whence I imagined, that detaining the Washington was no longer necessary; and it was certainly incumbent on us to give Congress as early an account as possible of our proceedings, who will think it extremely strange to hear of them by other means, without a line from us. I acquainted your Excellency, however, with our intention of despatching that ship, supposing you might possibly have something to send by her.

Nothing has been agreed in the preliminaries contrary to the interests of France; and no peace is to take place between us and England, till you have concluded yours. Your observation is, however, apparently just, that, in not consulting you before they were signed, we been guilty of neglecting a point of *bienséance*. But, as this was not from want of respect for the King, whom we all love and honour, we hope it will be excused, and that the great work, which has hitherto been so happily conducted, is so nearly brought to perfection, and is so glorious to his reign, will not be ruined by a single indiscretion of ours. And certainly the whole edifice sinks to the ground immediately, if you refuse on that account to give us any further assistance.

We have not yet despatched the ship, and I beg leave to wait upon you on Friday for your answer.

It is not possible for any one to be more sensible than I am, of what I and every American owe to the King, for the many and great benefits and favours he has bestowed upon us. All my letters to America are proofs of this; all tending to make the same impressions on the minds of my countrymen, that I felt in my own. And I believe, that no Prince was ever more beloved and respected by his own subjects, than the King is by the people of the United States. *The English, I just now learn, flatter themselves they have already divided us.* I hope this little misunderstanding will therefore be kept a secret, and that they will find themselves totally mistaken.

4. The Treaty of Paris

The American peace commissioners, with the exception of Laurens who was in England, signed the definitive Treaty of Paris on September 3, 1783. Source: Miller (ed.), Treaties and Other International Acts . . . , II, 151–155.

In the Name of the most Holy & undivided Trinity.

It having pleased the divine Providence to dispose the Hearts of the most Serene and most Potent Prince George the third, by the

Grace of God, King of Great Britain, France & Ireland, Defender of the Faith, Duke of Brunswick and Lunebourg, Arch Treasurer, and Prince Elector of the Holy Roman Empire &cᵃ and of the United States of America, to forget all past Misunderstandings and Differences that have unhappily interrupted the good Correspondence and Friendship which they mutually wish to restore; and to establish such a beneficial and satisfactory Intercourse between the two Countries upon the Ground of reciprocal Advantages and mutual Convenience as may promote and secure to both perpetual Peace & Harmony, and having for this desirable End already laid the Foundation of Peace & Reconciliation by the Provisional Articles signed at Paris on the 30ᵗʰ of Novʳ 1782. by the Commissioners empower'd on each Part, which Articles were agreed to be inserted in and to constitute the Treaty of Peace proposed to be concluded between the Crown of Great Britain and the said United States, but which Treaty was not to be concluded until Terms of Peace should be agreed upon between Great Britain & France, And his Britannic Majesty should be ready to conclude such Treaty accordingly: and the Treaty between Great Britain & France having since been concluded, His Britannic Majesty & the United States of America, in Order to carry into full Effect the Provisional Articles abovementioned, according to the Tenor thereof, have constituted & appointed, that is to say His Britannic Majesty on his Part, David Hartley Esqʳ, Member of the Parliament of Great Britain; and the said United States on their Part, John Adams Esqʳ, late a Commissioner of the United States of America at the Court of Versailles, late Delegate in Congress from the State of Massachusetts and Chief Justice of the said State, and Minister Plenipotentiary of the said United States to their High Mightinesses the States General of the United Netherlands; Benjamin Franklin Esqʳᵉ late Delegate in Congress from the State of Pennsylvania, President of the Convention of the sᵈ State, and Minister Plenipotentiary from the United States of America at the Court of Versailles; John Jay Esqʳᵉ late President of Congress, and Chief Justice of the State of New-York & Minister Plenipotentiary from the said United States at the Court of Madrid; to be the Plenipotentiaries for the concluding and signing the Present Definitive Treaty; who after having reciprocally communicated their respective full Powers have agreed upon and confirmed the following Articles.

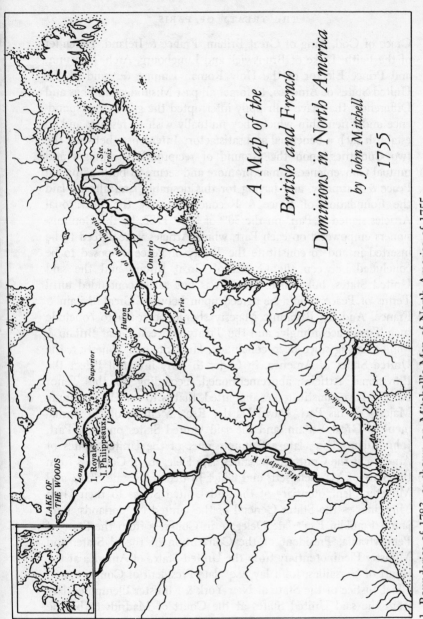

1. Boundaries of 1783, as shown on Mitchell's Map of North America of 1755.

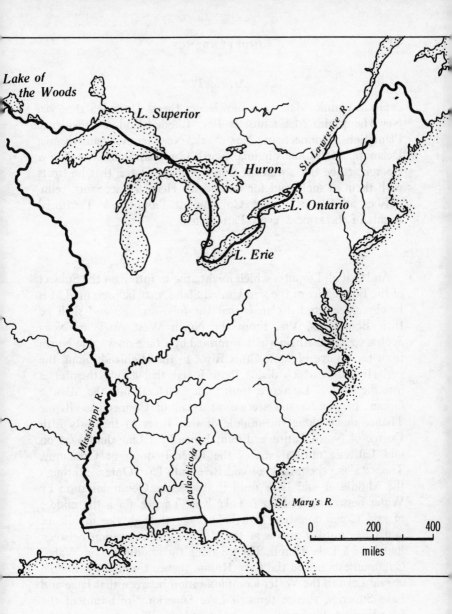

2. Boundaries of 1783, as shown on a modern map.

Article 1st

His Britannic Majesty acknowledges the s^d United States, viz. New-Hampshire Massachusetts Bay, Rhode-Island & Providence Plantations, Connecticut, New York, New Jersey, Pennsylvania, Delaware, Maryland, Virginia, North Carolina, South Carolina & Georgia, to be free sovereign & Independent States; that he treats with them as such, and for himself his Heirs & Successors, relinquishes all Claims to the Government Propriety & Territorial Rights of the same & every Part thereof.

Article 2^d

And that all Disputes which might arise in future on the Subject of the Boundaries of the said United States, may be prevented, it is hereby agreed and declared, that the following are and shall be their Boundaries, Viz. From the North West Angle of Nova Scotia, viz. That Angle which is formed by a Line drawn due North from the Source of Saint Croix River to the Highlands along the said Highlands which divide those Rivers that empty themselves into the River St Lawrence, from those which fall into the Atlantic Ocean, to the Northwestern-most Head of Connecticut River: Thence down along the middle of that River to the forty fifth Degree of North Latitude; From thence by a Line due West on said Latitude until it strikes the River Iroquois or Cataraquy; Thence along the middle of said River into Lake Ontario; through the Middle of said Lake until it strikes the Communication by Water between that Lake & Lake Erie; Thence along the middle of said Communication into Lake Erie; through the middle of said Lake, until it arrives at the Water Communication between that Lake & Lake Huron; Thence along the middle of said Water-Communication into the Lake Huron, thence through the middle of said Lake to the Water Communication between that Lake and Lake Superior, thence through Lake Superior Northward of the Isles Royal & Phelipeaux to the Long Lake; Thence through the Middle of said Long-Lake, and the Water Communication between it & the Lake of the Woods, to the said Lake of the Woods; Thence through the said Lake to the most Northwestern Point thereof, and from thence on a due West Course to the River Mississippi, Thence by a Line to be drawn along the Middle of the said River Mississippi until it shall intersect the Northernmost Part of the thirty first Degree of North Latitude. South, by a Line to be drawn due East from the Determination of the Line last mentioned, in the Latitude of thirty one Degrees North of the Equator to the middle of the River Apalachicola or Catahouche. Thence along the middle thereof to its Junction with the Flint River; Thence strait to the Head of St Mary's River, and thence down along the middle of St Mary's River to the Atlantic Ocean. East, by a Line to be drawn along the Middle of the River St Croix from its Mouth in the Bay of Fundy to its Source; and from its Source directly North to the aforesaid Highlands, which divide the Rivers that fall into the Atlantic Ocean, from those which fall into the River St Lawrence; comprehending all Islands within twenty Leagues of any Part of the Shores of the United States, & lying between Lines to be drawn due East from the Points where the aforesaid Boundaries between Nova Scotia on the one Part and East Florida on the other, shall respectively touch the Bay of Fundy and the Atlantic Ocean, excepting such Islands as now are or heretofore have been within the Limits of the said Province of Nova Scotia.

Article 3^d

It is agreed that the People of the United States shall continue to enjoy unmolested the Right to take Fish of every kind on the Grand Bank and on all the other Banks of New-foundland, also in the Gulph of St Lawrence, and at all other Places in the Sea where the Inhabitants of both Countries used at any time heretofore to fish. And also that the Inhabitants of the United States shall have Liberty to take Fish of every Kind on such Part of the Coast of New-foundland as British Fishermen shall use, (but not to dry or cure the same on that Island) And also on the Coasts Bays & Creeks of all other of his Britannic Majesty's Dominions in America, and that the American Fishermen shall have Liberty to dry and cure Fish in any of the unsettled Bays Harbours and Creeks of Nova Scotia, Magdalen Islands, and Labrador, so long as the same shall remain unsettled but so soon as the same or either of them shall be settled, it shall not be lawful for the said Fishermen to dry or cure Fish at such Settlement without a previous Agreement for that purpose with the Inhabitants, Proprietors or Possessors of the Ground.

Article 4ᵗʰ

It is agreed that Creditors on either Side shall meet with no lawful Impediment to the Recovery of the full Value in Sterling Money of all bona fide Debts heretofore contracted.

Article 5ᵗʰ

It is agreed that the Congress shall earnestly recommend it to the Legislatures of the respective States to provide for the Restitution of all Estates, Rights and Properties which have been confiscated belonging to real British Subjects; and also of the Estates Rights and Properties of Persons resident in Districts in the Possession of his Majesty's Arms, and who have not borne Arms against the said United States. And that Persons of any other Description shall have free Liberty to go to any Part or Parts of any of the thirteen United States and therein to remain twelve Months unmolested in their Endeavours to obtain the Restitution of such of their Estates Rights & Properties as may have been confiscated. And that Congress shall also earnestly recommend to the several States, a Reconsideration and Revision of all Acts or Laws regarding the Premises, so as to render the said Laws or Acts perfectly consistent, not only with Justice and Equity, but with that Spirit of Conciliation, which, on the Return of the Blessings of Peace should universally prevail. And that Congress shall also earnestly recommend to the several States, that the Estates, Rights and Properties of such last mentioned Persons shall be restored to them, they refunding to any Persons who may be now in Possession, the Bonâ fide Price (where any has beene given) which such Persons may have paid on purchasing any of the said Lands, Rights or Properties, since the Confiscation.

And it is agreed that all Persons who have any Interest in confiscated Lands, either by Debts, Marriage Settlements, or otherwise, shall meet with no lawful Impediment in the Prosecution of their just Rights.

Article 6ᵗʰ

That there shall be no future Confiscations made nor any Prosecutions commenc'd against any Person or Persons for or by Reason of the Part, which he or they may have taken in the present War, and that no Person shall on that Account suffer any future Loss or Damage, either in his Person Liberty or Property; and that those who may be in Confinement on such Charges at the Time of the Ratification of the Treaty in America shall be immediately set at Liberty, and the Prosecutions so commenced be discontinued.

Article 7th

There shall be a firm and perpetual Peace between his Britannic Majesty and the said States and between the Subjects of the one, and the Citizens of the other, wherefore all Hostilities both by Sea and Land shall from henceforth cease: All Prisoners on both Sides shall be set at Liberty, and his Britannic Majesty shall with all convenient speed, and without causing any Destruction, or carrying away any Negroes or other Property of the American Inhabitants, withdraw all his Armies, Garrisons & Fleets from the said United States, and from every Port, Place and Harbour within the same; leaving in all Fortifications the American Artillery that may be therein: And shall also Order & cause all Archives, Records, Deeds & Papers belonging to any of the said States, or their Citizens, which in the Course of the War may have fallen into the Hands of his Officers, to be forthwith restored and deliver'd to the proper States and Persons to whom they belong.

Article 8th

The Navigation of the River Mississippi, from its source to the Ocean shall for ever remain free and open to the Subjects of Great Britain and the Citizens of the United States. . . .

III

Commerce

The French memorandum of January 1778 quoted in Part II, re-marked with acumen that the United States "took up arms only in order to establish and defend their independence and the freedom of their commerce." That latter purpose was second in importance to independence. The Americans wished to establish their positions in the world as a great carrier of commerce, which meant gaining access to the imperial trade of Spain, France, and Great Britain. They wished not merely peacetime access, but freedom to trade with the European nations and empires even in time of European war. War naturally would bring some restriction on the trade of vessels belonging to the neutral United States, but the Americans desired belligerents to proceed toward neutral commerce in as restricted a manner as possible.

5. The treaty plans of 1776 and 1784

Ever since the late Middle Ages a body of legal claims and precedents had been accumulating to protect merchants upon the seas in time of war, and the Americans at the outset of independence moved to support these "neutral rights." The small-navy powers of the eighteenth century, including France, favored liberal trading rights for neutrals in wartime. The British demurred, as any stiffening of international law—which had to occur, of course, either in bilateral treaties of so-called leagues of neutrals—would reduce the importance of British seapower. The plan of September 17, 1776, was a model treaty for negotiation with the king of France, "the most Christian King." Its articles are rather technical, hence their prefacing with bracketed explanations. The reader should bear in mind that no prospective neutral in a future war, even the ambitious Americans, claimed a right to trade in contraband goods or in blockaded ports. Source: Carlton Savage (ed.), Policy of the United States toward Maritime Commerce in War (2 vols., Washington, D.C., 1934), I, 132–134.

... [Free (that is, neutral) ships make free goods, with exception of contraband] The Merchant Ship of either of the Parties, which shall be making into a Port belonging to the Enemy of the other Ally, and concerning whose Voyage, and the Species of Goods on board her, there shall be just Grounds of Suspicion, shall be obliged to exhibit, as well upon the high Seas as in the Ports and Havens, not only her Passports, but like wise Certificates, expressly shewing that her Goods are not of the Number of those which have been prohibited, as Contraband.

. . . If by the exhibiting of the above Certificates, the other Party discover there are any of those Sorts of Goods, which are prohibited and declared Contraband, and consigned for a Port under the obedience of his Enemies, it shall not be lawfull to break up the Hatches of such Ship, or to open any Chest, Coffers, Packs, Casks, or any other Vessells found therein or to remove the smallest Parcells of her Goods, whether such Ship belong to the subjects of France, or the Inhabitants of the said United States, unless the lading be brought on Shore in the Presence of the officers of the Court of Admiralty, and an Inventory thereof made; but there shall be no allowance to sell, exchange, or alienate the same in any manner, untill after that due and lawfull Process shall have been had against such prohibited Goods, and the Courts of Admiralty shall, by a Sentence pronounced, have confiscated the same, saving always as well the Ship itself, as any other Goods found therein, which by this Treaty, are to be esteemed free, neither may they be detained on Pretence of their being as it were infected by the prohibited Goods, much less shall they be confiscated as lawfull Prize: But if not the whole Cargo, but only Part thereof shall consist of prohibited or contraband Goods, and the Commander of the Ship shall be ready and willing to deliver them to the Captor who has discovered them, in such Case the Captor having received those Goods, shall forthwith discharge the Ship, and not hinder her by any Means freely to prosecute the Voyage on which she was bound.

. . . [Enemy ships make enemy goods, unless neutrals are unaware of a declaration of war] On the Contrary, it is agreed, that whatever shall be found to be laden by the Subjects and Inhabitants of either Party, on any Ship belonging to the Enemy of the other, or to his Subjects, although it be not of the Sort of prohibited Goods, may be confiscated in the same Manner as if it belonged to the Enemy himself, except such Goods and Merchandise as were put on board such Ship before the Declaration of War, or even after such

Declaration, if so be it were done without Knowledge of such Declaration. So that the Goods of the Subjects or People of either Party, whether they be of the Nature of such as are prohibited, or otherwise which, as is aforesaid, were put on board any Ship belonging to an Enemy before the War, or after the Declaration of it, without the Knowledge of it, shall no wise be liable to Confiscation, but shall well and truly be restored without delay to the Proprietors demanding the same; but so as that if the said Merchandises be contraband, it shall not be any Ways lawfull to carry them afterwards to any Ports belonging to the Enemy.

. . . [Right of neutrals to trade with belligerents, even from one belligerent port to another] It shall be lawfull for all and Singular the Subjects of the most Christian King, and the Citizens, People, and Inhabitants of the said States, to Sail with their Ships, with all manner of Liberty and Security; no distinction being made, who are the Proprietors of the Merchandizes laden thereon from any Port, to the Places of those who now are, or hereafter shall be at Enmity with the most Christian King, or the United States. It shall likewise be lawfull for the Subjects and Inhabitants aforesaid, to sail with the Ships and Merchandizes aforementioned; and to trade with the same Liberty, and Security, from the Places, Ports, and Havens of those who are Enemies of both or either Party, without any opposition or Disturbance whatsoever, not only directly from the Places of the Enemy aforementioned to neutral Places; but also from one Place belonging to an Enemy, to another Place belonging to an Enemy, whether they be under the Jurisdiction of the same Prince or under Several: And it is hereby Stipulated that free Ships shall also give a Freedom to Goods, and that every Thing shall be deemed to be free and exempt, which shall be found on board the Ships, belonging to the Subjects of either of the Confederates; although the whole Lading or any Part thereof, should appertain to the Enemies of Either, Contraband Goods being always excepted. It is also agreed in like manner, that the same Liberty, be extended to Persons, who are on board a free Ship with this Effect, that although they be Enemies to both or either Party, they are not to be taken out of that free Ship, unless they are Soldiers, and in actual Service of the Enemies.

. . . [Tight definition of contraband, excluding foodstuffs and naval stores] This Liberty of Navigation and Commerce shall extend to all Kinds of Merchandizes, excepting those only which are distinguished by the Name of Contraband: and under this Name of Contraband, or prohibited Goods, shall be comprehended Arms, Great Guns, Bombs with their Fuzees, and other Things belonging to them; Fire Balls, Gunpowder, Match, Cannon Ball, Pikes, Swords, Lances, Spears, Halberds, Mortars, Petards, Granadoes, Saltpetre, Musketts, Muskett Balls, Helmets, Head Pieces, Breast Plates, Coats of Mail, and the like Kind of Arms proper for arming Soldiers, Muskett rests, Belts, Horses with their Furniture, and all other war like Instruments whatsoever. These Merchandizes which follow, shall not be reckoned among Contraband or prohibited Goods; that is to Say, all Sorts of Cloths, and all other Manufactures woven of any Wool, Flax, Silk, Cotton, or any other Material whatever; all Kinds of Wearing apparell, together with the Species whereof they are used to be made; Gold and Silver, as well coined as uncoined, Tin, Iron, Lead, Copper, Brass, Coals; as also Wheat and Barley, and any other Kind of Corn and Pulse; Tobacco, and likewise all manner of Spices; Salted and Smoked Flesh, Salted Fish, Cheese and Butter, Beer, Oils, Wines, Sugars, and all Sorts of Salt; and in general, all Provisions which Serve for the Nourishment of Mankind, and the Sustenance of Life: Furthermore, all Kinds of Cotton, Hemp, Flax, Tar, Pitch, Ropes, Cables, Sails, Sail Cloth, Anchors, and any Parts of Anchors; also Ships' Masts, Planks, Boards, and Beams, of what Tree Soever; and all other Things proper either for building or repairing Ships, and all other Goods whatsoever which have not been worked into the Form of any Instrument or Thing prepared for War, by Land or by Sea, shall not be reputed Contraband, much less such as have been already wrought and made up for any other use; all which shall wholly be reckoned among free Goods; as likewise all other Merchandizes and Things which are not comprehended, and particularly mentioned in the foregoing Enumeration of Contraband Goods; So that they may be transported and carried in the freest Manner by the Subjects of both Confederates, even to Places belonging to an Enemy, such Towns and Places being only excepted as are at that time besieged, blocked up, or invested.

The treaty plan of May 7, 1784, sought to define blockade. Source: ibid., 159.

. . . [A blockade means "imminent danger"] And that to ascertain what shall constitute the blockade of any place or port, it shall be understood to be in such predicament, when the assailing power shall have taken such a station as to expose to imminent danger any ship or ships that would attempt to sail in or out of the said port . . .

6. The French treaty

The first commercial treaty negotiated by diplomats of the United States was with France, signed on February 6, 1778, the same day as the alliance. Not unexpectedly, it recognized the American view of neutral rights. Source: Miller (ed.), Treaties and Other International Acts . . . , II, 3–5, 8–9, 12–17, 19–23, 26. Article 31 led to the consular convention of 1788, for which see ibid., 228–241.

The most Christian King, and the thirteen United States of North America, to wit, New-Hampshire, Massachusetts Bay, Rhodeisland, Connecticut, New York, New-Jersey, Pennsylvania, Delaware, Maryland, Virginia, North-Carolina, South Carolina, & Georgia, willing to fix in an equitable and permanent manner the Rules which ought to be followed relative to the Correspondence & Commerce which the two Parties desire to establish between their respective Countries, States, and Subjects, his most Christian Majesty and the said United States have judged that the said End could not be better obtained than by taking for the Basis of their Agreement the most perfect Equality and Reciprocity, and by carefully avoiding all those burthensome Preferences, which are usually Sources of Debate, Embarrasment and Discontent; by leaving also each Party at Liberty to make, respecting Commerce and Navigation, those interior Regulations which it shall find most convenient to itself; and by founding the Advantage of Commerce solely upon reciprocal Utility, and the just Rules of free Intercourse; reserving withal to each Party the Liberty of admitting at its pleasure other Nations to a Participation of the same Advantages. It is in the Spirit of this Intention, and to fulfil these Views, that his said Majesty having named and appointed for his Plenipotentiary Conrad Alexander Gerard, Royal *Sindic* of the City of Strasbourg, Secretary of his Majesty's Council of State, and the United States on their Part, having fully impower'd Benjamin Franklin Deputy from the State of Pennsylvania to the general Congress, and President of the Convention of said State, Silas Deane late Deputy from the State of Connecticut to the said Congress, and Arthur Lee Councellor at Law; The said respective Plenipotentiaries after exchanging their Powers, and after mature Deliberation, have concluded and agreed upon the following Articles. . . .

Art. 2

The most Christian King, and the United States engage mutually not to grant any particular Favour to other Nations in respect of Commerce and Navigation, which shall not immediately become common to the other Party, who shall enjoy the same Favour, freely, if the Concession was freely made, or on allowing the same Compensation, if the Concession was Conditional. . . .

Art. 8

The most Christian King will employ his good Offices and Interposition with the King or Emperor of Morocco or Fez, the Regencies of Algier, Tunis and Tripoli, or with any of them, and also with every other Prince, State or Power of the Coast of Barbary in Africa, and the Subjects of the said King Emperor, States and Powers, and each of them; in order to provide as fully and efficaciously as possible for the Benefit, Conveniency and Safety of the said United States, and each of them, their Subjects, People, and Inhabitants, and their Vessels and Effects, against all Violence, Insult, Attacks, or Depredations on the Part of the said Princes and States of Barbary, or their Subjects. . . .[1]

Art. 14

The merchant Ships of either of the Parties, which shall be making into a Port belonging to the Enemy of the other Ally and concerning whose Voyage & the Species of Goods on board her there shall be just Grounds of Suspicion shall be obliged to exhibit as well upon the high Seas as in the Ports and Havens not only her

[1] One of the problems of American independence was the forfeiture of British protection against the Barbary pirates. The United States at first sought to invoke non-British protection—from France in 1778, and perhaps from Spain (see John Jay's address to Congress in 1786, below, pp. 73–74) —and then tried appeasement and eventually sent out naval squadrons both before and after the War of 1812, with success after the latter conflict.

Passports, but likewise Certificates expressly shewing that her Goods are not of the Number of those, which have been prohibited as contraband.

Art. 15

If by the exhibiting of the above said Certificates, the other Party discover there are any of those Sorts of Goods, which are prohibited and declared contraband and consigned for a Port under the Obedience of his Enemies, it shall not be lawful to break up the Hatches of such Ship, or to open any Chest, Coffers, Packs, Casks, or any other Vessels found therein, or to remove the smallest Parcels of her Goods, whether such Ship belongs to the Subjects of France or the Inhabitants of the said United States, unless the lading be brought on Shore in the presence of the Officers of the Court of Admiralty and an Inventory thereof made; but there shall be no allowance to sell, exchange, or alienate the same in any manner, untill after that due and lawful Process shall have been had against such prohibited Goods, and the Court of Admiralty shall, by a Sentence pronounced, have confiscated the same: saving always as well the Ship itself as any other Goods found therein, which by this Treaty are to be esteemed free: neither may they be detained on pretence of their being as it were infected by the prohibited Goods, much less shall they be confiscated as lawful Prize: But if not the whole Cargo, but only part thereof shall consist of prohibited or contraband Goods and the Commander of the Ship shall be ready and willing to deliver them to the Captor, who has discovered them, in such Case the Captor having received those Goods shall forthwith discharge the Ship and not hinder her by any means freely to prosecute the Voyage, on which she was bound. But in Case the Contraband Merchandises, cannot be all receiv'd on board the Vessel of the Captor, then the Captor may, notwithstanding the Offer of delivering him the Contraband Goods, carry the Vessel into the nearest Port agreable to what is above directed.

Art. 16

On the contrary it is agreed, that whatever shall be found to be laden by the Subjects and Inhabitants of either Party on any Ship belonging to the Enemys of the other or to their Subjects, the whole although it be not of the Sort of prohibited Goods may be confiscated in the same manner, as if it belonged to the Enemy, except such Goods and Merchandizes as were put on board such Ship before the Declaration of War, or even after such Declaration, if so be it were done without knowledge of such Declaration. So that the Goods of the Subjects and People of either Party, whether they be of the Nature of such as are prohibited or otherwise, which, as is aforesaid were put on board any Ship belonging to an Enemy before the War, or after the Declaration of the same, without the Knowledge of it, shall no ways be liable to confiscation, but shall well and truely be restored without Delay to the proprietors demanding the same; but so as that, if the said Merchandizes be contraband, it shall not be any Ways lawful to carry them afterwards to any Ports belonging to the Enemy. The two contracting Parties agree, that the Term of two Months being passed after the Declaration of War, their respective Subjects, from whatever Part of the World they come, shall not plead the Ignorance mentioned in this Article. . . .

Art. 19

It shall be lawful for the Ships of War of either Party & Privateers freely to carry whithersoever they please the Ships and Goods taken from their Enemies, without being obliged to pay any Duty to the Officers of the Admiralty or any other Judges; nor shall such Prizes be arrested or seized, when they come to and enter the Ports of either Party; nor shall the Searchers or other Officers of those Places search the same or make examination concerning the Lawfulness of such Prizes, but they may hoist Sail at any time and depart and carry their Prizes to the Places express'd in their Commissions, which the Commanders of such Ships of War shall be obliged to shew: On the contrary no Shelter or Refuge shall be given in their Ports to such as shall have made Prize of the Subjects, People or Property of either of the Parties; but if such shall come in, being forced by Stress of Weather or the Danger of the Sea, all proper means shall be vigorously used that they go out and retire from thence as soon as possible. . . .

Art. 24

It shall not be lawful for any foreign Privateers, not belonging to Subjects of the most Christian King nor Citizens of the said United States, who have Commissions from any other Prince or

State in enmity with either Nation to fit their Ships in the Ports of either the one or the other of the aforesaid Parties, to sell what they have taken or in any other manner whatsoever to exchange their Ships, Merchandizes or any other lading; neither shall they be allowed even to purchase victuals except such as shall be necessary for their going to the next Port of that Prince or State from which they have Commissions.

Art. 25

It shall be lawful for all and singular the Subjects of the most Christian King and the Citizens People and Inhabitants of the said United States to sail with their Ships with all manner of Liberty and Security; no distinction being made, who are the Proprietors of the Merchandizes laden thereon, from any Port to the places of those who now are or hereafter shall be at Enmity with the most Christian King or the United States. It shall likewise be Lawful for the Subjects and Inhabitants aforesaid to sail with the Ships and Merchandizes aforementioned and to trade with the same Liberty and security from the Places, Ports and Havens of those who are Enemies of both or either Party without any Opposition or disturbance whatsoever, not only directly from the Places of the Enemy afore mentioned to neutral Places; but also from one Place belonging to an Enemy to another place belonging to an Enemy, whether they be under the Jurisdiction of the same Prince or under several; And it is hereby stipulated that free Ships shall also give a freedom to Goods, and that every thing shall be deemed to be free and exempt, which shall be found on board the Ships belonging to the Subjects of either of the Confederates, although the whole lading or any Part thereof should appertain to the Enemies of either, contraband Goods being always excepted. It is also agreed in like manner that the same Liberty be extended to Persons, who are on board a free Ship, with this Effect, that although they be Enemies to both or either Party, they are not to be taken out of that free Ship, unless they are Soldiers and in actual Service of the Enemies.

Art. 26

This Liberty of Navigation and Commerce shall extend to all kinds of Merchandizes, excepting those only which are distinguished by the name of contraband; And under this Name of

Contraband or prohibited Goods shall be comprehended, Arms, great Guns, Bombs with the fuzes, and other things belonging to them, Cannon Ball, Gun powder, Match, Pikes, Swords, Lances, Spears, halberds, Mortars, Petards, Granades Salt Petre, Muskets, Musket Ball, Bucklers, Helmets, breast Plates, Coats of Mail and the like kinds of Arms proper for arming Soldiers, Musket rests, belts, Horses with their Furniture, and all other Warlike Instruments whatever. These Merchandizes which follow shall not be reckoned among Contraband or prohibited Goods, that is to say, all sorts of Cloths, and all other Manufactures woven of any wool, Flax, Silk, Cotton or any other Materials whatever; all kinds of wearing Apparel together with the Species, whereof they are used to be made; gold & Silver as well coined as uncoin'd, Tin, Iron, Latten, Copper, Brass Coals, as also Wheat and Barley and any other kind of Corn and pulse; Tobacco and likewise all manner of Spices; salted and smoked Flesh, salted Fish, Cheese and Butter, Beer, Oils, Wines, Sugars and all sorts of Salts; & in general all Provisions, which serve for the nourishment of Mankind and the sustenence of Life; furthermore all kinds of Cotton, hemp, Flax, Tar, Pitch, Ropes, Cables, Sails, Sail Cloths, Anchors and any Parts of Anchors; also Ships Masts, Planks, Boards and Beams of what Trees soever; and all other Things proper either for building or repairing Ships, and all other Goods whatever, which have not been worked into the form of any Instrument or thing prepared for War by Land or by Sea, shall not be reputed Contraband, much less such as have been already wrought and made up for any other Use; all which shall be wholly reckoned among free Goods: as likewise all other Merchandizes and things, which are not comprehended and particularly mentioned in the foregoing enumeration of contraband Goods: so that they may be transported and carried in the freest manner by the Subjects of both Confederates even to Places belonging to an Enemy such Towns or Places being only excepted as are at that time beseiged, blocked up or invested. . . .

Art. 31

The two contracting Parties grant mutually the Liberty of having each in the Ports of the other, Consuls, Vice Consuls, Agents and Commissaries, whose Functions shall be regulated by a particular Agreement. . . .

7. Pressing the British

The czarina of Russia, Catherine II, in 1780 suggested an "armed neutrality" among the Baltic neutrals. This proposition held serious problems for the British, because a combination of the Danish, Swedish, and Russian navies would have been formidable. The czarina quickly abandoned the idea, and soon cynically was describing it as an armed nullity. Congress meanwhile in a resolution of September 26, 1780, jumped at the prospect of European support for neutral rights. Source: Worthington C. Ford, et al. (eds.), Journals of the Continental Congress: 1774–1789 (34 vols., Washington, D.C., 1904–37), XVIII, 864–866.

Congress took into consideration the report of the committee on the motion of Mr. [Samuel] Adams;

The Committee to whom was referred the motion of Mr Adams, Report that,

Whereas her Imperial Majesty of all the Russias, animated with the clearest sentiments of Justice, equity and moderation, and a strict regard to the unquestionable rights of neutrality and the most perfect freedom of Commerce that can consist with such neutrality has notified both to the belligerent and neutral Powers, the following propositions to which his Most Christian Majesty, the Illustrious ally of these United States and his Catholic Majesty two of the Belligerent Powers, and most of the neutral maritime Powers in Europe have acceded, to wit:

1. That Neutral vessels may sail, without being liable to molestation from port to port and along the coasts of nations at war.

2. That the effects belonging to the subjects of powers at war should be free in neutral vessels, excepting only contraband.

3. That in ascertaining what shall be deemed contraband the Empress will hold herself bound by that which is declared in the 10 and 11 articles of her Treaty of Commerce with Great Britain, and extend the obligations contained in those articles to all the powers at war.

4. That to determine when a port shall be said to be blocked up, this term shall only be applied to that where a sufficient number of vessels belonging to the power that invests it are stationed so near as evidently to render the entrance into it hazardous.

5. That the principles above stated ought to serve as a rule in all proceedings whenever there is a question concerning the legality of captures. . . .

Congress have considered the declaration of the Empress of all the Russias, relative to the rights of neutral vessels. The regulations it contains are useful, wise and just. The acts of a sovereign who promotes the happiness of her subjects and extends her views to the welfare of nations, who forms laws for a vast empire and corrects the great code of the world, claim the earliest attention of a rising republick; therefore,

Resolved, That the Board of Admiralty report instructions for the commanders of armed vessels commissioned by the United States, conformable to the principles contained in the said declaration.

Resolved, That copies of the above resolution be transmitted to the Ministers of the United States respectively, and to Monsr de Marbois, chargé des affaires, from his Most Christian Majesty.

At the end of the Revolution the American government hoped to make a commercial treaty with Great Britain. Difficulties arose, as the minister to London, John Adams, wrote to Secretary for Foreign Affairs John Jay, August 6, 1785. Source: Adams (ed.), The Works of John Adams, VIII, 289–291.

I find the spirit of the times very different from that which you and I saw, when we were here together, in the months of November and December, 1783.

Then, the commerce of the United States had not fully returned to these kingdoms; then, the nation had not digested its system, nor determined to adhere so closely to its navigation acts, relatively to the United States; then, it was common, in conversation, to hear a respect and regard for America professed and even boasted of.

Now, the boast is, that our commerce has returned to its old channels, and that it can follow in no other; now, the utmost contempt of our commerce is freely expressed in pamphlets, gazettes, coffee-houses, and in common street talk. I wish I could not add to this the discourses of cabinet counsellors and ministers of state, as well as members of both houses of parliament.

The national judgment and popular voice is so decided in favor of the navigation acts, that neither administration nor opposition dare avow a thought of relaxing them farther than has been already done. This decided cast has been given to the public opinion and the national councils by two facts, or rather presumptions. The first is, that in all events this country is sure of the American commerce. Even in case of war, they think that British manufactures will find their way to the United States through France, Holland, the Austrian low countries, Spain, Portugal, Sweden, the French and Dutch West Indies, and even through Canada and Nova Scotia. The second is, that the American States are not, and cannot be united. The landed interest will never join with the commercial nor the southern States with the northern, in any measures of retaliation or expressions of resentment. These things have been so often affirmed to this people by the refugees, and they have so often repeated them to one another, that they now fully believe them; and, I am firmly persuaded, they will try the experiment as long as they can maintain the credit of their stocks. It is our part, then, to try our strength. You know better than I do, whether the States will give congress the power, and whether congress, when they have the power, will judge it necessary or expedient to exert it, in its plenitude.

You were present in congress, sir, in 1774, when many members discussed in detail the commercial relations between the United States, then United Colonies, and Great Britain, Ireland, the British West Indies, and all other parts of the British empire, and showed to what a vast amount the wealth, power, and revenue of Great Britain would be affected by a total cessation of exports and imports. The British revenue is now in so critical a situation, that it might be much sooner and more essentially affected than it could be then. You remember, however, sir, that although the theory was demonstrated, the practice was found very difficult.

Britain has ventured to begin commercial hostilities. I call them hostilities, because their direct object is not so much the increase of their own wealth, ships, or sailors, as the diminution of ours. A jealousy of our naval power is the true motive, the real passion which actuates them; they consider the United States as their rival, and the most dangerous rival they have in the world. I see clearly they are less afraid of an augmentation of French ships and sailors than American.

They think they foresee, that if the United States had the same fisheries, the same carrying trade, and the same market for ready built ships, which they had ten years ago, they would be in so respectable a posture, and so happy in their circumstances, that their own seamen, manufacturers, and merchants, too, would hurry over to them.

If Congress should enter in earnest into this commercial war, it must necessarily be a long one, before it can fully obtain the victory; and it may excite passions on both sides which may break out into a military war. It is to be hoped, therefore, that the people and their councils will proceed with all the temperance and circumspection which such a state of things requires. I would not advise to this commercial struggle, if I could see a prospect of justice without it; but I do not; every appearance is on the contrary.

I have not, indeed, obtained any direct evidence of the intentions of the ministry, because I have received no answer to any of my letters to Lord Carmarthen; and, it seems to me, to press them at this juncture, with any great appearance of anxiety, would not be good policy. Let them hear a little more news from Ireland, France, and, perhaps, Spain, as well as America, which I think will operate in our favor.

An opportunity to press the British government into a treaty of commerce appeared momentarily in 1789–90. Organization of the new federal government under the Constitution gave Americans the ability to lay a tariff against British manufactures. Then the British were embarrassed by the prospect of a war with Spain over the Nootka Sound affair, wherein the Spanish had seized a British fur-trading establishment on Vancouver Island. President Washington commissioned Gouverneur Morris, then in Europe, to sound the British on a treaty. Morris spoke sharply to the ministry of William Pitt the younger, if we may judge from Morris's account of the London talks. But the Americans gained nothing. The Nootka crisis blew over; the Spanish gave in to an ultimatum from London. It is interesting that in the course of the crisis the American secretary of the treasury, Alexander Hamilton, held some conversation in New York with Major George Beckwith, a representative of the governor general of Canada. Toward the end of September 1790, Beckwith reported in cipher to his chief, Lord Dorchester, who sent the message on to London. Source: Julian P. Boyd, Number 7: Alexander Hamilton's Secret Attempts to Control American Foreign Policy (Princeton University Press: Princeton, N.J., 1964), pp. 156–158.

. . . 7. [Alexander Hamilton] 23. [Gouverneur Morris] is a man of capacity, but apt at particular times to give himself up too much to the impressions of his own mind.

From the Duke of Leeds's reply to 23.'s first application I confess I did not think favorably of the prospect, although it was far from being conclusive. The June packet brought us accounts of his interviews with Mr. Pitt, and from 23.'s own detail of what passed, there was a something in his conduct on that occasion, which I confess I do not altogether approve.

[Beckwith] "It strikes me as possible that 23. has been ocassionally out of England, has he been in France?"

[Hamilton] Not that I know of, and if 23. has cultivated an intimacy with the Ministers of any other power in Europe, or has caused suspicion on that ground with respect to France, or elsewhere, he has had no authority, for so doing; it occurs to me, that he was very intimate with Monsr. de La Luzerne the Ambassador of France now in London, when he was Minister in this country, possibly from that circumstance he may have been more frequently there, than prudence ought to have dictated, and the knowledge of this circumstance may have produced a greater reserve on the part of Your administration; these ideas strike me, although I have no grounds to go upon.

[Beckwith] "Do you wish to have a West India Island?"

[Hamilton] I answer without hesitation No, we do not, it is not in our contemplation. We wish the liberty of trading in that quarter, at least this is decidedly my own opinion, we should consider the Sovereignty of a West India island as a burthen. Our territories are already very extensive, and I can assure you, the idea of having possessions further to the northward than our present boundaries would be esteemed an incumbrance, with an exception to the Forts. On that score therefore I cannot foresee any solid grounds for a national difference with you; to the southward the case is very different. We look forward to procuring the means of an export for our western country, and we must have it. We cannot suffer the navigation of the Mississippi to remain long in its present state. That country is at this moment ready to open it if they met with the smallest encouragement, and undoubtedly we look forward to the possession of New Orleans.

[Beckwith] "Since my arrival here I have made it a point to preserve the strictest silence with respect to (23) yet I have more than once had occasion to hear his name mentioned by his relations and their acquaintances; it came out in their conversations that 23 is greatly liked in London, that he is frequently with the French Ambassador Monsieur de la Luzerne, and with Mr. Fox, who had expressed himself to be greatly pleased with his character and company."

[Hamilton] Yes, it is so reported; I believe it in some measure to be true; I am the more inclined to be of this way of thinking from extracts of letters, which I have seen of 23., in which he throws out, that such and such were Mr. Fox's opinions on partitcular subjects, and from the former intimacy, which subsisted here between 23 and Monsieur de la Luzerne, as well as from Mr. Fox's line of politics during the war, his general character, and from my knowledge of 23 himself.

I do not question this gentleman's sincerity in following up those objects committed to his charge, but to deal frankly with you, I have some doubts of his prudence; this is the point in which he is deficient, for in other respects he is a man of great genius, liable however to be occasionally influenced by his fancy, which sometimes outruns his discretion.

[Beckwith] "Mr. Fox is a very able man, very generally respected, and his character as a stateman is known in the world; but professing every possible respect for Mr. Fox, and for Mr. de la Luzerne likewise, it is for your consideration, how far a gentleman in 23. situation ought to form intimacies with persons in public political situations, excepting they are in administration."

[Hamilton] I am quite of your opinion, and this amongst other causes led me to remark, that it is greatly desirable, that this negotiation should be transferred to our seat of Government. However we have no reason on the whole to question Mr. Pitt's good dispositions towards us, on the contrary he seemed personally disposed to grant us more, than other members of your Cabinet thought advisable for your general commercial interests.

In a report to Washington dated December 15, 1790, Secretary of State Jefferson summed up the British position. Source: Paul Leicester Ford (ed.), The Writings of Thomas Jefferson (10 vols., New York, 1892–99), V, 261–263.

The Secretary of State having had under consideration the two letters of October 13th, 1789, from the President of the United States to Mr. Gouverneur Morris; and those of Mr. Morris to the President, of January 22d, April 7th, 13th, May 1st, 29th, July 3d, August 16th, and September 18th, referred to him by the President, makes the following report thereon:

The President's letter of January 22d, authorized Mr. Morris to enter into conference with the British ministers in order to discover their sentiments on the following subjects:

1. Their retention of the western posts contrary to the treaty of peace.

2. Indemnification for the negroes carried off against the stipulations of the same treaty.

3. A treaty for the regulation of the commerce between the two countries.

4. The exchange of a minister.

The letters of Mr. Morris before mentioned state the communications, oral and written, which have passed between him and the ministers; and from these the Secretary of State draws the following inferences:

1. That the British court is decided not to surrender the post[s] in any event; and that they will urge as a pretext that though our courts of justice are now open to British subjects, they were so long shut after the peace as to have defeated irremediably the recovery of debts in many cases. They suggest, indeed, the idea of an indemnification on our part. But probably were we disposed to admit their right to indemnification, they would take care to set it so high as to insure a disagreement.

2. That as to indemnification for the negroes, their measures for concealing them were in the first instance so efficacious, as to reduce our demand for them, so far as we can support it by direct proof, to be very small indeed. Its smallness seems to have kept it out of discussion. Were other difficulties removed, they would probably make none of this article.

3. That they equivocate on every proposal of a treaty of commerce, and authorize in their communications with Mr. Morris the same conclusions which have been drawn from those they had had from time to time with Mr. Adams, and those through Major Beckwith; to wit, that they do not mean to submit their present advantages in commerce to the risk which might attend a discussion of them, whereon some reciprocity could not fail to be demanded. Unless, indeed, we would agree to make it a treaty of alliance as well as commerce, so as to undermine our obligations with France. This method of stripping that rival nation of its alliances, they tried successfully with Holland, endeavored at it with Spain, and have plainly and repeatedly suggested to us. For this they would probably relax some of the rigors they exercise against our commerce.

4. That as to a minister, their Secretary for foreign affairs is dis-

posed to exchange one, but meets with opposition in his cabinet, so as to render the issue uncertain.

From the whole of which, the Secretary of State is of opinion that Mr. Morris' letters remove any doubts which might have been entertained as to the intentions and dispositions of the British cabinet.

That it would be dishonorable to the United States, useless and even injurious, to renew the propositions for a treaty of commerce, or for the exchange of a minister; and that these subjects should now remain dormant, till they shall be brought forward earnestly by them.

That the demands of the posts, and of indemnification for the negroes should not be again made till we are in readiness to do ourselves the justice which may be refused.

That Mr. Morris should be informed that he fulfilled the object of his agency to the satisfaction of the President, inasmuch as he has enabled him to judge of the real views of the British cabinet, and that it is his pleasure that the matters committed to him be left in the situation in which the letter shall find them.

That a proper compensation be given to Mr. Morris for his services herein, which having been begun on the 22d of January, and ended the 18th of September, comprehend a space of near eight months; that the allowance to an agent may be properly fixed anywhere between the half and the whole of what is allowed to a Chargé d'affaires; which, according to the establishment of the United States at the time of this appointment, was at the rate of $3,000 a year; consequently, that such a sum of between one and two thousand dollars be allowed him as the President shall deem proper, on a view of the interference which this agency may have had with Mr. Morris' private pursuits in Europe.

8. Jay's Treaty

A year after outbreak of general war in Europe the Washington administration dispatched Chief Justice Jay to London. The resultant commercial treaty, dated November 19, 1794, was highly unpopular. Source: Miller (ed.), Treaties and Other International Acts . . . , II, 246–247, 249–250, 252, 254–255, 258–259, 262, 264, 266–267. Historians have held varying opinions of the treaty. Henry Adams in his Life of Albert Gallatin (Philadelphia, 1879) wrote "that Mr. Jay's treaty was a bad one few persons even then ventured to dispute; no one would venture on its merits to defend it now." Charles A. Beard pilloried the treaty in his Economic Origins of Jeffersonian Democracy (New York, 1915). But Samuel Flagg Bemis's definitive Jay's Treaty (New York, 1923; rev. ed., New Haven, 1962) makes the common-sense point that the treaty ensured survival of the new federal government, revenues for which came from customs duties. Bradford Perkins, The First Rapprochement (Philadelphia, 1955) comments that the treaty inaugurated a decade of comparatively favorable relations with Great Britain. It gave time and put off the inevitable confrontation. The treaty contained an interesting innovation, four mixed commissions—half Britishers, half Americans—for settlement of disputes over British spoliations on American shipping after outbreak of the war in Europe in 1793, to fix fair compensation for the unpaid private debts contracted by citizens of the United States prior to the Treaty of Paris of 1783, and to close the gaps in the boundaries stipulated by the treaty of 1783 between Maine and Canada and to the west of Lake Superior. For the article concerning the Maine boundary, see below, pp. 189–191.

Article 2

His Majesty will withdraw all His Troops and Garrisons from all Posts and Places within the Boundary Lines assigned by the Treaty of Peace to the United States. This Evacuation shall take place on or before the first Day of June One thousand seven hundred and ninety six . . .

Article 3

It is agreed that it shall at all Times be free to His Majesty's Subjects, and to the Citizens of the United States, and also to the Indians dwelling on either side of the said Boundary Line freely to pass and repass by Land, or Inland Navigation, into the respective Territories and Countries of the Two Parties on the Continent of America (the Country within the Limits of the Hudson's Bay Company only excepted) and to navigate all the Lakes, Rivers, and waters thereof, and freely to carry on trade and commerce with each other. But it is understood, that this Article does not extend to the admission of Vessels of the United States into the Sea Ports, Harbours, Bays, or Creeks of His Majesty's said Territories; nor into such parts of the Rivers in His Majesty's said Territories as are between the mouth thereof, and the highest Port of Entry from the

Sea, except in small vessels trading bona fide between Montreal and Quebec, under such regulations as shall be established to prevent the possibility of any Frauds in this respect. Nor to the admission of British vessels from the Sea into the Rivers of the United States, beyond the highest Ports of Entry for Foreign Vessels from the Sea. The River Mississippi, shall however, according to the Treaty of Peace be entirely open to both Parties; And it is further agreed, That all the ports and places on its Eastern side, to whichsoever of the parties belonging, may freely be resorted to, and used by both parties, in as ample a manner as any of the Atlantic Ports or Places of the United States, or any of the Ports or Places of His Majesty in Great Britain. . . .

Article 6

Whereas it is alledged by divers British Merchants and others His Majesty's Subjects, that Debts to a considerable amount which were bona fide contracted before the Peace, still remain owing to them by Citizens or Inhabitants of the United States, and that by the operation of various lawful Impediments since the Peace, not only the full recovery of the said Debts has been delayed, but also the Value and Security thereof, have been in several instances impaired and lessened, so that by the ordinary course of Judicial proceedings the British Creditors, cannot now obtain and actually have and receive full and adequate Compensation for the losses and damages which they have thereby sustained: It is agreed that in all such Cases where full Compensation for such losses and damages cannot, for whatever reason, be actually obtained had and received by the said Creditors in the ordinary course of Justice, The United States will make full and complete Compensation for the same to the said Creditors . . .

Article 7

Whereas Complaints have been made by divers Merchants and others, Citizens of the United States, that during the course of the War in which His Majesty is now engaged they have sustained considerable losses and damage by reason of irregular or illegal Captures or Condemnations of their vessels and other property under Colour of authority or Commissions from His Majesty, and that from various Circumstances belonging to the said Cases adequate

Compensation for the losses and damages so sustained cannot now be actually obtained, had and received by the ordinary Course of Judicial proceedings; It is agreed that in all such Cases where adequate Compensation cannot for whatever reason be now actually obtained, had and received by the said Merchants and others in the ordinary course of Justice, full and Complete Compensation for the same will be made by the British Government to the said Complainants. ...

Article 11

It is agreed between His Majesty and the United States of America, that there shall be a reciprocal and entirely perfect Liberty of Navigation and Commerce, between their respective People, in the manner, under the Limitations, and on the Conditions specified in the following Articles.

Article 12

His Majesty Consents that it shall and may be lawful, during the time hereinafter Limited, for the Citizens of the United States, to carry to any of His Majesty's Islands and Ports in the West Indies from the United States in their own Vessels, not being above the burthen of Seventy Tons, any Goods or Merchandizes, being of the Growth, Manufacture, or Produce of the said States, which it is, or may be lawful to carry to the said Islands or Ports from the said States in British Vessels, and that the said American Vessels shall be subject there to no other or higher Tonnage Duties or Charges, than shall be payable by British Vessels, in the Ports of the United States; and that the Cargoes of the said American Vessels, shall be subject there to no other or higher Duties or Charges, than shall be payable on the like Articles if imported there from the said States in British vessels.

And His Majesty also consents that it shall be lawful for the said American Citizens to purchase, load and carry away, in their said vessels to the United States from the said Islands and Ports, all such articles being of the Growth, Manufacture or Produce of the said Islands, as may now by Law be carried from thence to the said States in British Vessels, and subject only to the same Duties and Charges on Exportation to which British Vessels and their Cargoes are or shall be subject in similar circumstances.

Provided always that the said American vessels do carry and land their Cargoes in the United States only, it being expressly agreed and declared that during the Continuance of this article, the United States will prohibit and restrain the carrying any Melasses, Sugar, Coffee, Cocoa or Cotton in American vessels, either from His Majesty's Islands or from the United States, to any part of the World, except the United States, reasonable Sea Stores excepted. Provided also, that it shall and may be lawful during the same period for British vessels to import from the said Islands into the United States, and to export from the United States to the said Islands, all Articles whatever being of the Growth, Produce or Manufacture of the said Islands, or of the United States respectively, which now may, by the Laws of the said States, be so imported and exported. And that the Cargoes of the said British vessels, shall be subject to no other or higher Duties or Charges, than shall be payable on the same articles if so imported or exported in American Vessels.

It is agreed that this Article, and every Matter and Thing therein contained, shall continue to be in Force, during the Continuance of the war in which His Majesty is now engaged; and also for Two years from and after the Day of the signature of the Preliminary or other Articles of Peace by which the same may be terminated. . . .

Article 17

It is agreed that, in all Cases where Vessels shall be captured or detained on just suspicion of having on board Enemy's property or of carrying to the Enemy, any of the articles which are Contraband of war; The said Vessel shall be brought to the nearest or most convenient Port, and if any property of an Enemy, should be found on board such Vessel, that part only which belongs to the Enemy shall be made prize, and the Vessel shall be at liberty to proceed with the remainder without any Impediment . . .

Article 18

In order to regulate what is in future to be esteemed Contraband of war, it is agreed that under the said Denomination shall be comprized all Arms and Implements serving for the purposes of war by Land or Sea; such as Cannon, Muskets, Mortars, Petards, Bombs, Grenades Carcasses, Saucisses, Carriages for Cannon,

Musket rests, Bandoliers, Gunpowder, Match, Saltpetre, Ball, Pikes, Swords, Headpieces Cuirasses Halberts Lances Javelins, Horsefurniture, Holsters, Belts and, generally all other Implements of war, as also Timber for Ship building, Tar or Rosin, Copper in Sheets, Sails, Hemp, and Cordage, and generally whatever may serve directly to the equipment of Vessels, unwrought Iron and Fir planks only excepted, and all the above articles are hereby declared to be just objects of Confiscation, whenever they are attempted to be carried to an Enemy.

And Whereas the difficulty of agreeing on the precise Cases in which alone Provisions and other articles not generally contraband may be regarded as such, renders it expedient to provide against the inconveniences and misunderstandings which might thence arise: It is further agreed that whenever any such articles so becoming Contraband according to the existing Laws of Nations, shall for that reason be seized, the same shall not be confiscated, but the owners thereof shall be speedily and completely indemnified; and the Captors, or in their default the Government under whose authority they act, shall pay to the Masters or Owners of such Vessels the full value of all such Articles, with a reasonable mercantile Profit thereon, together with the Freight, and also the Demurrage incident to such Detension. . . .

Article 24

It shall not be lawful for any Foreign Privateers (not being Subjects or Citizens of either of the said Parties) who have Commissions from any other Prince or State in Enmity with either Nation, to arm their Ships in the Ports of either of the said Parties, nor to sell what they have taken, nor in any other manner to exchange the same, nor shall they be allowed to purchase more provisions than shall be necessary for their going to the nearest Port of that Prince or State from whom they obtained their Commissions.

Article 25

It shall be lawful for the Ships of war and Privateers belonging to the said Parties respectively to carry whithersoever they please the Ships and Goods taken from their Enemies without being obliged to pay any Fee to the Officers of the Admiralty, or to any Judges whatever; nor shall the said Prizes when they arrive at, and enter the Ports of the said Parties be detained or seized, neither shall the Searchers or other Officers of those Places visit such Prizes (except for the purpose of preventing the Carrying of any part of the Cargo thereof on Shore in any manner contrary to the established Laws of Revenue, Navigation or Commerce) nor shall such Officers take Cognizance of the Validity of such Prizes; but they shall be at liberty to hoist Sail, and depart as speedily as may be, and carry their said Prizes to the place mentioned in their Commissions or Patents, which the Commanders of the said Ships of war or Privateers shall be obliged to shew. No Shelter or Refuge shall be given in their Ports to such as have made a Prize upon the subjects or Citizens of either of the said Parties; but if forced by stress of weather or the Dangers of the Sea, to enter therein, particular care shall be taken to hasten their departure, and to cause them to retire as soon as possible. Nothing in this Treaty contained shall however be construed or operate contrary to former and existing Public Treaties with other Sovereigns or States. But the Two parties agree, that while they continue in amity neither of them will in future make any Treaty that shall be inconsistent with this or the preceding article. . . .

Article 28

It is agreed that the first Ten Articles of this Treaty shall be permanent and that the subsequent Articles except the Twelfth shall be limited in their duration to Twelve years to be computed from the Day on which the Ratifications of this Treaty shall be exchanged . . .

Additional Article

It is further agreed between the said contracting parties, that the operation of so much of the twelfth Article of the said Treaty as respects the trade which his said Majesty thereby consents may be carried on between the United States and his Islands in the West Indies, in the manner and on the terms and conditions therein specified, shall be suspended.

IV

The Mississippi Question

In seeking freedom of commerce the Americans had to consider the question of access to the Mississippi River—the early diplomats hoped to obtain assurance from whatever European nation held New Orleans and Louisiana that American settlers and traders could use the great river and its tributaries. This was a serious issue. John Jay during the Revolution told the Spanish foreign minister, José de Moñino y Redondo, Count of Floridablanca, that "the Americans, almost to a man, believed that God Almighty had made that river a highway for the people of the upper country to go to the sea by."

9. Revolutionary diplomacy

Jay was the unrecognized minister of the United States to Spain from 1779 to 1782, and received the following instruction from Congress under the date September 29, 1779. Source: Wharton (ed.), The Revolutionary Diplomatic Correspondence of the United States, III, 352–353. The reader must remember that the king of France was "his most Christian majesty" and the king of Spain "his Catholic majesty."

By the treaties subsisting between his most Christian majesty and the United States of America a power is reserved to his Catholic majesty to accede to the said treaties, and to participate in their stipulations at such time as he shall judge proper, it being well understood, nevertheless, that if any of the stipulations of the said treaties are not agreeable to the court of Spain, his Catholic majesty may propose other conditions analogous to the principal aim of the alliance, and conformable to the rules of equality, reciprocity, and friendship. Congress is sensible of the friendly regard to these States manifested by his most Christian majesty in reserving a power to his Catholic majesty of acceding to the alliance entered into between his most Christian majesty and these United States; and therefore, that nothing may be wanting on their part to facilitate the views of his most Christian majesty, and to obtain a treaty of alliance and of amity and commerce with his Catholic majesty, have thought proper to anticipate any propositions which his Catholic majesty might make on that subject by yielding up to him those objects which they conclude he may have principally in view; and for that purpose have come to the following resolution:

"That if his Catholic majesty shall accede to the said treaties, and, in concurrence with France and the United States of America, continue the present war with Great Britain for the purpose expressed in the treaties aforesaid, he shall not thereby be precluded from securing to himself the Floridas; on the contrary, if he shall obtain the Floridas from Great Britain, these United States will guaranty the same to his Catholic majesty; provided always, that the United States shall enjoy the free navigation of the river Mississippi into and from the sea."

You are therefore to communicate to his most Christian majesty the desire of Congress to enter into a treaty of alliance and of amity and commerce with his Catholic majesty, and to request his favorable interposition for that purpose. At the same time, you are to make such proposal to his Catholic majesty as in your judgment, from circumstances, will be proper for obtaining for the United States of America equal advantages with those which are secured to them by the treaties with his most Christian majesty; observing always the resolution aforesaid as the ultimatum of the United States.

You are particularly to endeavor to obtain some convenient port or ports below the thirty-first degree of north latitude on the river Mississippi for all merchant vessels, goods, wares, and merchandises belonging to the inhabitants of these States.

The distressed state of our finances and the great depreciation of our paper money inclined Congress to hope that his Catholic majesty, if he shall conclude a treaty with these States, will be induced to lend them money; you are therefore to represent to him the great distress of these States on that account, and to solicit a loan of five millions of dollars upon the best terms in your power, not exceeding six per cent per annum, effectually to enable them to co-operate with the allies against the common enemy. But before you make any propositions to his Catholic majesty for a loan you are to endeavor to obtain a subsidy in consideration of the guaranty aforesaid.

Additional instructions went out to Jay dated October 4, 1780. Source: ibid., IV, 78–79.

On the report of a committee to whom were referred certain instructions to the delegates of Virginia by their constituents, and a letter of the 26th of May from the honorable John Jay, Congress unanimously agreed to the following instructions to the honorable John Jay, minister plenipotentiary of the United States of America at the court of Madrid:

That the said minister adhere to his former instructions respecting the right of the United States of America to the free navigation of the river Mississippi into and from the sea; which right, if an express acknowledgment of it can not be obtained from Spain, is not by any stipulation on the part of America to be relinquished. To render the treaty to be concluded between the two nations permanent, nothing can more effectually contribute than a proper attention not only to the present but the future reciprocal interests of the contracting powers.

The river Mississippi being the boundary of several States in the Union, and their citizens, while connected with Great Britain, and since the Revolution, having been accustomed to the free use thereof in common with the subjects of Spain, and no instance of complaint or dispute having resulted from it, there is no reason to fear that the future mutual use of the river by the subjects of the two nations, actuated by friendly dispositions, will occasion any interruption of that harmony which it is the desire of America, as well as of Spain, should be perpetual. That if the unlimited freedom of the navigation of the river Mississippi, with a free port or ports below the thirty-first degree of north latitude, accessible to merchant ships, can not be obtained from Spain, the said minister in that case be at liberty to enter into such equitable regulations as may appear a necessary security against contraband; provided the right of the United States to the free navigation of the river be not relinquished, and a free port or ports as above described be stipulated to them.

That with respect to the boundary alluded to in his letter of the 26th of May last, the said minister be, and hereby is, instructed to adhere strictly to the boundaries of the United States as already fixed by Congress. Spain having by the treaty of Paris ceded to Great Britain all the country to the northeastward of the Mississippi, the people inhabiting these States, while connected with Great Britain, and also since the Revolution, have settled themselves at divers places to the westward near the Mississippi, are friendly to the Revolution, and being citizens of these United States, and subject to the laws of those to which they respectively belong, Congress can not assign them over as subjects to any other power.

That the said minister be further informed that in case Spain shall eventually be in possession of East and West Florida at the termination of the war, it is of the greatest importance to these United States to have the use of the waters running out of Georgia through West Florida into the Bay of Mexico for the purpose of navigation; and that he be instructed to endeavor to obtain the same, subject to such regulations as may be agreed on between the contracting parties; and that, as a compensation for this, he be, and hereby is, empowered to guaranty the possession of the said Floridas to the crown of Spain.

In communicating the following instructions dated February 15, 1781, Jay carefully placed a time limit on Congress's concession. To his annoyance the government of Charles III, "his most Supine Majesty," did nothing, one way or the other. Source: ibid., 257.

. . . Congress having since their instructions to you of the 29th September, 1779, and 4th October, 1780, relative to the claim of the United States to the free navigation of the river Mississippi, and to a free port or ports below the 31st degree of north latitude, resumed the consideration of that subject; and being desirous to manifest to all the world, and particularly to his Catholic majesty, the moderation of their views, the high value they place on the friendship of his Catholic majesty, and their disposition to remove every reasonable obstacle to his accession to the alliance subsisting between his most Christian majesty, and these United States, in order to unite the more closely in their measures and operations three powers who have so great a unity of interests, and thereby to compel the common enemy to a speedy, just, and honorable peace, have resolved, and you are hereby instructed, to recede from the instructions above referred to, so far as they insist on the free navigation of that part of the river Mississippi which lies below the 31st degree of north latitude and on a free port or ports below the same, provided such cession shall be unalterably insisted on by Spain, and provided the free navigation of the said river above the said degree of north latitude shall be acknowledged and guaranteed by his Catholic majesty to the citizens of the United States in common with his own subjects. It is the order of Congress at the same time that you exert every possible effort to obtain from his Catholic majesty the use of the river aforesaid with a free port or ports below the said 31st degree of north latitude for the citizens of the United States under such regulations and restrictions only as may be a necessary safeguard against illicit commerce.

10. The first Jay Treaty

Giving way to the pleas of the new Spanish minister to the United States, Diego de Gardoqui, Jay as secretary for foreign affairs made a proposal to Congress on August 3, 1786. Source: Ford, et al. (eds.), Journals of the Continental Congress, XXXI, 473–476, 479–483. In the course of his speech he advised a mixed commission to settle the Spanish-American border, the first advocacy by an American negotiator of a form of settlement akin to arbitration. He wrote this idea into Article 5 of his treaty with Great Britain of 1794 (see below, pp. 189–191).

Every person to whom is committed the management of a negotiation, from which many good or ill consequences will probably result, must find himself placed in a very delicate and responsible Situation. In that point of light I consider our present Negotiations with Spain, and that my sentiments on the subject may be conveyed to Congress with precision, and authentick evidence of them preserved, I have reduced them to writing as concisely and accurately as I could find leisure to do since I received notice to attend this day.

It appears to me, that a proper Commercial treaty with Spain would be of more importance to the United States than any they have formed, or can form, with any other Nation. I am led to entertain this opinion from the influence which Spain may and will have both on our politicks and Commerce.

France, whom we consider as our Ally, and to whom we shall naturally turn our eyes for aid in case of war, &c. is strongly bound to Spain by the family compact; and the advantages she derives from it are so various and so great, that it is questionable whether she could ever remain neutre in case of a rupture between us and his Catholic Majesty. Besides, we are well apprized of the sentiments of France relative to our Western Claims; in which I include that of freely navigating the river Mississippi. I take it for granted that, while the compact in question exists, France will invariably think it her interest to prefer the good will of Spain to the good will of America; and altho' she would very reluctantly give umbrage to either, yet, if driven to take part with one or the other, I think it would not be in our favour. Unless we are friends with Spain, her influence, whether more or less, on the Counsels of Versailles, will always be against us.

The intermarriages between Spain and Portugal, which have taken place in this and the late Reigns, have given the former a degree of influence at the Court of the latter which she never before possessed; and leading men in both those Kingdoms seem disposed to bury former jealousies and apprehensions in mutual confidence and good offices. How far this system may be perfected, or how long continue, is uncertain; while it lasts, we must expect good or evil from it, according as we stand well or ill with Spain.

Britain would be rejoiced to find us at variance with Spain on any points. She remembers that we were once her Subjects, and loves us not. She perceives that we are her most important rivals in the Spanish trade, and that her nursery of Seamen on the banks of Newfoundland will prosper or otherwise, as ours of the like kind shall encrease or diminish; and it will encrease or diminish in proportion as we may or may not undersell them at foreign Markets, among which that of Spain is the most advantageous.

If Spain should be disposed to sink that scale in favour of Britain, there is little reason to doubt but that the latter will offer her powerful inducements to grant and perpetuate valuable preferences to her.

It is hard to say how far these inducements may extend, or how far they might *both* think it their interest to join in every measure tending to impair our strength, and thereby quiet those fears, with which uneasy Borderers and discontented neighbours usually inspire each other.

Recent transactions tell us that the influence of Spain in Barbary is not contemptible. When time shall have cast a thicker veil over the memory of past and long continued hostilities; when the convenience of Spanish money and Spanish favors shall become better known, and more felt at Fez, Algiers, &c. it is more than probable that those powers will be little inclined to disoblige a nation, whose arms have given them much trouble, and from whose gratuities they derive more wealth and advantages than they have ever been able to reap from depredations and from plunder often hardly gained.

The influence which the Catholic King will and must have, in greater or lesser degrees in Italy, with several of whose Sovereigns he is allied by blood, as well as by treaties, merits some consideration. The trade of the Mediterranean deserves our notice; and Spain has convenient ports in that Sea.

In various ways, therefore, may Spain promote or oppose our political interests with several other Countries; and we shall, I think, either find her in America a very convenient Neighbour, or a very troublesome one.

They who are acquainted with the Commerce of that Country, can be at no loss in perceiving or estimating its value.

It is well known that they consume more than they export, and consequently that the balance of trade is and must be against them. Hence it is that the Millions they yearly bring from the Mines of America, so soon disappear, flying out of Spain by every road and port in it.

Details would be tedious, and considering where I am, unnecessary. It is sufficient to observe, that there is scarcely a single production of this Country but what may be advantageously exchanged in the Spanish European ports for Gold and Silver. These advantages, however, must depend on a Treaty; for Spain, like other Nations, may admit Foreigners to trade with her or not, and on such terms only as she may think proper. . . .

My attention is chiefly fixed on two obstacles, which at present divide us, viz. the Navigation of the Mississippi, and the territorial limits between them and us.

My Letters written from Spain, when our affairs were the least promising, evince my opinion respecting the Mississippi, and oppose every idea of our relinquishing our right to navigate it. I entertain the same sentiments of that right, and of the importance of retaining it, which I then did.

Mr. Gardoqui strongly insists on our relinquishing it. We have had many Conferences and much reasoning on the subject, not necessary now to detail. His concluding answer to all my Arguments has steadily been, that the King will never yield that point, nor consent to any compromise about it; for that it always has been, and continues to be, one of their Maxims of policy, to exclude all Mankind from their American shores.

I have often reminded him that the adjacent Country was filling fast with people; and that the time must and would come, when they would not submit to seeing a fine river flow before their doors without using it as a high way to the sea for the transportation of their productions; that it would therefore be wise to look forward to that event, and take care not to sow in the treaty any seeds of future discord. He said that the time alluded to was far distant; and that treaties were not to provide for contingencies so remote and future. For his part he considered the rapid settlement of that Country as injurious to the States, and that they would find it necessary to check it. Many fruitless Arguments passed between us; and tho' he would admit that the only way to make treaties and friendship permanent, was for neither party to leave the other any thing to complain of; yet he would still insist, that the Mississippi must be shut against us. The truth is, that Courts never admit the force of any reasoning or Arguments but such as apply in their favor; and it is equally true, that even if our right to that Navigation, or to any thing else, was expressly declared in Holy Writ, we should be able to provide for the enjoyment of it no otherwise than by being in capacity to repel force by force.

Circumstanced as we are, I think it would be expedient to agree that the treaty should be limited to twenty five or thirty years, and that one of the Articles should stipulate that the United States would forbear to use the Navigation of that River below their territories to the Ocean. Thus the duration of the treaty and of the forbearance in question would be limited to the same period. . . .

Spain now excludes us from that Navigation, and with a strong hand holds it against us. She will not yield it peaceably, and therefore we can only acquire it by War. Now as we are not prepared for a War with any power; as many of the States would be little inclined to a War with Spain for that object at this day; and as such a War would for those and a variety of obvious reasons be inexpedient, it follows, that Spain will, for a long space of time yet to come, exclude us from that Navigation. Why therefore should we not (for a valuable Consideration too) consent to forbear to use what we know is not in our power to use. . . .

With respect to territorial limits, it is clear to me that Spain can justly claim nothing East of the Mississippi but what may be comprehended within the bounds of the Floridas.[1] How far those bounds extend, or ought to extend, may prove a question of more difficulty to negotiate than to decide. Pains I think should be taken to conciliate and settle all such matters amicably; and it would be better even to yield a few Acres, than to part in ill humour.

If their demands, when ascertained, should prove too extravagant, and too pertinaciously adhered to, one mode of avoiding a rupture will still be left, viz. referring that dispute to impartial Commissioners. I do not mean by this, that any third sovereign should be called in to mediate or arbitrate about the matter. They make troublesome Arbitrators, and not always the most impartial. I mean private men for Commissoners; and to me there appears little difficulty in finding proper ones; for not being prepared for War, I think it much our interest to avoid placing ourselves in such a situation, as that our forbearing hostilities may expose us to indignities.

It is much to be wished that all these matters had lain dormant for years yet to come; but such wishes are vain; these disputes are agitating; they press themselves upon us, and must terminate in accommodation, or War, or disgrace. The last is the worst that can happen; the second we are unprepared for; and therefore our attention and endeavours should be bent to the first. . . .

11. Pinckney's Treaty

*Thomas Pinckney signed a treaty with Spain on October 27, 1795. Source: Miller (ed.), Treaties and Other International Acts . . . , I*i, *319–322, 328–331, 337.*

Art. II

To prevent all disputes on the subject of the boundaries which separate the territories of the two High contracting Parties, it is

[1] See below, p. 133.

hereby declared and agreed as follows: to wit: The Southern boundary of the United States which divides their territory from the Spanish Colonies of East and West Florida, shall be designated by a line beginning on the River Mississippi at the Northermost part of the thirty first degree of latitude North of the Equator, which from thence shall be drawn due East to the middle of the River Apalachicola or Catahouche, thence along the middle thereof to its junction with the Flint, thence straight to the head of St Mary's River, and thence down the middle there of to the Atlantic Occean. . . .

Art. IV

It is likewise agreed that the Western boundary of the United States which separates them from the Spanish Colony of Louissiana, is in the middle of the channel or bed of the River Mississipi from the Northern boundary of the said States to the completion of the thirty first degree of latitude North of the Equator; and his Catholic Majesty has likewise agreed that the navigation of the said River in its whole breadth from its source to the Occean shall be free only to his Subjects, and the Citizens of the United States, unless he should extend this privilege to the Subjects of other Powers by special convention.

Art. V

The two High contracting Parties shall by all the means in their power maintain peace and harmony among the several Indian Nations who inhabit the country adjacent to the lines and Rivers which by the preceeding Articles form the boundaries of the two Floridas; and the beter to obtain this effect both Parties oblige themselves expressly to restrain by force all hostilities on the part of the Indian Nations living within their boundaries: so that Spain will not suffer her Indians to attack the Citizens of the United States, nor the Indians inhabiting their territory; nor will the United States permit these last mentioned Indians to commence hostilities against the Subjects of his Catholic Majesty, or his Indians in any manner whatever. . . .

Art. XV

It shall be lawful for all and singular the Subjects of his Catholic Mayesty, and the Citizens, People, and inhabitants of the said

United States to sail with their Ships with all manner of liberty and security, no distinction being made who are the propietors of the merchandizes laden thereon from any Port to the Places of those who now are or hereafter shall be at enmity with his Catholic Majesty or the United States. It shall be likewise lawful for the Subjects and inhabitants aforesaid to sail with the Ships and merchandizes aforementioned, and to trade with the same liberty and security from the Places, Ports, and Havens of those who are Enemies of both or either Party without any opposition or disturbance whatsoever, not only directly from the Places of the Enemy aforementioned to neutral Places but also from one Place belonging to an Enemy to another Place belonging to an Enemy, whether they be under the jurisdiction of the same Prince or under several, and it is hereby stipulated that Free Ships shall also give freedom to goods, and that every thing shall be deemed free and exempt which shall be found on board the Ships belonging to the Subjects of either of the contracting Parties although the whole lading of any part thereof should appartain to the Enemies of either; contraband goods being always excepted. It is also agreed that the same liberty be extended to persons who are on board a free Ship, so that, although they be Enemies to either Party they shall not be made Prisoners or taken out of that free Ship unless they are Soldiers and in actual service of the Enemies.

Art. XVI

This liberty of navigation and commerce shall extend to all kinds of merchandizes excepting those only which are distinguished by the name of contraband; and under this name of contraband or prohibited goods shall be comprehended arms, great guns, bombs, with the fusees, and other things belonging to them, cannon ball, gun powder, match, pikes, swords, lances, speards, halberds, mortars, petards, granades, salpetre, muskets, musket ball bucklers, helmets, breast plates, coats of mail, and the like kind of arms proper for arming soldiers, musket rests, belts, horses with their furniture and all other warlike instruments whatever. These merchandizes which follows shall not be reckoned among contraband or prohibited goods; that is to say, all sorts of cloths and all other manufactures woven of any wool, flax, silk, cotton, or any other materials whatever, all kinds of wearing aparel together with all species whereof they are used to be made, gold and silver as well coined as uncoined, tin, iron, latton, copper, brass, coals, as also wheat, barley, oats, and any other kind of corn and pulse: tobacco and likewise all manner of spices, salted and smoked flesh, salted fish, cheese and butter, beer, oils, wines, sugars, and all sorts of salts, and in general all provisions which serve for the sustenance of life. Furthermore all kinds of cotton, hemp, flax, tar, pitch, ropes, cables, sails, sail cloths, anchors, and any parts of anchors, also ships masts, planks, wood of all kind, and all other things proper either for building or repairing ships, and all other goods whatever which have not been worked into the form of any instrument prepared for war by land or by sea, shall not be reputed contraband, much less such as have been already wrought and made up for any other use: all which shall be wholy reckoned among free goods, as likewise all other merchandizes and things which are not comprehended and particularly mentioned in the foregoing enumeration of contraband goods: so that they may be transported and carried in the freest manner by the subjects of both parties, even to Places belonging to an Enemy, such towns or Places being only excepted as are at that time besieged, blocked up, or invested. . . .

Art. XXII

. . . his Catholic Majesty will permit the Citizens of the United States for the space of three years from this time to deposit their merchandize and effects in the Port of New Orleans, and to export them from thence without paying any other duty than a fair price for the hire of the stores, and his Majesty promises either to continue this permission if he finds during that time that it is not prejudicial to the interests of Spain, or if he should not agree to continue it there, he will assign to them on another part of the banks of the Mississipi an equivalent establishment.

V

Neutrality and Quasi War

It was sheer coincidence, and for the United States a wonderful piece of luck, that the year in which the French Revolution began, 1789, saw in America the inauguration of the new national government under the Constitution. How different might have been the fate of the United States if the nation had continued the weak Articles of Confederation into the 1790's, the era when the inflamed patriotism of the French people turned all Europe into war. To invert Samuel Flagg Bemis's thesis, Europe's distress would not have been America's advantage. One of the belligerents, France or Britain, might have converted the United States into a sort of self-supporting colony. The future of the North American continent would have changed, and in the nineteenth century there would have appeared a series of North American republics, probably at first under protection of a European nation, then independent like the nations of South America. Instead, the American republic with new vigor maintained its neutrality in the 1790's, despite ill treatment of its commerce by Britain and France.

12. The Constitution on foreign affairs

The Founding Fathers had seen European politics at first hand. Their stipulations on foreign affairs in the great document of 1787 represented no closet philosophy.

We the people of the United States, in Order to form a more perfect Union, establish Justice, insure domestic Tranquility, provide for the common defence, promote the general Welfare, and secure the Blessings of Liberty to ourselves and our Posterity, do ordain and establish this Constitution for the United States of America.

Article I

. . . Section 7. All Bills for raising Revenue shall originate in the House of Representatives; but the Senate may propose or concur with Amendments as on other Bills.

Every Bill which shall have passed the House of Representatives and the Senate, shall, before it become a Law, be presented to the President of the United States; If he approve he shall sign it, but if not he shall return it, with his Objections to that House in which it shall have originated, who shall enter the Objections at large on their Journal, and proceed to reconsider it. If after such Reconsideration two thirds of that House shall agree to pass the Bill, it shall be sent, together with the Objections, to the other House, by which it shall likewise be reconsidered, and if approved by two thirds of that House, it shall become a Law. But in all such Cases the Votes of both Houses shall be determined by yeas and Nays, and the Names of the Persons voting for and against the Bill shall be entered on the Journal of each House respectively. If any Bill shall not be returned by the President within ten Days (Sundays excepted) after it shall have been presented to him, the Same shall be a Law, in like Manner as if he had signed it, unless the Congress by their Adjournment prevent its Return, in which Case it shall not be a Law.

Every Order, Resolution, or Vote to which the Concurrence of the Senate and House of Representatives may be necessary (except on a question of Adjournment) shall be presented to the President of the United States; and before the Same shall take Effect, shall be approved by him, or being disapproved by him, shall be re-passed by two thirds of the Senate and House of Representatives, according to the Rules and Limitations prescribed in the Case of a Bill.

Section 8. The Congress shall have Power To lay and collect Taxes, Duties, Imposts and Excises, to pay the Debts and provide for the common Defence and general Welfare of the United States; but all Duties, Imposts, and Excises shall be uniform throughout the United States;

To borrow Money on the credit of the United States;

To regulate Commerce with foreign Nations, and among the several States, and with the Indian Tribes;

To establish an uniform Rule of Naturalization, and uniform Laws on the subject of Bankruptcies throughout the United States;

To coin Money, regulate the Value thereof, and of foreign Coin, and fix the Standard of Weights and Measures; . . .

To define and punish Piracies and Felonies committed on the high Seas, and Offences against the Law of Nations;

To declare War, grant Letters of Marque and Reprisal, and make Rules concerning Captures on Land and Water;

To raise and support Armies, but no Appropriation of Money to that Use shall be for a longer Term than two Years;

To provide and maintain a Navy;

To make Rules for the Government and Regulation of the land and naval Forces;

To provide for calling forth the Militia to execute the Laws of the Union, suppress Insurrections and repel Invasions;

To provide for organizing, arming, and disciplining, the Militia, and for governing such Part of them as may be employed in the Service of the United States, reserving to the States respectively, the Appointment of the Officers, and the Authority of training the Militia according to the discipline prescribed by Congress; . . .

To make all Laws which shall be necessary and proper for carrying into Execution the foregoing Powers, and all other Powers vested by this Constitution in the Government of the United States, or in any Department or Officer thereof.

Section 9. The Migration or Importation of such Persons as any of the States now existing shall think proper to admit, shall not be prohibited by the Congress prior to the year one thousand eight hundred and eight, but a Tax or duty may be imposed on such Importation, not exceeding ten dollars for each Person. . . .

No Tax or Duty shall be laid on Articles exported from any State.

No Preference shall be given by any Regulation of Commerce or Revenue to the Ports of one State over those of another: nor shall Vessels bound to, or from, one State, be obliged to enter, clear, or pay Duties in another. . . .

No Title of Nobility shall be granted by the United States: And no Person holding any Office of Profit or Trust under them, shall, without the Consent of the Congress, accept of any present, Emolument, Office, or Title, of any kind whatever, from any King, Prince, or foreign State.

Section 10. No State shall enter into any Treaty, Alliance, or Confederation; grant Letters of Marque and Reprisal; coin Money; emit Bills of Credit; make any Thing but gold and silver Coin a Tender in Payment of Debts; pass any Bill of Attainder, ex post facto Law, or Law impairing the Obligation of Contracts, or grant any Title of Nobility.

No State shall, without the Consent of the Congress, lay any Imposts or Duties on Imports or Exports, except what may be absolutely necessary for executing it's inspection Laws: and the net Produce of all Duties and Imposts, laid by any State on Imports or Exports, shall be for the Use of the Treasury of the United States; and all such Laws shall be subject to the Revision and Controul of the Congress.

No State shall, without the Consent of Congress, lay any Duty of Tonnage, keep Troops, or Ships of War in time of Peace, enter into any Agreement or Compact with another State, or with a foreign Power, or engage in War, unless actually invaded, or in such imminent Danger as will not admit of delay.

Article II

Section 1. The executive Power shall be vested in a President of the United States of America. . . .

Section 2. The President shall be Commander in Chief of the Army and Navy of the United States, and of the Militia of the several States, when called into the actual Service of the United States; he may require the Opinion, in writing, of the principal Officer in each of the executive Departments, upon any Subject relating to the Duties of their respective Offices, and he shall have Power to grant Reprieves and Pardons for Offences against the United States, except in Cases of Impeachment.

He shall have Power, by and with the Advice and Consent of the Senate, to make Treaties, provided two thirds of the Senators present concur; and he shall nominate, and by and with the Advice and Consent of the Senate, shall appoint Ambassadors, other public Ministers and Consuls, Judges of the supreme Court, and all other Officers of the United States, whose Appointments are not herein otherwise provided for, and which shall be established by Law: but the Congress may by Law vest the Appointment of such inferior Officers, as they think proper, in the President alone, in the Courts of Law, or in the Heads of Departments.

The President shall have Power to fill up all Vacancies that may happen during the Recess of the Senate, by granting Commissions which shall expire at the End of their next Session.

Section 3. He . . . shall receive Ambassadors and other public Ministers . . . and shall Commission all the Officers of the United States. . . .

Article III

Section 1. The judicial Power of the United States, shall be vested in one supreme Court, and in such inferior Courts as the Congress may from time to time ordain and establish. The Judges, both of the supreme and inferior Courts, shall hold their Offices during good Behaviour, and shall, at stated Times, receive for their Services, a Compensation, which shall not be diminished during their Continuance in Office.

Section 2. The judicial Power shall extend to all Cases, in Law and Equity, arising under this Constitution, the Laws of the United States, and Treaties made, or which shall be made, under their Authority;—to all Cases affecting Ambassadors, other public Ministers and Consuls;—to all Cases of admiralty and maritime Jurisdiction;—to Controversies to which the United States shall be a Party;—to Controversies between two or more States;—between a State and Citizens of another State;—between Citizens of different States,—between Citizens of the same State claiming Lands under Grants of different States, and between a State, or the Citizens thereof, and foreign States, Citizens or Subjects.

In all Cases affecting Ambassadors, other public Ministers and Consuls, and those in which a State shall be Party, the supreme Court shall have original Jurisdiction. In all the other cases before mentioned, the supreme Court shall have appellate Jurisdiction, both as to Law and Fact, with such exceptions, and under such Regulations as the Congress shall make. . . .

Section 3. Treason against the United States, shall consist only in levying War against them, or in adhering to their Enemies, giving them Aid and Comfort. No Person shall be convicted of Treason unless on the Testimony of two Witnesses to the same overt Act, or on Confession in open Court.

The Congress shall have Power to declare the Punishment of Treason, but no Attainder of Treason shall work Corruption of Blood, or Forfeiture except during the Life of the Person attainted.

Article IV

. . . *Section 2.* The Citizens of each State shall be entitled to all Privileges and immunities of Citizens in the several States.

A person charged in any State with Treason, Felony, or other

Crime, who shall flee from from Justice, and be found in another State, shall on Demand of the executive Authority of the State from which he fled, be delivered up, to be removed to the State having Jurisdiction of the Crime. . . .

Section 3. . . . The Congress shall have Power to dispose of and make all needful Rules and Regulations respecting the Territory or other Property belonging to the United States; and nothing in this Constitution shall be so construed as to Prejudice any Claims of the United States, or of any particular State.

Section 4. The United States shall guarantee to every State in this Union a Republican Form of Government, and shall protect each of them against Invasion; and on Application of the Legislature, or of the Executive (when the Legislature cannot be convened) against domestic Violence. . . .

Article VI

All Debts contracted and Engagements entered into, before the Adoption of this Constitution, shall be as valid against the United States under this Constitution, as under the Confederation.

This Constitution, and the Laws of the United States which shall be made in Pursuance thereof; and all Treaties made, or which shall be made, under the Authority of the United States, shall be the supreme Law of the Land; and the Judges in every State shall be bound thereby, any Thing in the Constitution or Laws of any State to the Contrary notwithstanding. . . .

Amendment XI

The Judicial power of the United States shall not be construed to extend to any suit in law or equity, commenced or prosecuted against one of the United States by Citizens of another State, or by Citizens or Subjects of any Foreign State. . . .

13. The heritage of George Washington

Soon after the European war broke out, Washington on April 18, 1793, submitted the following questions to his cabinet. Source: John C. Fitz-

patrick (ed.), The Writings of George Washington (39 vols., Washington, D.C., 1931–44), XXXII, 419–420.

Question I. Shall a proclamation issue for the purpose of preventing interferences of the Citizens of the United States in the War between France and Great Britain &ca.? Shall it contain a declaration of Neutrality or not? What shall it contain?

Questn. II. Shall a Minister from the Republic of France be received?

Quest. III. If received shall it be absolutely or with qualifications; and if with qualifications, of what kind?

Quest. IV. Are the United States obliged by good faith to consider the Treaties heretofore made with France as applying to the present situation of the parties. May they either renounce them, or hold them suspended 'till the Government of France shall be *established.*

Questn. V. If they have the right is it expedient to do either, and which?

Questn. VI. If they have an option, would it be a breach of Neutrality to consider the Treaties still in operation?

Quest. VII. If the Treaties are to be considered as now in operation is the Guarantee in the Treaty of Alliance applicable to a defensive war only, or to War either offensive or defensive?

VIII. Does the War in which France is engaged appear to be offensive or defensive on her part? or of a mixed and equivocal character?

IX. If of a mixed and equivocal character does the Guarantee in any event apply to such a War?

X. What is the effect of a Guarantee such as that to be found in the Treaty of Alliance between the United States and France?

XI. Does any Article in either of the Treaties prevent Ships of War, other than Privateers, of the Powers opposed to France, from coming into the Ports of the United States to act as Convoys to their own Merchantment? or does it lay any other restraint upon them more than wd. apply to the Ships of War of France?

Quest. XII. Should the future Regent of France send a Minister to the United States ought he to be received?

XIII. Is it necessary or advisable to call together the two Houses of Congress with a view to the present posture of European Affairs? If it is, what should be the particular object of such a call?

Hamilton replied in two memoranda. Source: Henry Cabot Lodge (ed.), The Works of Alexander Hamilton (9 vols., New York, 1885–86), IV, 79, 97–98, 112.

[April 1793] . . . This great and important question arises out of the facts which have been stated:

Are the United States bound, by the principles of the laws of nations, to consider the treaties heretofore made with France as in present force and operation between them and the actual governing powers of the French nation? or may they elect to consider their operation as suspended, reserving also a right to judge finally whether any such changes have happened in the political affairs of France as may justify a renunciation of those treaties?

It is believed that they have an option to consider the operation of those treaties as suspended, and will have eventually a right to renounce them, if such changes shall take place as can *bona fide* be pronounced to render a continuance of the connections which result from them disadvantageous or dangerous. . . .

In national questions, the general conduct of nations has great weight. When all Europe is, or is likely to be, armed in opposition to the authority of the present government of France, would it not be to carry theory to an extreme, to pronounce that the United States are *under* an *absolute*, indispensable obligation, not only to acknowledge respectfully the authority of that government, but to admit the immediate operation of treaties, which would constitute them at once its ally?

Prudence, at least, seems to dictate the course of *reserving* the question in order that further reflection and a more complete development of circumstances shall enable us to make a decision both *right* and *safe*. It does not appear necessary to precipitate the fixing of our relations to France beyond the possibility of retraction. It is putting too suddenly too much to hazard. . . .

[May 2] . . . The result from what has been said is, that the war in which France is engaged is in *fact* an offensive war on her part against all the Powers with which she is engaged, except one; and in *principle*, to speak in the most favorable terms for her, is *at least* a mixed case—a case of mutual aggression.

The inference from this state of things is as plain as it is important. The *casus foederis* of the guaranty in the treaty of alliance between the United States and France cannot take place, though her West India Islands should be attacked.

The express denomination of this treaty is "Traité d' Alliance eventuelle et defensive"—Treaty of Alliance eventual and defensive.

The second article of the treaty also calls it a "defensive alliance." This, then, constitutes the leading feature, the characteristic quality of the treaty. By this principle every stipulation in it is to be judged.

Secretary Jefferson's written reply was dated April 28. Source: Ford (ed.), Writings of Thomas Jefferson, VI, 220, 224, 231.

. . . I consider the people who constitute a society or nation as the source of all authority in that nation, as free to transact their common concerns by any agents they think proper, to change these agents individually, or the organisation of them in form or function whenever they please: that all the acts done by those agents under the authority of the nation, are the acts of the nation, are obligatory on them, & enure to their use, & can in no wise be annulled or affected by any change in the form of the government, or of the persons administering it. Consequently the Treaties between the US. and France, were not treaties between the US. & Louis Capet, but between the two nations of America & France, and the nations remaining in existence, tho' both of them have since changed their forms of government, the treaties are not annulled by these changes. . . .

But I go further & deny that the most explicit declaration made at this moment that we acknolege the obligation of the treatys could take from us the right of non-compliance at any future time when compliance would involve us in great & inevitable danger.

I conclude then that few of these sources threaten any danger at all; and from none of them is it inevitable: & consequently none of them give us the right at this moment of releasing ourselves from our treaties. . . .

Upon the whole I conclude

That the treaties are still binding, notwithstanding the change of government in France: that no part of them, but the clause of guarantee, holds up danger, even at a distance.

And consequently that a liberation from no other part could be proposed in any case: that if that clause may ever bring danger, it is neither extreme, nor imminent, nor even probable: that the authority for renouncing a treaty, when *useless* or *disagreeable*, is either misunderstood, or in opposition to itself, to all their writers, & to every moral feeling: that were it not so, these treaties are in fact neither useless nor disagreeable.

That the receiving a Minister from France at this time is an act of no significance with respect to the treaties, amounting neither to an admission nor a denial of them, forasmuch as he comes not under any stipulation in them:

That were it an explicit admission, or were an express declaration of this obligation now to be made, it would not take from us that right which exists at all times of liberating ourselves when an adherence to the treaties would be *ruinous* or *destructive* to the society: and that the not renouncing the treaties now is so far from being a breach of neutrality, that the doing it would be the breach, by giving just cause of war to France.

In the somewhat formal manner of the eighteenth century, President Washington on September 17, 1796, submitted to his countrymen a "farewell address," which was not a speech but a statement to the newspaper press. By the end of his second term Washington had endured nearly four years of European war, and in the address he and his literary collaborator Hamilton produced some often-quoted thoughts on the true course of American policy. The interpretation of the address recently has been a subject of some controversy. In a book entitled Entangling Alliance (1958) Alexander De Conde drew the address as a piece of domestic political propaganda to ensure the election to the presidency of Washington's chosen successor, John Adams. Shortly after De Conde's book appeared, the then president of the American Historical Association, Samuel Flagg Bemis, pointedly reaffirmed Washington's nonpartisanship in an "editorial" in the American Historical Review, without taking specific issue with De Conde. For the address, see Fitzpatrick (ed.), The Writings of George Washington, XXXV, 219.

. . . Citizens by birth or choice, of a common country, that country has a right to concentrate your affections. The name of AMERICAN, which belongs to you, in your national capacity, must always exalt the just pride of Patriotism, more than any appellation derived from local discriminations. With slight shades of difference, you have the same Religeon, Manners, Habits and political Principles. You have in a common cause fought and triumphed together. The independence and liberty you possess are the work of joint councils, and joint efforts; of common dangers, sufferings and successes.

But these considerations, however powerfully they address themselves to your sensibility are greatly outweighed by those which apply more immediately to your Interest. Here every portion of our country finds the most commanding motives for carefully guarding and preserving the Union of the whole. . . .

In contemplating the causes wch. may disturb our Union, it occurs as matter of serious concern, that any ground should have been furnished for characterizing parties by *Geographical* discriminations: *Northern* and *Southern*; *Atlantic* and *Western*; whence designing men may endeavour to excite a belief that there is a real difference of local interests and views. One of the expedients of Party to acquire influence, within particular districts, is to misrepresent the opinions and aims of other Districts. You cannot shield yourselves too much against the jealousies and heart burnings which spring from these misrepresentations. They tend to render Alien to each other those who ought to be bound together by fraternal affection. The Inhabitants of our Western country have lately had a useful lesson on this head. They have seen, in the Negociation by the Executive, and in the unanimous ratification by the Senate, of the Treaty with Spain, and in the universal satisfaction at that event, throughout the United States, a decisive proof how unfounded were the suspicions propagated among them of a policy in the General Government and in the Atlantic States unfriendly to their Interests in regard to the MISSISSIPPI. They have been witnesses to the formation of two Treaties, that with G: Britain and that with Spain, which secure to them every thing they could desire, in respect to our Foreign relations, towards confirming their prosperity. Will it not be their wisdom to rely for the preservation of [sic] these advantages on the UNION by wch. they were procured? Will they not henceforth be deaf to those advisers, if such there are, who would sever them from their Brethren and connect them with Aliens?

To the efficacy and permanency of Your Union, a Government for the whole is indispensable. No Alliances however strict between the parts can be an adequate substitute. They must inevitably experience the infractions and interruptions which all Alliances in all times have experienced. Sensible of this momentous truth, you have improved upon your first essay, by the adoption of a Constitution of Government, better calculated than your former for an intimate Union, and for the efficacious management of your common concerns. This government, the offspring of our own choice uninfluenced and unawed, adopted upon full investigation and mature deliberation, completely free in its principles, in the distribution of its powers, uniting security with energy, and containing within itself a provision for its own amendment, has a just claim to your confidence and your support. . . .

Observe good faith and justice towds. all Nations. Cultivate peace and harmony with all. Religion and morality enjoin this conduct; and can it be that good policy does not equally enjoin it? It will be worthy of a free, enlightened, and, at no distant period, a great Nation, to give to mankind the magnanimous and too novel example of a People always guided by an exalted justice and benevolence. Who can doubt that in the course of time and things the fruits of such a plan would richly repay any temporary advantages wch. might be lost by a steady adherence to it? Can it be, that Providence has not connected the permanent felicity of a Nation with its virtue? The experiment, at least, is recommended by every sentiment which ennobles human Nature. Alas! is it rendered impossible by its vices?

In the execution of such a plan nothing is more essential than that permanent, inveterate antipathies against particular Nations and passionate attachments for others should be excluded; and that in place of them just and amicable feelings towards all should be cultivated. The Nation, which indulges towards another an habitual hatred, or an habitual fondness, is in some degree a slave. It is a slave to its animosity or to its affection, either of which is sufficient to lead it astray from its duty and its interest. Antipathy in one Nation against another, disposes each more readily to offer insult and injury, to lay hold of slight causes of umbrage, and to be haughty and intractable, when accidental or trifling occasions of dispute occur. Hence frequent collisions, obstinate envenomed and bloody contests. The Nation, prompted by illwill and resentment sometimes impels to War the Government, contrary to the best calculations of policy. The Government sometimes participates in the national propensity, and adopts through passion what reason would reject; at other times, it makes the animosity of the Nation subservient to projects of hostility instigated by pride, ambition and other sinister and pernicious motives. The peace often, sometimes perhaps the Liberty, of Nations has been the victim.

So likewise, a passionate attachment of one Nation for another produces a variety of evils. Sympathy for the favourite nation, facilitating the illusion of an imaginary common interest, in cases where no real common interest exists, and infusing into one the enmities of the other, betrays the former into a participation in the quarrels and Wars of the latter, without adequate inducement or justification: It leads also to concessions to the favourite Nation of priviledges denied to others, which is apt doubly to injure the Nation making the concessions; by unnecessarily parting with what ought to have been retained; and by exciting jealousy, ill will, and a disposition to retaliate, in the parties from whom eql. priviledges are withheld: And it gives to ambitious, corrupted, or deluded citizens (who devote themselves to the favourite Nation) facility to betray, or sacrifice the interests of their own country, without odium, sometimes even with popularity; gilding with the appearances of a virtuous sense of obligation a commendable deference for public opinion, or a laudable zeal for public good, the base or foolish compliances of ambition corruption or infatuation.

As avenues to foreign influence in innumerable ways, such attachments are particularly alarming to the truly enlightened and independent Patriot. How many opportunities do they afford to tamper with domestic factions, to practice the arts of seduction, to mislead public opinion, to influence or awe the public Councils! Such an attachment of a small or weak, towards a great and powerful Nation, dooms the former to be the satellite of the latter.

Against the insidious wiles of foreign influence, (I conjure you to believe me fellow citizens) the jealousy of a free people ought to be *constantly* awake; since history and experience prove that foreign influence is one of the most baneful foes of Republican Government. But that jealousy to be useful must be impartial; else it becomes the instrument of the very influence to be avoided, instead of a defence against it. Excessive partiality for one foreign nation and excessive dislike of another, cause those whom they actuate to see danger only on one side, and serve to veil and even second the arts of influence on the other. Real Patriots, who may resist the intriegues of the favourite, are liable to become suspected and odious; while its tools and dupes usurp the applause and confidence of the people, to surrender their interests.

The Great rule of conduct for us, in regard to foreign Nations is in extending our commercial relations to have with them as little *political* connection as possible. So far as we have already formed engagements let them be fulfilled, with perfect good faith. Here let us stop.

Europe has a set of primary interests, which to us have none, or a very remote relation. Hence she must be engaged in frequent controversies, the causes of which are essentially foreign to our concerns. Hence therefore it must be unwise in us to implicate ourselves, by artificial ties, in the ordinary vicissitudes of her politics, or the ordinary combinations and collisions of her friendships, or enmities:

Our detached and distant situation invites and enables us to pursue a different course. If we remain one People, under an efficient government, the period is not far off, when we may defy material injury from external annoyance; when we may take such an attitude as will cause the neutrality we may at any time resolve upon to be scrupulously respected; when belligerent nations, under the impossibility of making acquisitions upon us, will not lightly hazard the giving us provocation; when we may choose peace or war, as our interest guided by our justice shall Counsel.

Why forego the advantages of so peculiar a situation? Why quit our own to stand upon foreign ground? Why, by interweaving our destiny with that of any part of Europe, entangle our peace and prosperity in the toils of European Ambition, Rivalship, Interest, Humour or Caprice?

'Tis our true policy to steer clear of permanent Alliances, with any portion of the foreign world. So far, I mean, as we are now at liberty to do it, for let me not be understood as capable of patronising infidility to existing engagements (I hold the maxim no less applicable to public than to private affairs, that honesty is always the best policy). I repeat it therefore, let those engagements be observed in their genuine sense. But in my opinion, it is unnecessary and would be unwise to extend them.

Taking care always to keep ourselves, by suitable establishments, on a respectably defensive posture, we may safely trust to temporary alliances for extraordinary emergencies.

Harmony, liberal intercourse with all Nations, are recommended by policy, humanity and interest. But even our Commercial policy should hold an equal and impartial hand: neither seeking nor granting exclusive favours or preferences; consulting the natural course of things; diffusing and deversifying by gentle means the streams of Commerce, but forcing nothing; establishing with

Powers so disposed; in order to give to trade a stable course, to define the rights of our Merchants, and to enable the Government to support them; conventional rules of intercourse, the best that present circumstances and mutual opinion will permit, but temporary, and liable to be from time to time abandoned or varied, as experience and circumstances shall dictate; constantly keeping in view, that 'tis folly in one Nation to look for disinterested favors from another; that it must pay with a portion of its Independence for whatever it may accept under that character; that by such acceptance, it may place itself in the condition of having given equivalents for nominal favours and yet of being reproached with ingratitude for not giving more. There can be no greater error than to expect, or calculate upon real favours from Nation to Nation. 'Tis an illusion which experience must cure, which a just pride ought to discard.

In offering to you, my Countrymen these counsels of an old and affectionate friend, I dare not hope they will make the strong and lasting impression, I could wish; that they will controul the usual current of the passions, or prevent our Nation from running the course which has hitherto marked the Destiny of Nations: But if I may even flatter myself, that they may be productive of some partial benefit, some occasional good; that they may now and then recur to moderate the fury of party spirit, to warn against the mischiefs of foreign Intrigue, to guard against the Impostures of pretended patriotism; this hope will be a full recompence for the solicitude for your welfare, by which they have been dictated.

How far in the discharge of my Official duties, I have been guided by the principles which have been delineated, the public Records and other evidences of my conduct must Witness to You and to the world. To myself, the assurance of my own conscience is, that I have at least believed myself to be guided by them.

In relation to the still subsisting War in Europe, my Proclamation of the 22d. of April 1793 is the index to my Plan.[1] Sanctioned by your approving voice and by that of Your Representatives in both Houses of Congress, the spirit of that measure has continually

---

[1] Washington's proclamation of neutrality (he did not use the word "neutrality") remarked that the United States was at peace with France and Great Britain, and warned American citizens against acts of hostility toward any of the belligerent powers.

governed me; uninfluenced by any attempts to deter or divert me from it. . . .

14. XYZ

The quasi war with France of 1798–99 stemmed from the refusal of the French government of the time, the Directory, to show even a modicum of respect for the United States—this despite the continued existence of the alliance of 1778. It was a question of war or humiliation. When Minister James Monroe left Revolutionary France he was succeeded in 1797 by Charles Cotesworth Pinckney, whom the Directory refused to receive. President Adams thereupon moved with care. Because of the need to obtain unity in domestic politics, to avoid any feeling among the lovers or haters of Revolutionary France that the United States government had failed of proper behavior toward the erstwhile ally, Adams chose a geographically representative commission to reopen negotiations in Paris: C. C. Pinckney (South Carolina), John Marshall (Virginia), and Elbridge Gerry (Massachusetts). This diplomatic trinity reported their reception in the French capital, in some astonishment, to Secretary of State Timothy Pickering on October 22, 1797. President Adams was deeply angered, and sent this dispatch and subsequent dispatches to Congress as he received them, substituting for Talleyrand's intermediaries the initials of "X" and "Y" and "Z." Walter Lowrie and Matthew St. Clair Clarke (eds.), American State Papers: Foreign Relations (6 vols., Washington, D.C., 1832–59), II, 158–160 is the source usually cited for the famous dispatch of October 22. This published version is rather unreliable, and following is the original from the archives of the Department of State.

. . . In the morning of October the eighteenth, Mr. Hubbard, of the House of Van Stophorsts and Hubbard of Amsterdam called on general Pinckney and informed him that a Mr. Hottinguer who was in Paris and whom the Gen[l] had seen at Amsterdam was a gentleman of considerable credit and reputation; that he had formerly been a banker . . . . . [these dots are in the manuscript] at Paris, and had settled his [?] affairs with honor; that he had then formed connections in America, had married a [?] of that country; intended to settle there; was supported by some capital [?] houses in Holland; and that we might place great reliance on him.

In the evening of the same day, M. Hottinguer called on Gen[l] Pinckney; and after having sat some time in a room full of company, whispered him that he had a message from M. Talleyrand to communicate when he was at leisure. General Pinckney immediately withdrew with him into another room; and when they were alone, M. Hottinguer said that he was charged with a business in which he was a novice; that he had been acquainted with M. Talleyrand in America; and that he was sure that he had a great regard for that country and its citizens; and was very desirous that a reconciliation should be brought about with France: that to effectuate that end, he was ready, if it was thought proper, to suggest a plan, confidentially, that M. Talleyrand expected would answer the purpose. Gen[l] Pinckney said he should be glad to hear it. M. Hottinguer replied, that the Directory, and particularly two of the members of it, were exceedingly irritated at some passages of the President's speech, and desired that they should be softened; and that this step would be necessary previous to our reception: that besides this, a sum of money was required for the pocket of the Directory and ministers, which would be at the disposal of M. Talleyrand: and that a loan would also be insisted on. M. Hottinguer said if we acceded to these measures, M. Talleyrand had no doubt that all our differences with France might be accommodated. On enquiry, M. Hottinguer could not point out the particular passages of the speech that had given offence, nor the quantum of the loan, but mentioned that the douceur for the pocket was twelve hundred thousand livres,—about fifty thousand pounds sterling. Gen[l] Pickney told him, his colleagues and himself, from the time of their arrival here, had been treated with great slight and disrespect; that they earnestly wished for peace and reconciliation with France; & had been entrusted by their country with very great powers to obtain these ends, on honorable terms; that with regard to the propositions made, he could not even consider of them before he had communicated them to his colleagues; that after he had done so, he should hear from him. After a communication and consultation had, it was agreed that General Pinckney should call on M. Hottinguer, and request him to make his propositions to us all; and, for fear of mistake or misapprehension, that he should be requested to reduce the heads into writing. Accordingly, on the morning of October the nineteenth, General Pinckney called on M. Hottinguer, who consented to see his colleagues in the evening, and to reduce his propositions to writing. He said his communication was not immediately with M. Talleyrand, but thro' another gentleman, in whom M. Talleyrand had great confidence: this proved afterwards to be M. Bellamy, a native of Geneva, of the house of Bellamy Riccia and Company of Hamburg.

... Mr. Bellami stated to us explicitly and repeatedly that he was clothed with no authority; that he was not a diplomatic character; that he was not even a Frenchman; he was only the friend of M. Talleyrand, and trusted by him. That with regard to himself he had landed property in America, on which he hoped his children would reside; and that he earnestly wished well to the UStates. He then took out of his pocket a French translation of the President's speech, the parts of which, objected to by the Directory, were marked agreeably to our request to M. Hottinguer, and are contained in the exhibit A. Then he made us the second set of propositions ...

But, said he, gentlemen, I will not disguise from you, that this satisfaction, being made, the essential part of the treaty remains to be adjusted: "il faut de l'argent—il faut beaucoup d'argent." You must pay money—you must pay a great deal of money. He spoke much of the force, the honor, and the jealous republican pride of France; and represented to us strongly the advantages which we should derive from the neutrality thus to be purchased. He said that the receipt of the money might be so disguised as to prevent its being considered as a breach of neutrality by England; and thus save us from being embroiled with that power. . . .

He spoke of the respect which the Directory required, and repeated, that it would exact as much as was paid to the antient kings. We answered that America had demonstrated to the world, and especially to France, a much greater respect for her present government than for her former monarchy; and that there was no evidence of this disposition which ought to be required, that we were not ready to give. He said that we should certainly not be received; and seemed to shudder at the consequences. We told him that America had made every possible effort to remain on friendly terms with France; that she was still making them: that if France would not hear us, but would make war on the Ustates; nothing remained for us, but to regret the unavoidable necessity of defending ourselves. . . .

VI

The Louisiana Purchase

No one in the United States in 1803 was more astonished than President Jefferson when he learned that his ministers in Paris, Livingston and Monroe, had bought all of Louisiana. He had instructed them to buy the "island" of New Orleans and if possible the Floridas, East and West. Their mission's outcome was extraordinary. A later generation would describe the Louisiana Purchase as an evidence of "manifest destiny." In the year 1803 that phrase was two generations into the future, and Jefferson could only consider it a result of the chapter of accidents.

The President quickly accepted this turn of fortune, whatever damage the purchase did to his dearest principle of political science, the strict construction of the Constitution.

15. A small view of a large opportunity

In the months after the secret Franco-Spanish Treaty of San Ildefonso of October 1, 1800, the retrocession of Louisiana from Spain to France was rumored in the chancellories of Europe, and at last it took on almost the full color of truth. Jefferson indited a famous letter of April 18, 1802, to Livingston. Source: 57th Congress, 2d Session, House Executive Document No. 431, State Papers and Correspondence bearing upon the Purchase of the Territory of Louisiana (Washington, D.C., 1903), pp. 15–18.

The cession of Louisiana and the Floridas by Spain to France, works most sorely on the United States. On this subject the Secretary of State has written to you fully, yet I cannot forbear recurring to it personally, so deep is the impression it makes on my mind. It completely reverses all the political relations of the United States, and will form a new epoch in our political course. Of all nations of any consideration, France is the one which, hitherto, has offered the fewest points on which we could have any conflict of right, and the most points of a communion of interests. From these causes, we have ever looked to her as our *natural friend*, as one with which we never could have an occasion of difference. Her growth, therefore, we viewed as our own, her misfortunes ours. There is on the globe one single spot, the possessor of which is our natural and habitual enemy. It is New Orleans, through which the produce of three-eighths of our territory must pass to market, and from its fertility it will ere long yield more than half of our whole produce, and contain more than half of our inhabitants. France, placing herself in that door, assumes to us the attitude of defiance. Spain might have retained it quietly for years. Her pacific dispositions, her feeble state, would induce her to increase our facilities there, so that her possession of the place would be hardly felt by us, and it would not, perhaps, be very long before some circumstance might arise, which might make the cession of it to us the price of something of more worth to her. Not so can it ever be in the hands of France: the impetuosity of her temper, the energy and restlessness of her character, placed in a point of eternal friction with us, and our character, which, though quiet and loving peace and the pursuit of wealth, is high-minded, despising wealth in competition with insult or injury, enterprising and energetic as any nation on earth; these circumstances render it impossible that France and the United States can continue long friends, when they meet in so irritable a position. They, as well as we, must be blind if they do not see this; and we must be very improvident if we do not begin to make arrangements on that hypothesis. The day that France takes possession of New Orleans, fixes the sentence which is to restrain her forever within her low-water mark. It seals the union of two nations, who, in conjunction, can maintain exclusive possession of the ocean. From that moment, we must marry ourselves to the British fleet and nation. We must turn all our attention to a maritime force, for which our resources place us on very high ground; and having formed and connected together a power which may render reinforcement of her settlements here impossible to France, make the first cannon which shall be fired in Europe the signal for the tearing up any settlement she may have made, and for holding the two continents of America in sequestration for the common purposes of the United British and American nations. This is not a state of things we seek or desire. It is one which this measure, if adopted by France, forces on us as necessarily, as any other cause, by the laws of nature, brings on its necessary effect.

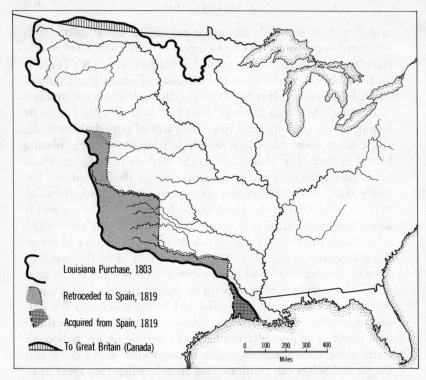

3. The Louisiana Purchase.

It is not from a fear of France that we deprecate this measure proposed by her. For however greater her force is than ours, compared in the abstract, it is nothing in comparison of ours, when to be exerted on our soil. But it is from a sincere love of peace, and a firm persuasion, that bound to France by the interests and the strong sympathies still existing in the minds of our citizens, and holding relative positions which insure their continuance, we are secure of a long course of peace. Whereas, the change of friends, which will be rendered necessary if France changes that position, embarks us necessarily as a belligerent power in the first war of Europe. In that case, France will have held possession of New Orleans during the interval of a peace, long or short, at the end of which it will be wrested from her. Will this short-lived possession have been an equivalent to her for the transfer of such a weight into the scale of her enemy? Will not the amalgamation of a young, thriving nation, continue to that enemy the health and force which are at present so evidently on the decline? And will a few years' possession of New Orleans add equally to the strength of France? She may say she needs Louisiana for the supply of her West Indies. She does not need it in time of peace, and in war she could not depend on them, because they would be so easily intercepted. I should suppose that all these considerations might, in some proper form, be brought into view of the Government of France. Though stated by us, it ought not to give offence; because we do not bring them forward as a menace, but as consequences not controllable by us, but inevitable from the course of things. We mention them, not as things which we desire by any means, but as things we deprecate; and we beseech a friend to look forward and to prevent them for our common interest.

If France considers Louisiana, however, as indispensable for her views, she might perhaps be willing to look about for arrangements which might reconcile it to our interests. If anything could do this, it would be the ceding to us the island of New Orleans and the Floridas. This would certainly, in a great degree, remove the causes of jarring and irritation between us, and perhaps for such a length of time, as might produce other means of making the measure permanently conciliatory to our interests and friendships. It would, at any rate, relieve us from the necessity of taking immediate measures for countervailing such an operation by arrangements in another quarter. But still we should consider New Orleans and the Floridas as no equivalent for the risk of a quarrel with France, produced by her vicinage.

I have no doubt you have urged these considerations, on every proper occasion, with the government where you are. They are such as must have effect, if you can find means of producing thorough reflection on them by that government. The idea here is, that the troops sent to St. Domingo, were to proceed to Louisiana after finishing their work in that island. If this were the arrangement, it will give you time to return again and again to the charge. For the conquest of St. Domingo will not be a short work. It will take considerable time, and wear down a great number of soldiers. Every eye in the United States is now fixed on the affairs of Louisiana. Perhaps nothing since the revolutionary war, has produced more uneasy sensations through the body of the nation. Notwithstanding temporary bickerings have taken place with France, she has still a strong hold on the affections of our citizens generally. I have thought it not amiss, by way of supplement to the letters of the Secretary of State, to write you this private one, to impress you with the importance we affix to this transaction. I pray you to cherish Dupont. He has the best disposition for the continuance of friendship between the two nations, and perhaps you may be able to make a good use of him.

Nothing if not clever, the President on April 25, 1802, arranged for the powder maker, Dupont de Nemours, to carry the Livingston letter to Paris. Source: ibid., pp. 18–19.

The week being now closed, during which you had given me a hope of seeing you here, I think it safe to enclose you my letters for Paris, lest they should fail of the benefit of so desirable a conveyance. They are addressed to Kosciugha, Madame de Corney, Mrs. Short, and Chancellor Livingston. You will perceive the unlimited confidence I repose in your good faith, and in your cordial dispositions to serve both countries, when you observe that I leave the letters for Chancellor Livingston open for your perusal. The first page respects a cypher, as do the loose sheets folded with the letter. These are interesting to him and myself only, and therefore are not for your perusal. It is the second, third, and fourth pages which I wish you to read to possess yourself of completely, and then seal the letter with wafers stuck under the flying seal, that it may be seen by nobody else if any accident should happen to you. I wish you to be possessed of the subject, because you may be able to impress on the government of France the inevitable consequences of their taking possession of Louisiana; and though, as I here mention, the cession of New Orleans and the Floridas to us would be a palliation, yet I believe it would be no more, and that this measure will cost France, and perhaps not very long hence, a war which will annihilate her on the ocean, and place that element under the despotism of two nations, which I am not reconciled to the more because my own would be one of them. Add to this the exclusive appropriation of both continents of America as a consequence. I wish the present order of things to continue, and with a view to this I value highly a state of friendship between France and us. You know too well how sincere I have ever been in these dispositions to doubt them. You know, too, how much I value peace, and how unwillingly I should see any event take place which would render war a necessary resource; and that all our movements should change their character and object. I am thus open with you,. because I trust that you will have it in your power to impress on that government considerations, in the scale against which the possession of Louisiana is nothing. In Europe, nothing but Europe is seen, or supposed to have any right in the affairs of nations; but this little event, of France's possessing herself of Louisiana, which is thrown in as nothing, as a mere make-weight in the general settlement of accounts,—this speck which now appears as an almost invisible point in the horizon, is the embryo of a tornado which will burst on the countries on both sides of the Atlantic, and involve in its effects their highest destinies. That it may yet be avoided is my sincere prayer; and if you can be the means of informing the wisdom of Bonaparte of all its consequences, you have deserved well of both countries. Peace and abstinence from European interferences are our objects, and so will continue while the present order of things in America remain uninterrupted. There is another service you can render. I am told that Talleyrand is personally hostile to us. This, I suppose, has been occasioned by the X Y Z history. But he should consider that that was the artifice of a party, willing to sacrifice him to the consolidation of their power. This nation has done him justice by dismissing them; that those in power are precisely those who disbelieved that story, and saw in it nothing but an attempt to deceive our country; that we entertain towards him personally the most friendly dispositions; that as to the government of France, we know too little of the state of things there to understand what it is, and have no inclination to meddle in their settlement. Whatever government they establish, we wish to be well with it. One more request,—that you deliver the letter to Chancellor Livingston with your own hands, and, moreover, that you charge Madam Dupont, if any accident happen to you, that she deliver the letter with her own hands. If it passes only through her's and your's, I shall have perfect confidence in its safety. Present her my most sincere respects, and accept yourself assurances of my constant affection, and my prayers, that a genial sky and propitious gales may place you, after a pleasant voyage, in the midst of your friends.

16. Purchase

The European wars which had begun in 1793 ended with a truce in
1801, made formal by the Treaty of Amiens of 1802. But Amiens was
a truce, for the young Napoleon Bonaparte was anxious for some sort
of action. When the troops designated to occupy Louisiana were unable
to sail late in 1802 because of the freezing of the Dutch Channel port
of Sluis, the first consul—France had changed its form of government
to a Consulate—apparently began to consider renewing the European
struggle. Livingston at this time was writing essays on the general
worthlessness of territory in the New World, which he believed Napoleon read, and with a certain pride he had sent copies to Secretary
of State James Madison. Livingston evidently suspected Madison of not
reading the essays. In any event the time for essays was passing, as the
minister wrote in the following remarkable document to Jefferson dated
March 12, 1803. Source: ibid., pp. 145–146.

Mr. Madison has never told me whether he has received two
little essays, calculated, the one to raise our importance in the
views of this Government as a naval Power; and the other to disgust
them with Louisiana, preparatory to our future negotiations. They
were both read with considerable attention by the First Consul,
having had them translated for that purpose.

I broke off this part of my letter to attend Madame Bonaparte's
drawing-room, where a circumstance happened of sufficient importance to merit your attention. . . . After the First Consul
had gone the circuit of one room, he turned to me, and made some
of the common inquiries usual on those occasions. He afterwards
returned, and entered into a further conversation. When he quitted
me, he passed most of the other Ministers merely with a bow,
went up to Lord Whitworth, and, after the first civilities, said: "I
find, my Lord, your nation wants war again." L. W. "No, sir, we
are very desirous of peace." First Consul. "You have just finished
a war of fifteen years." L. W. "It is true, sir, and that was
fifteen years too long." Consul. "But you want another war of
fifteen years." L. W. "Pardon, me, sir, we are very desirous of
peace." Consul. "I must either have Malta or war." L. W. "I am
not prepared, sir, to speak on that subject; and I can only assure
you, citizen First Consul, that we wish for peace."

The prefect of the palace, at this time, came up to the Consul, and informed him that there were ladies in the next room, and asked him to go in. He made no reply, but, bowing hastily to the company, retired immediately to his cabinet, without entering the other room. Lord Whitworth came up to me, and repeated the conversation as I now give it to you. I asked Lord Whitworth whether there were any pending negotiations relative to Malta. He told me that there were; that the conduct of France having convinced them that they still had views upon Egypt, and the guaranties to which they were entitled, with respect to Malta, not having been executed, they thought they could not surrender it with safety. But what brought on the business to-day was, a message from the King of Great Britain to the Parliament on the 1st, which has just been received here, speaking with distrust of the armaments in the French ports, and, in fact, preparing them for war.

This you will have sooner by the way of England than this letter. It is, then, highly probable that a new rupture will take place, since it is hardly possible that the First Consul would commit himself so publicly, unless his determination had been taken. I am fearful that this may again throw some impediment in the way of our claims, which I believed in so prosperous a train. In other views it may serve us, and I shall give all my attention to avail myself of circumstances as they arise; in which I hope shortly to receive the assistance of Mr. Monroe.

I must pray you, sir, to furnish Mr. Madison with such an extract from this letter as ought to be on his file of correspondence with me; since the fear of losing the opportunity, and the necessity of the greater activity at this interesting moment, will deprive me of the pleasure of writing further to him by this conveyance.

On Easter Sunday, April 10, 1803, or thereabouts, the first consul made up his mind to sell Louisiana, and commissioned his minister of foreign affairs, Talleyrand, to talk to Livingston. Next day the American minister was debating the edges of the problem, such as the closure of the port of New Orleans by the Spanish official Morales, contrary to the terms of Pinckney's Treaty, when Talleyrand asked him the question. The following account is taken from a letter by Livingston to Madison, written that epochal day, Monday, April 11. Source: ibid., pp. 157–159.

My note will tell you how far I have officially pressed the Government on the subject of Louisiana. I have omitted no means, in conversation, of eradicating their prejudices in its favor; and I informed you that I had reason to think that I had been successful with all, unless it was the First Consul, to whom I addressed myself in the letter and essays that you have seen, and which were attentively read by him, as well as several informal notes to his brother. I had reason to think that he began to waver; but we had nothing to offer but money, and commercial advantages: of the latter, I did not think myself entitled to be liberal; and of the first, I found in them a certain degree of reluctance to treat, as derogatory to the dignity of the Government. The affair of New Orleans gave me two very important strings to touch: I endeavored to convince the Government that the United States would avail themselves of the breach of the treaty to possess themselves of New Orleans and the Floridas; that Britain would never suffer Spain to grant the Floridas to France, even were she so disposed, but would immediately seize upon them as soon as the transfer was made; that without the Floridas, Louisiana would be indefensible, as it possesses not one port even for frigates; and I showed the effect of suffering that important country to fall into the hands of the British, both as it affected our country, and the naval force of all Europe.

These reasons, with the probability of war, have had, I trust, the desired effect. M. Talleyrand asked me this day, when pressing the subject, whether we wished to have the whole of Louisiana. I told him no; that our wishes extended only to New Orleans and the Floridas; that the policy of France should dictate (as I had shown in an official note) to give us the country above the river Arkansas, in order to place a barrier between them and Canada. He said, that if they gave New Orleans the rest would be of little value; and that he would wish to know "what we would give for the whole." I told him it was a subject I had not thought of; but that I supposed we should not object to twenty millions, provided our citizens were paid. He told me that this was too low an offer; and that he would be glad if I would reflect upon it, and tell him to-morrow. I told him that, as Mr. Monroe would be in town in two days, I would delay my further offer until I had the pleasure of introducing him. He added, that he did not speak from authority, but that the idea had struck him. . . .

P. S., 12th.—Orders are gone this day to stop the sailing of vessels from the French ports; war is inevitable; my conjecture as to their determination to sell is well founded; Mr. Monroe is just arrived here.

The minister of the treasury, François Barbé-Marbois, took over the negotiation from Talleyrand, presumably because the Americans in 1797 had had an unpleasant experience with the foreign minister's personal concern for money. Livingston wrote Madison on Wednesday midnight, April 13, 1803. Source: ibid., pp. 159–163.

PARIS, *April 13, 1803, midnight.*

I have just come from the Minister of the Treasury. Our conversation was so important, that I think it necessary to write it, while the impressions are strong upon my mind; and the rather, as I fear I shall not have time to copy and send this letter, if I defer it till morning.

By my letter of yesterday, you learned that the Minister had asked me whether I would agree to purchase Louisiana, &c. On the 12th, I called upon him to press this matter further. He then thought proper to declare that his proposition was only personal, but still requested me to make an offer; and, upon declining to do so, as I expected Mr. Monroe the next day, he shrugged up his shoulders, and changed the conversation. Not willing, however, to lose sight of it, I told him I had been long endeavoring to bring him to some point; but, unfortunately, without effect: that I wished merely to have the negotiation opened by any proposition on his part; and, with that view, had written him a note which contained that request, grounded upon my apprehension of the consequence of sending General Bernadotte without enabling him to say a treaty was begun. He told me he would answer my note, but that he must do it evasively, because Louisiana was not theirs. I smiled at this assertion, and told him I had seen the treaty recognizing it; that I knew the Consul had appointed officers to govern the country, and that he had himself told me that General Victor was to take possession; that, in a note written by the express order of the First Consul, he had told me that General Bernadotte was to treat relative to it in the United States, &c. He still persisted that they had it in contemplation to obtain it, but had it not. I told him that I was very well pleased to understand this from him, because, if so, we should not commit ourselves with them in taking it from Spain, to whom, by his account, it still belonged; and that, as we had just cause of complaint against her, if

Mr. Monroe concurred in opinion with me, we should negotiate no further on the subject, but advise our Government to take possession. He seemed alarmed at the boldness of the measure, and told me he would answer my note, but that it would be evasively. I told him I should receive with pleasure any communication from him, but that we were not disposed to trifle; that the times were critical, and though I did not know what instructions Mr. Monroe might bring, I was perfectly satisfied that they would require a precise and prompt notice; that I was very fearful, from the little progress I had made, that my Government would consider me as a very indolent negotiator. He laughed, and told me that he would give me a certificate that I was the most importunate he had met with.

There was something so extraordinary in all this, that I did not detail it to you till I found some clue to the labyrinth, which I have done, as you will find before I finish this letter; and the rather, as I was almost certain that I could rely upon the intelligence I had received of the resolution to dispose of this country.

This day Mr. Monroe passed with me in examining my papers; and while he and several other gentlemen were at dinner with me, I observed the Minister of the Treasury walking in my garden. I sent out Colonel Livingston to him; he told him he would return when we had dined. While we were taking coffee he came in; and, after being some time in the room, we strolled into the next room, when he told me he heard I had been at his house two days before, when he was at St. Cloud; that he thought I might have something particular to say to him, and had taken the first opportunity to call on me. I saw that this was meant as an opening to one of those free conversations which I had frequently had with him. I accordingly began on the subject of the debt, and related to him the extraordinary conduct of the Minister, &c. He told me that this led to something important, that had been cursorily mentioned to him at St. Cloud; but as my house was full of company, he thought I had better call on him any time before 11 that night. He went away, and, a little after, when Mr. Monroe took leave, I followed him. He told me that he wished me to repeat what I had said relative to M. Talleyrand's requesting a proposition from me as to the purchase of Louisiana. I did so; and concluded with the extreme absurdity of his evasions of that day, and stated the consequence of any delay on this subject, as it would enable Britain to take posses-

sion, who would readily relinquish it to us. He said that this proceeded upon a supposition of her making so successful a war as to
be enabled to retain her conquests. I told him that it was probable
that the same idea might suggest itself to the United States; in
which case, it would be their interest to contribute to render her
successful, and I asked whether it was prudent to throw us into
her scale? This led to long discussions of no moment to repeat. We
returned to the point: he said, that what I had told him led him
to think that what the Consul had said to him on Sunday, at St.
Cloud, (the day on which, as I told you, the determination had
been taken to sell,) had more of earnest than he thought at the
time; that the Consul had asked him what news from England? . . .

He (Marbois) then took occasion to mention his sorrow that any
cause of difference should exist between our countries. The Consul
told him, in reply, "Well, you have the charge of the treasury; let
them give you one hundred millions of francs, and pay their own
claims, and take the whole country." Seeing, by my looks, that I
was surprised at so extravagant a demand, he added that he considered the demand as exorbitant, and had told the First Consul
that the thing was impossible; that we had not the means of raising
that. The Consul told him we might borrow it. I now plainly saw
the whole business: first, the Consul was disposed to sell; next, he
distrusted Talleyrand, on account of the business of the supposed
intention to bribe, and meant to put the negotiation into the hands
of Marbois, whose character for integrity is established. I told him
that the United States were anxious to preserve peace with France;
that, for that reason, they wished to remove them to the west side
of the Mississippi; that we would be perfectly satisfied with New
Orleans and the Floridas, and had no disposition to extend across
the river; that, of course, we would not give any great sum for the
purchase; that he was right in his idea of the extreme exorbitancy
of the demand, which would not fall short of one hundred and
twenty-five millions; that, however, we would be ready to purchase,
provided the sum was reduced to reasonable limits. He then
pressed me to name the sum. I told him that this was not worth
while, because, as he only treated the inquiry as a matter of curiosity,
any declaration of mine would have no effect. If a negotiation was
to be opened, we should (Mr. Monroe and myself) make the offer
after mature reflection. This compelled him to declare, that,
though he was not authorized expressly to make the inquiry from

me, yet, that, if I could mention any sum that came near the mark, that could be accepted, he would communicate it to the First Consul. I told him that we had no sort of authority to go to a sum that bore any proportion to what he mentioned; but that, as he himself considered the demand as too high, he would oblige me by telling me what he thought would be reasonable. He replied that, if we would name sixty millions, and take upon us the American claims, to the amount of twenty more, he would try how far this would be accepted. I told him that it was vain to ask anything that was so greatly beyond our means; that true policy would dictate to the First Consul not to press such a demand; that he must know that it would render the present Government unpopular, and have a tendency, at the next election, to throw the power into the hands of men who were most hostile to a connection with France; and that this would probably happen in the midst of a war. I asked him whether the few millions acquired at this expense would not be too dearly bought?

He frankly confessed that he was of my sentiments; but that he feared the Consul would not relax. I asked him to press this argument upon him, together with the danger of seeing the country pass into the hands of Britain. I told him that he had seen the ardor of the Americans to take it by force, and the difficulty with which they were restrained by the prudence of the President; that he must easily see how much the hands of the war party would be strengthened, when they learned that France was upon the eve of a rupture with England. He admitted the weight of all this: "But," says he, "you know the temper of a youthful conqueror; everything he does is rapid as lightning; we have only to speak to him as an opportunity presents itself, perhaps in a crowd, when he bears no contradiction. When I am alone with him, I can speak more freely, and he attends; but this opportunity seldom happens, and is always accidental. Try, then, if you can not come up to my mark. Consider the extent of the country, the exclusive navigation of the river, and the importance of having no neighbors to dispute you, no war to dread." I told him that I considered all these as important considerations, but there was a point beyond which we could not go, and that fell far short of the sum he mentioned.

. . . I speak now without reflection, and without having seen Mr. Monroe, as it was midnight when I left the Treasury Office, and is now near 3 o'clock. It is so very important that you should be apprized that a negotiation is actually opened, even before Mr. Monroe has been presented, in order to calm the tumult which the news of war will renew, that I have lost no time in communicating it. We shall do all we can to cheapen the purchase; but my present sentiment is that we shall buy. Mr. Monroe will be presented to the Minister to-morrow, when we shall press for as early an audience as possible from the First Consul. I think it will be necessary to put in some proposition to-morrow: the Consul goes in a few days to Brussels, and every moment is precious.

17. Loose construction in foreign affairs

A principle of eighteenth-century political science which has lingered into the twentieth is that the best government is the least. Strict construction of the Constitution was both philosophically attractive and politically expedient, once Jefferson passed into opposition against the Hamiltonians, especially in the era of the quasi war with France when Jefferson inspired the Virginia and Kentucky Resolutions. After the Louisiana Purchase the President, on August 12, 1803, wrote to Senator John Breckinridge of Kentucky, a close friend and supporter. Source: ibid., pp. 233–235.

The enclosed letter, though directed to you, was intended to me also, and was left open with a request, that when forwarded, I would forward it to you. It gives me occasion to write a word to you on the subject of Louisiana, which being a new one, an interchange of sentiments may produce correct ideas before we are to act on them.

Our information as to the country is very incomplete; we have taken measures to obtain it full as to the settled part, which I hope to receive in time for Congress. The boundaries, which I deem not admitting question, are the high lands on the western side of the Mississippi enclosing all its waters, the Missouri of course, and terminating in the line drawn from the northwestern point of the Lake of the Woods to the nearest source of the Mississippi, as lately settled between Great Britain and the United States. We have some claims, to extend on the seacoast westwardly to the Rio Norte or Bravo, and better, to go eastwardly to the Rio Perdido, between Mobile and Pensacola, the ancient boundary of Louisiana. These claims will be a subject of negotiation with Spain, and if, as soon as she is at war, we push them strongly with one hand, holding out a price in the other, we shall certainly obtain the Floridas, and all in good time. In the meanwhile, without waiting for permission, we shall enter into the exercise of the natural right we have always insisted on with Spain, to-wit, that of a nation holding the upper part of streams, having a right of innocent passage through them to the ocean. We shall prepare her to see us practice on this, and she will not oppose it by force.

Objections are raising to the eastward against the vast extent of our boundaries, and propositions are made to exchange Louisiana, or a part of it, for the Floridas. But, as I have said, we shall get the Floridas without, and I would not give one inch of the waters of the Mississippi to any nation, because I see in a light very important to our peace the exclusive right to its navigation, and the admission of no nation into it, but as into the Potomac or Delaware, with our consent and under our police. These federalists see in this acquisition the formation of a new confederacy, embracing all the waters of the Mississippi, on both sides of it, and a separation of its eastern waters from us. These combinations depend on so many circumstances which we can not foresee, that I place little reliance on them. We have seldom seen neighborhood produce affection among nations. The reverse is almost the universal truth. Besides, if it should become the great interest of those nations to separate from this, if their happiness should depend on it so strongly as to induce them to go through that convulsion, why should the Atlantic States dread it? But especially why should we, their present inhabitants, take side in such a question? When I view the Atlantic States, procuring for those on the eastern waters of the Mississippi friendly instead of hostile neighbors on its western waters, I do not view it as an Englishman would the procuring future blessings for the French nation, with whom he has no relations of blood or affection. The future inhabitants of the Atlantic and Mississippi States will be our sons. We leave them in distinct but bordering establishments. We think we see their happiness in their union, and we wish it. Events may prove it otherwise; and if they see their interest in separation, why should we take side with our Atlantic rather than our Mississippi descendants? It is the elder and the younger son differing. God bless them both, and keep them in union, if it be for their good, but separate them, if it be better. The inhabited part of Louisiana, from Point Coupée to the sea, will of course be immediately a territorial government, and soon a State. But above that, the best use we can make of the country for some time, will be to give establishments in it to the Indians on the east side of the Mississippi, in exchange for their present country, and open land offices in the last, and thus make this acquisition the means of filling up the eastern side, instead of drawing off its population. When we shall be full on this side, we may lay off a range of States on the western bank from the head to the mouth, and so, range after range, advancing compactly as we multiply.

This treaty must of course be laid before both Houses, because both have important functions to exercise respecting it. They, I presume, will see their duty to their country in ratifying and paying for it, so as to secure a good which would otherwise probably be never again in their power. But I suppose they must then appeal to *the nation* for an additional article to the Constitution, approving and confirming an act which the nation had not previously authorized. The Constitution has made no provision for our holding foreign territory, still less for incorporating foreign nations into our Union. The executive in seizing the fugitive occurrence which so much advances the good of their country, have done an act beyond the Constitution. The Legislature in casting behind them metaphysical subtleties, and risking themselves like faithful servants, must ratify and pay for it, and throw themselves on their country for doing for them unauthorized, what we know they would have done for themselves had they been in a situation to do it. It is the case of a guardian investing the money of his ward in purchasing an important adjacent territory; and saying to him when of age, I did this for your good; I pretend to no right to bind you: you may disavow me, and I must get out of the scrape as I can: I thought it my duty to risk myself for you. But we shall not be disavowed by the nation, and their act of indemnity will confirm and not weaken the Constitution, by more strongly marking out its lines.

VII

War of 1812

American entrance into the Napoleonic wars in 1812, like her entrance into the First World War in 1917, came from many reasons, but chief of the reasons both in 1812 and 1917 was the defense of neutral rights. If one were to cut the neutral rights controversy out of the eras before 1812 or 1917 with a pair of unhistorical scissors, there probably (although who can prove it?) would have been no resort to war. In the years before 1812, Americans held many grievances against the British: western desire for Canada, southern desire for the Floridas, western land hunger, frontier anger against British support of the Indians from Canada and Spain's inability to prevent Indian raids out of the Floridas, an agricultural depression in the West and South which stirred frontiersmen into ascribing their woes to Britain's restrictive maritime measures. Woodrow Wilson, a well-known scholar at the turn of the twentieth century, announced in 1902 that the causes of the War of 1812 were "singularly uncertain." But from the viewpoint of the latter twentieth century, neutral rights do stand out as the chief cause of the War of 1812.

18. Europe's restrictions

President Jefferson's first term almost completed the circle of his felicities (to use one of his expressions), but his second administration beginning in March 1805 saw a succession of calamities. It was not his fault but that of the belligerents of Europe. The dismal year 1805 produced not merely the Essex decision, in which a court in London virtually closed the American wartime trade to the French and British colonies; the Battle of Trafalgar gave Britain supremacy on sea, and Austerlitz ensured Napoleon—now emperor—supremacy on land. Both belligerents soon fell upon neutral commerce, which was mainly that of the United States. The American treaty plan of 1784 had set out the formula of "imminent danger" as a definition of blockade. The British *government found it more convenient to declare a "paper blockade" of European ports, and capture neutral violators on the high seas, either on the trade routes or in the narrow places such as the Channel. A major British pronouncement came on May 16, 1806, setting out a blockade of the coast, rivers, and ports of the Continent from the Elbe River to the port of Brest, both inclusive. Although on September 25 the ministry announced discontinuance of the blockade of the coast, rivers, and ports from the Elbe to the Ems River, both inclusive, Napoleon from his "imperial camp" in Berlin retaliated with a decree of November 21, 1806. Source: 10th Cong., 2d Sess., Annals of Congress, pp. 1749–1750.*

Napoleon, Emperor of the French and King of Italy, considering:

1. That England does not admit the right of nations as universally acknowledged by all civilized people;

2. That she declares as an enemy every individual belonging to an enemy State, and, in consequence, makes prisoners of war, not only the crews of armed vessels, but also of merchant vessels, and even the supercargoes of the same;

3. That she extends or applies to merchant vessels, to articles of commerce, and to the property of individuals, the right of conquest, which can only be applied or extended to what belongs to an enemy State;

4. That she extends to ports not fortified, to harbors and mouths of rivers, the right of blockade, which, according to reason and the usage of civilized nations, is applicable only to strong or fortified ports;

5. That she declares blockaded, places before which she has not a single vessel of war, although a place ought not to be considered blockaded but when it is so invested as that no approach to it can be made without imminent hazard; that she declares even places blockaded which her united forces would be incapable of doing, such as entire coasts, and a whole empire;

6. That this unequalled abuse of the right of blockade has no other object than to interrupt the communications of different nations, and to extend the commerce and industry of England upon the ruin of those of the Continent;

4. Europe in the Age of Napoleon, 1806.

Kingdom
of
Sweden

St. Petersburg

Moscow

RUSSIA

Mecklenburg

Tilsit

Friedland

Eylau

BRANDENBURG-
PRUSSIA

Berlin

Warsaw

Saxony

Austerlitz

HAPSBURG EMPIRE

Vienna   Pressburg

Buda

Kingdom
of
ssia

dom
of Italy

OTTOMAN EMPIRE

EUROPE in 1806

0   100   200   300

miles

Malta

7. That this being the evident design of England, whoever deals on the Continent in English merchandise favors that design and becomes an accomplice;

8. That this conduct in England (worthy only of the first ages of barbarism,) has benefited her, to the detriment of other nations;

9. That it being right to oppose to an enemy the same arms she makes use of, to combat as she does, when all ideas of justice and every liberal sentiment (the result of civilization among men) are disregarded;

We have resolved to enforce against England the usages which she has consecrated in her maritime code.

The present decree shall be considered as the fundamental law of the Empire, until England has acknowledged that the rights of war are the same on the land as at sea; that it cannot be extended to any private property whatever, nor to persons who are not military, and until the right of blockade be restrained to fortified places, actually invested by competent forces.

Art. 1. The British islands are declared in a state of blockade.

Art. 2. All commerce and correspondence with the British islands are prohibited.

The British replied with an order in council of January 7, 1807—that is, an executive decision of the British cabinet taken in council with the sovereign. Source: ibid., pp. 1695–1696.

Whereas the French Government has issued certain orders, which, in violation of the usages of war, purport to prohibit the commerce of all neutral nations with His Majesty's dominions, and also to prevent such nations from trading with any other country in any articles the growth, produce, or manufacture of His Majesty's dominions; and whereas the said Government has also taken upon itself to declare all His Majesty's dominions to be in a state of blockade at the time when the fleets of France and her allies are themselves confined within their own ports by the superior valor and discipline of the British navy; and whereas such attempts, on the part of the enemy, would give to His Majesty an unquestionable right of retaliation, and would warrant His Majesty in enforcing the same prohibition of all commerce with France, which that Power vainly hopes to effect against the commerce of His Majesty's subjects, a prohibition which the superiority of His Majesty's naval forces might enable him to support by actually investing the ports and coasts of the enemy with numerous squadrons and cruisers, so as to make the entrance or approach thereto manifestly dangerous; and whereas His Majesty, though unwilling to follow the example of his enemies by proceeding to an extremity so distressing to all nations not engaged in the war, and carrying on their accustomed trade, yet feels himself bound, by due regard to the just defence of the rights and interests of his people not to suffer such measures to be taken by the enemy, without taking some steps on his part to restrain this violence, and to retort upon them the evils of their own injustice: His Majesty is thereupon pleased, by and with the advice of his Privy Council, to order, and it is hereby ordered, that no vessels shall be permitted to trade from one port to another, both which ports shall belong to or be in the possession of France or her allies, or shall be so far under their control as that British vessels may not trade freely thereat. . . .

The British minister in Washington, David M. Erskine, on June 26, 1807, communicated the following advice to Secretary Madison. Source: ibid., p. 1696.

I have the honor to inform you that His Majesty has judged it expedient to re-establish the most rigorous blockade at the entrances of the rivers Ems, Weser, and Elbe, inclusive, in consequence of the present position of the enemy upon the Continent, which enables him to command the navigation of those rivers.

More orders in council followed on November 11, 1807. Source: ibid., pp. 1698–1699, 1703. The licensing system therein announced eventually proved so lenient—many thousands of licenses were to be granted, for trade almost anywhere—that it removed most of the restrictions of the orders, but at the time it appeared formidable enough.

Whereas certain orders, establishing an unprecedented system of warfare against this Kingdom, and aimed especially at the destruction of its commerce and resources, were, sometime since, issued by the Government of France, by which "the British islands were declared to be in a state of blockade," thereby subjecting to capture and condemnation all vessels, with their cargoes, which should continue to trade with His Majesty's dominions:

And whereas, by the same order, "all trading in English merchandise is prohibited, and every article of merchandise belonging to England, or coming from her colonies, or of her manufacture, is declared lawful prize:"

And whereas the nations in alliance with France, and under her control, were required to give, and have given, and do give, effect to such orders:

And whereas His Majesty's order of the 7th of January last has not answered the desired purpose, either of compelling the enemy to recall those orders, or of inducing neutral nations to interpose, with effect, to obtain their revocation, but, on the contrary, the same have been recently enforced with increased rigor:

And whereas His Majesty, under these circumstances, finds himself compelled to take further measures for asserting and vindicating his just rights, and for supporting that maritime power which the exertions and valor of his people have, under the blessing of Providence, enabled him to establish and maintain; and the maintenance of which is not more essential to the safety and prosperity of His Majesty's dominions, than it is to the protection of such States as still retain their independence, and to the general intercourse and happiness of mankind:

His Majesty is therefore pleased, by and with the advice of his Privy Council, to order, and it is hereby ordered, that all the ports and places of France and her allies, or of any other contry at war with His Majesty, and all other ports or places in Europe, from which, although not at war with His Majesty, the British flag is excluded, and all ports or places in the colonies belonging to His Majesty's enemies, shall, from henceforth, be subject to the same restrictions in point of trade and navigation, with the exceptions hereinafter mentioned, as if the same were actually blockaded by His Majesty's naval forces, in the most strict and rigorous manner . . .

And it is further ordered, that all vessels which shall arrive at any port of the United Kingdom, or at Gibraltar, or Malta . . . shall be allowed, in respect to all articles which may be on board the same, except sugar, coffee, wine, brandy, snuff, and tobacco, to clear out to any port whatever, to be specified in such clearance; and, with respect to the last mentioned articles, to export the same to such ports, and under such conditions and regulations only, as His Majesty, by any license to be granted for that purpose, may direct. . . .

Whereas the sale of ships by a belligerent to a neutral is considered by France to be illegal:

And whereas a great part of the shipping of France and her

allies has been protected from capture during the present hostilities by transfers, or pretended transfers, to neutrals:

And whereas it is fully justifiable to adopt the same rule, in this respect, towards the enemy, which is applied by the enemy to this country:

His Majesty is pleased, by and with the advice of his Privy Council to order, and it is hereby ordered, that, in future, the sale to a neutral of any vessel belonging to His Majesty's enemies shall not be deemed to be legal, nor in any manner to transfer the property, nor to alter the character of such vessel; and all vessels now belonging, or which shall hereafter belong, to any enemy of His Majesty, notwithstanding any sale, or pretended sale, to a neutral, after a reasonable time shall have elapsed for receiving information of this His Majesty's order at the place where such sale, or pretended sale, was effected, shall be captured and brought in, and shall be adjudged as lawful prize to the captors. . . .

From "our royal palace at Milan" Napoleon retaliated on December 17, 1807. Source: ibid., pp. 1751–1752.

Napoleon, Emperor of the French, King of Italy, and Protector of the Rhenish Confederation:

Observing the measures adopted by the British Government, on the 11th November last, by which vessels belonging to neutral, friendly, or even Powers the allies of England, are made liable, not only to be searched by English cruisers, but to be compulsorily detained in England, and to have a tax laid on them of so much per cent. on the cargo, to be regulated by the British Legislature:

Observing that, by these acts, the British Government denationalizes ships of every nation in Europe; that it is not competent for any Government to detract from its own independence and rights, all the Sovereigns of Europe having in trust the sovereignties and independence of the flag; that if, by an unpardonable weakness, and which in the eyes of posterity would be an indelible stain, if such a tyranny was allowed to be established into principles, consecrated by usage, the English would avail themselves of it to assert it as a right, as they have availed themselves of the tolerance of Government to establish the infamous principle that the flag of a nation does not cover goods and to have to their right of blockade an arbitrary extension, and which infringes on the sovereignty of every

State; we have decreed and do decree as follows:

Art. 1. Every ship, to whatever nation it may belong, that shall have submitted to be searched by an English ship, or to a voyage to England, or shall have paid any tax whatsoever to the English Government, is thereby, and for that alone, declared to be denationalized, to have forfeited the protection of its King, and to have become English property.

Art. 3. The British islands are declared to be in a state of measures of the English Government enter into our ports, or those of our allies, or whether they fall into the hands of our ships of war, or of our privateers, they are declared to be good and lawful prize.

Art. 3. The British islands are declared to be in a state of blockade, both by land and sea. Every ship, of whatever nation, or whatsoever the nature of its cargo may so be, that sails from the ports of England, or those of the English colonies, and of the countries occupied by English troops, and proceeding to England, or to the English colonies, or to countries occupied by English troops, is good and lawful prize, as contrary to the present decree, and may be captured by our ships of war, or our privateers, and adjudged to the captor.

Art. 4. These measures, which are resorted to only in just retaliation of the barbarous system adopted by England, which assimilates its legislation to that of Algiers, shall cease to have any effect with respect to all nations who shall have the firmness to compel the English Government to respect their flag. . . .

19. America's prohibitions

Observing the pattern of American trade, seeing that so large a percentage of Britain's manufactures went to the United States, Jefferson and his advisers long had believed that it would be possible to coerce the British by cutting off their American markets, exactly as Napoleon was seeking to coerce the British through the continental system. In a sense this would resemble the nonimportation agreements before the American Revolution. The embargo of 1807–9 was nominally against both Britain and France, but its weight was on Britain. To the Jeffersonians an embargo had the added attraction of being a highly pacific measure, not likely to lead to war. The Embargo Act became law on December 22, 1807. Source: Statutes at Large, II, 451–453.

Be it enacted by the Senate and House of Representatives of the United States of America in Congress assembled, That an embargo be, and hereby is laid on all ships and vessels in the ports and places within the limits or jurisdiction of the United States, cleared or not cleared, bound to any foreign port or place; and that no clearance be furnished to any ship or vessel bound to such foreign port or place, except vessels under the immediate direction of the President of the United States: and that the President be authorized to give such instructions to the officers of the revenue, and of the navy and revenue cutters of the United States, as shall appear best adapted for carrying the same into full effect: *Provided,* that nothing herein contained shall be construed to prevent the departure of any foreign ship or vessel, either in ballast, or with the goods, wares and merchandise on board of such foreign ship or vessel, when notified of this act.

Sec. 2. *And be it further enacted,* That during the continuance of this act, no registered, or sea letter vessel, having on board goods, wares and merchandise, shall be allowed to depart from one port of the United States to any other within the same, unless the master, owner, consignee or factor of such vessel shall first give bond, with one or more sureties to the collector of the district from which she is bound to depart, in a sum of double the value of the vessel and cargo, that the said goods, wares, or merchandise shall be relanded in some port of the United States, dangers of the seas excepted, which bond, and also a certificate from the collector where the same may be relanded, shall by the collector respectively be transmitted to the Secretary of the Treasury. All armed vessels possessing public commissions from any foreign power, are not to be considered as liable to the embargo laid by this act.

Administratively the Embargo Act proved difficult. The bureaucratic machinery of the new United States just was not up to ensuring a total prohibition of foreign commerce. Nor, for that matter, were the machineries of any of the states of Europe; before the latter nineteenth century, none of the national bureaucracies was highly developed. To Jefferson's critics the Nonintercourse Act of March 1, 1809, which passed three days before Madison assumed the presidency, was an admission of defeat because—they said—it was impossible to check on vessels once departed from the Atlantic and Gulf harbors. Source: ibid., 528–533.

Be it enacted by the Senate and House of Representatives of the United States of America in Congress assembled, That from and after the passing of this act, the entrance of the harbors and waters of the United States and of the territories thereof, be, and the same is hereby interdicted to all public ships and vessels belonging to Great Britain or France, excepting vessels only which may be forced in by distress, or which are charged with despatches or business from the government to which they belong, and also packets having no cargo nor merchandise on board. . . .

Sec. 3. *And be it further enacted*, That from and after the twentieth day of May next, the entrance of the harbors and waters of the United States and the territories thereof be, and the same is hereby interdicted to all ships or vessels sailing under the flag of Great Britain or France, or owned in whole or in part by any citizen or subject of either; vessels hired, chartered or employed by the government of either country, for the sole purpose of carrying letters or despatches, and also vessels forced in by distress or by the dangers of the sea, only excepted. . . .

Sec. 4. *And be it further enacted*, That from and after the twentieth day of May next, it shall not be lawful to import into the United States or the territories thereof, any goods, wares or merchandise whatever, from any port or place situated in Great Britain or Ireland, or in any of the colonies or dependencies of Great Britain, nor from any port or place situated in France, or in any of her colonies or dependencies, nor from any port or place in the actual possession of either Great Britain or France. Nor shall it be lawful to import into the United States, or the territories thereof, from any foreign port or place whatever, any goods, wares or merchandise whatever, being of the growth, produce or manufacture of France, or of any of her colonies or dependencies, or being of the growth, produce or manufacture of Great Britain or Ireland, or of any of the colonies or dependencies of Great Britain, or being of the growth, produce or manufacture of any place or country in the actual possession of either France or Great Britain . . .

Sec. 11. *And be it further enacted*, That the President of the United States be, and he hereby is authorized, in case either France or Great Britain shall so revoke or modify her edicts, as that they shall cease to violate the neutral commerce of the United States, to declare the same by proclamation; after which the trade of the United States, suspended by this act, and by the act laying an embargo on all ships and vessels in the ports and harbors of the United States, and the several acts supplementary thereto, may be renewed with the nation so doing . . .

Sec. 12. *And be it further enacted,* That so much of the act laying an embargo on all ships and vessels in the ports and harbors of the United States, and of the several acts supplementary thereto, as forbids the departure of vessels owned by citizens of the United States, and the exportation of domestic and foreign merchandise to any foreign port or place, be, and the same is hereby repealed, after the fifteenth day of March, one thousand eight hundred and nine, except so far as they relate to Great Britain or France, or their colonies or dependencies, or places in the actual possession of either . . .

Sec. 13. *And be it further enacted,* That during the continuance of so much of the act laying an embargo on all ships and vessels in the ports and harbors of the United States, and of the several acts supplementary thereto, as is not repealed by this act, no ship or vessel bound to a foreign port, with which commercial intercourse shall, by virtue of this act, be again permitted, shall be allowed to depart for such port, unless the owner or owners, consignee or factor of such ship or vessel shall, with the master, have given bond with one or more sureties to the United States, in a sum double the value of the vessel and cargo, if the vessel is wholly owned by a citizen or citizens of the United States; and in a sum four times the value, if the vessel is owned in part or in whole by any foreigner or foreigners, that the vessel shall not leave the port without a clearance, nor shall, when leaving the port, proceed to any port or place in Great Britain or France, or in the colonies or dependencies of either, or in the actual possession of either, nor be directly or indirectly engaged during the voyage in any trade with such port, nor shall put any article on board of any other vessel . . .

Sec. 15. *And be it further enacted,* That during the continuance of so much of the act laying an embargo on all ships and vessels in the ports and harbors of the United States, and of the several acts supplementary thereto, as is not repealed by this act, no vessel owned by citizens of the United States, bound to another port of the said States or licensed for the coasting trade, shall be allowed to depart from any port of the United States, or shall receive a clearance, nor shall it be lawful to put on board any such vessel any specie or goods, wares, or merchandise, unless a permit shall have been previously obtained from the proper collector, or from a revenue officer, authorized by the collector to grant such permits; nor unless the owner, consignee, agent, or factor shall, with the master, give bond with one or more sureties, to the United States, in a sum double the value of the vessel and cargo, that the vessel shall not proceed to any foreign port or place, and that the cargo shall be relanded in some port of the United States . . .

Sec. 19. *And be it further enacted*, That this act shall continue and be in force until the end of the next session of Congress, and no longer . . .

The Nonintercourse Act lapsed at the end of the congressional session in the spring of 1810, and Congress conceived the idea of auctioning off American support between the two major belligerents. President Madison was by nature a theorist, and the stipulations of Macon's Bill Number 2, dated May 1, 1810, perhaps appealed to him. Source: ibid., 605–606.

Be it enacted by the Senate and House of Representatives of the United States of America in Congress assembled, That from and after the passage of this act, no British or French armed vessel shall be permitted to enter the harbors or waters under the jurisdiction of the United States; but every British and French armed vessel is hereby interdicted, except when they shall be forced in by distress, by the dangers of the sea, or when charged with despatches or business from their government, or coming as a public packet for the conveyance of letters . . .

Sec. 4. *And be it further enacted*, That in case either Great Britain or France shall, before the third day of March next [March 1811], so revoke or modify her edicts as that they shall cease to violate the neutral commerce of the United States, which fact the President of the United States shall declare by proclamation, and if the other nation shall not within three months thereafter so revoke or modify her edicts in like manner, then the . . . [nonintercourse articles of the Act of March 1, 1809] shall, from and after the expiration of three months from the date of the proclamation aforesaid, be revived and have full force and effect, so far as relates to the dominions, colonies and dependencies, and to the articles the growth, produce or manufacture of the dominions, colonies and dependencies of the nation thus refusing or neglecting to revoke or modify her edicts in the manner aforesaid. And the restrictions imposed by this act shall, from the date of such proclamation, cease and be discontinued in relation to the nation revoking or modifying her decrees in the manner aforesaid.

20. The descent into war

Where cleverness was involved, Napoleon was likely to prove more facile than President Madison. The emperor's foreign minister of the moment, the Duc de Cadore, sent the following letter dated August 5, 1810, to the American minister in Paris, General John Armstrong. Source: American State Papers: Foreign Relations, III, 386–387.

I have laid before His Majesty, the Emperor and King, the act of Congress of the 1st of May, taken from the Gazette of the United States, which you have sent to me.

His Majesty could have wished that this act, and all the other acts of the Government of the United States, which interest France, had always been officially made known to him. In general, he has only had a knowledge of them indirectly, and after a long interval of time. There have resulted from this delay serious inconveniences, which would not have existed if these acts had been promptly and officially communicated.

The Emperor had applauded the general embargo laid by the United States on all their vessels, because that measure, if it has been prejudicial to France, had in it at least nothing offensive to her honor. It has caused her to lose her colonies of Martinique, Guadaloupe, and Cayenne; the Emperor has not complained of it. He has made this sacrifice to the principle which had determined the Americans to lay the embargo, inspiring them with the noble resolution of interdicting to themselves the ocean, rather than to submit to the laws of those who wished to make themselves the tyrants of it.

The act of the 1st March has raised the embargo, and substituted for it a measure the most injurious to the interests of France.

This act, of which the Emperor knew nothing until very lately, interdicted to American vessels the commerce of France, at the time it authorized that to Spain, Naples, and Holland, that is to say, to the countries under French influence, and denounced confiscation against all French vessels which should enter the ports of America. Reprisal was a right, and commanded by the dignity of France, a circumstance on which it was impossible to make a compromise. The sequestration of all the American vessels in France has been the necessary consequence of the measure taken by Congress.

Now Congress retrace their steps, they revoke the act of the 1st of March; the ports of America are open to French commerce, and France is no longer interdicted to the Americans; in short, Congress engages to oppose itself to that one of the belligerent Powers which should refuse to acknowledge the rights of neutrals.

In this new state of things, I am authorized to declare to you, sir, that the decrees of Berlin and Milan are revoked, and that after the 1st of November they will cease to have effect; it being understood that, in consequence of this declaration, the English shall revoke their orders in council, and renounce the new principles of blockade, which they have wished to establish; or that the United States, conformably to the act you have just communicated, shall cause their rights to be respected by the English.

It is with the most particular satisfaction, sir, that I make known to you this determination of the Emperor. His Majesty loves the Americans. Their prosperity and their commerce are within the scope of his policy.

The independence of America is one of the principal titles of glory to France. Since that epoch, the Emperor is pleased in aggrandizing the United States, and, under all circumstances, that which can contribute to the independence, to the prosperity, and the liberty of the Americans, the Emperor will consider as conformable with the interests of his empire.

Not long after the Cadore letter, the congressional elections of 1810 returned a strident group of nationalists who in the House of Representatives elected the youthful Henry Clay as their Speaker. John Randolph, of course, described these men as war hawks. In the last weeks of 1811 the House gave vent to its anti-British feelings in a grand debate, and on December 31 the Speaker himself descended from the canopy to take part. Source: 12th Cong., 1st Sess., Annals of Congress, pp. 599–602.

. . . What are we to gain by war, has been emphatically asked? In reply, he would ask, what are we not to lose by peace?—commerce, character, a nation's best treasure, honor! If pecuniary considerations alone are to govern, there is sufficient motive for the war. Our revenue is reduced, by the operation of the belligerent edicts, to about six million of dollars, according to the Secretary of the Treasury's report. The year preceding the embargo, it was sixteen. Take away the Orders in Council, it will again mount up to sixteen millions. By continuing, therefore, in peace, if the mongrel state in which we are deserve that denomination, we lose annually, in revenue only, ten millions of dollars. Gentlemen will say; repeal the law of non-importation. He contended that, if the United States were capable of that perfidy, the revenue would not be restored to its former state, the Orders in Council continuing. Without an export trade, which those orders prevent, inevitable ruin would ensue, if we imported as freely as we did prior to the embargo. A nation that carries on an import trade without an export trade to support it, must, in the end, be as certainly bankrupt, as the individual would be, who incurred an annual expenditure, without an income.

He had no disposition to swell, or dwell upon the catalogue of injuries from England. He could not, however, overlook the impressment of our seamen; an aggression upon which he never reflected without feelings of indignation, which would not allow him appropriate language to describe its enormity. Not content with seizing upon all our property, which falls within her rapacious grasp, the personal rights of our countrymen—rights which forever ought to be sacred, are trampled upon and violated. The Orders in Council were pretended to have been reluctantly adopted as a measure of retaliation. The French decrees, their alleged basis, are revoked. England resorts to the expedient of denying the fact of the revocation . . . If, indeed, the aim of the French Emperor be universal dominion (and he was willing to allow it to the argument,) what a noble cause is presented to British valor. But, how is her philanthropic purpose to be achieved? By scrupulous observance of the rights of others; by respecting that code of public law, which she professes to vindicate, and by abstaining from self-aggrandizement. Then would she command the sympathies of the world. What are we required to do by those who would engage our feelings and wishes in her behalf? To bear the actual cuffs of her arrogance, that we may escape a chimerical French subjugation! We are invited, conjured to drink the potion of British poison actually presented to our lips, that we may avoid the imperial dose prepared by perturbed imaginations. We are called upon to submit to debasement, dishonor, and disgrace—to bow the neck to royal insolence, as a course of preparation for manly resistance to Gallic invasion! What nation, what individual was ever taught in the schools of ignominious submission, the patriotic lessons of freedom and independence? Let those who contend for this humiliating doctrine, read its refutation in the history of the very man against whose insatiable thirst of dominion we are warned. The experience of desolated Spain, for the last fifteen years, is worth volumes. Did she find her repose and safety in subserviency to the will of that man? Had she boldly stood forth and repelled the first attempt to dictate to her Councils, her Monarch would not now be a miserable captive at Marseilles. Let us come home to our own history. It was not by submission that our fathers achieved our independence. The patriotic wisdom that placed you, Mr. Chairman, said Mr. C., under that canopy, penetrated the designs of a corrupt Ministry, and nobly fronted encroachment on its first appearance. It saw beyond the petty taxes, with which it commenced, a long train of oppressive measures terminating in the total annihilation of liberty; and, contemptible as they were, did not hesitate to resist them. Take the experience of the last four or five years, and which, he was sorry to say, exhibited in appearance, at least, a different kind of spirit. He did not wish to view the past further than to guide us for the future. We were but yesterday contending for the indirect trade—the right to export to Europe the coffee and sugar of the West Indies. To-day we are asserting our claim to the direct trade—the right to export our cotton, tobacco, and other domestic produce to market. Yield this point, and to-morrow intercourse between New Orleans and New York—between the planters on James river and Richmond, will be interdicted. For, sir, the career of encroachment is never arrested by submission. It will advance while there remains a single privilege on which it can operate. Gentlemen say that this Government is unfit for any war, but a war of invasion. What, is it not equivalent to invasion, if the mouths of our harbors and outlets are blocked up, and we are denied egress from our own waters? Or, when the burglar is at our door, shall we bravely sally forth and repel his felonious entrance, or meanly skulk within the cells of the castle?

He contended that the real cause of British aggression, was not to distress an enemy but to destroy a rival. A comparative view of our commerce with England and the continent, would satisfy any one of the truth of this remark. Prior to the embargo, the balance of trade between this country and England, was between eleven and fifteen millions of dollars in favor of England. Our consumption of her manufactures was annually increasing, and had risen to nearly $50,000,000. We exported to her what she most wanted, provisions and raw materials for her manufactures, and received in return what she was most desirous to sell. Our exports to France, Holland, Spain, and Italy, taking an average of the years 1802, 3, and 4, amounted to about $12,000,000 of domestic, and about $18,000,000 of foreign produce. Our imports from the same countries amounted to about $25,000,000. The foreign produce exported consisted chiefly of luxuries from the West Indies. It is apparent that this trade, the balance of which was in favor, not of France, but of the United States, was not of very vital consequence to the enemy of England. Would she, therefore, for the sole purpose of depriving her adversary of this commerce, relinquish her valuable trade with this country, exhibiting the essential balance in her favor—nay, more; hazard the peace of the country? No, sir, you must look for an explanation of her conduct in the jealousies of a rival. She sickens at your prosperity, and beholds in your growth—your sails spread on every ocean, and your numerous seamen—the foundations of a Power which, at no very distant day, is to make her tremble for naval superiority.

21. Status quo ante bellum

The War of 1812 was hardly underway before President Madison was seeking an occasion to end it, and end it he did, albeit after months of uncertainty during which the American peace commissioners, hastily appointed, traipsed from St. Petersburg to Ghent, the Flemish town being the site chosen by the British. Fear of a revival of French power— Napoleon escaped from Elba barely two months after the Treaty of Ghent, and threw all Europe into an uproar which ended narrowly at Waterloo—persuaded the British to adjourn the American war. One of the American commissioners, Clay, described the Peace of Christmas Eve (it was concluded on December 24, 1814) as "a damned bad treaty," which perhaps it was; but the former war hawk signed it. The Senate approved it unanimously. Source: Miller (ed.), Treaties and Other International Acts . . . , II, 574–575, 581.

Article the First

There shall be a firm and universal Peace between His Britannic Majesty and the United States, and between their respective Countries, Territories, Cities, Towns, and People of every degree without exception of places or persons. All hostilities both by sea and land shall cease as soon as this Treaty shall have been ratified by both parties as hereinafter mentioned. All territory, places, and possessions whatsoever taken by either party from the other during the war, or which may be taken after the signing of this Treaty, excepting only the Islands hereinafter mentioned, shall be restored without delay and without causing any destruction or carrying away any of the Artillery or other public property originally captured in the said forts or places, and which shall remain therein upon the Exchange of the Ratifications of this Treaty, or any Slaves or other private property; And all Archives, Records, Deeds, and Papers, either of a public nature or belonging to private persons, which in the course of the war may have fallen into the hands of the Officers of either party, shall be, as far as may be practicable, forthwith restored and delivered to the proper authorities and persons to whom they respectively belong. Such of the Islands in the Bay of Passamaquoddy as are claimed by both parties shall remain in the possession of the party in whose occupation they may be at the time of the Exchange of the Ratifications of this Treaty until the decision respecting the title to the said Islands shall have been made in conformity with the fourth Article of this Treaty. No disposition made by this Treaty as to such possession of the Islands and territories claimed by both parties shall in any manner whatever be construed to affect the right of either. . . .

Article the Ninth

The United States of America engage to put an end immediately after the Ratification of the present Treaty to hostilities with all the Tribes or Nations of Indians with whom they may be at war at the time of such Ratification, and forthwith to restore to such Tribes or Nations respectively all the possessions, rights, and privileges which they may have enjoyed or been entitled to in one thousand eight hundred and eleven previous to such hostilities. Provided always that such Tribes or Nations shall agree to desist from all hostilities against the United States of America, their Citizens, and Subjects upon the Ratification of the present Treaty being notified to such Tribes or Nations, and shall so desist accordingly. And His Britannic Majesty engages on his part to put an end immediately after the Ratification of the present Treaty to hostilities with all the Tribes or Nations of Indians with whom He may be at war at the time of such Ratification, and forthwith to restore to such Tribes or Nations respectively all the possessions, rights, and privileges, which they may have enjoyed or been entitled to in one thousand eight hundred and eleven previous to such hostilities. Provided always that such Tribes or Nations shall agree to desist from all hostilities against His Britannic Majesty and His Subjects upon the Ratification of the present Treaty being notified to such Tribes or Nations, and shall so desist accordingly.

Article the Tenth

Whereas the Traffic in Slaves is irreconcilable with the principles of humanity and Justice, and whereas both His Majesty and the United States are desirous of continuing their efforts to promote its entire abolition, it is hereby agreed that both the contracting parties shall use their best endeavours to accomplish so desirable an object. . . .

VIII

Era of Good Feelings

In the United States the end of the War of 1812 brought a surge of nationalism more ambitious than the war's preliminary oratory, and in the next few years under Presidents Madison and (beginning in 1817) Monroe the nation stretched its pretensions to a size which the European powers considered either beyond or beneath contempt. It was bad enough, the Europeans thought, that after the wars of the French Revolution and Napoleon which had required four coalitions to send Bonaparte to St. Helena, that in the midst of organization of the Continent's peace by a series of congresses, the Americans should seek to force the hard-pressed Spanish monarch, Ferdinand VII, into consenting to an extraordinarily unfavorable (for Spain) boundary between Spanish and American possessions in the New World. Ferdinand may have been the most unreasonable man in Europe, as the quip had it, but even with his shortsightedness he could see that he had lost to the Americans. This sort of behavior, the Europeans felt, was bad enough. But the principles announced by Mr. Monroe in 1823 were so full of swagger and bluff that the only possible recourse was to ignore them. Or to convert them into a claim for one's own singular foresight and ingenuity, as Foreign Secretary George Canning did in 1826 before a House of Commons which, upon hearing Canning's boast, at first tittered uncertainly and then burst into a roar of applause.

To the American statesmen in the small town—it no longer was a village—of Washington, still remote in the American woods, these feelings and observations from the chancelleries of the Old World were the last squeakings and squawkings of a system so outmoded that it could not survive more than a generation or two. The United States recognized the Latin American republics of the New World beginning in 1821, and there was every evidence that before long the republics of Europe too would be clamoring for recognition.

22. The Transcontinental Treaty

Luis de Onís y Gonzales spent six years in the United States before the Madison administration cautiously recognized his presence as Spanish minister in 1815. Two years later he met President Monroe's secretary of state, John Quincy Adams, and the secretary soon was pressing the minister to cede the Floridas and to negotiate a boundary between Spanish Mexico and the Louisiana Purchase. The American claim to the Floridas was that West Florida—practically speaking, the portions of the present-day states of Alabama, Mississippi, and Louisiana below the thirty-first parallel, between the Perdido and Mississippi rivers—had been ceded to the United States in the Louisiana Purchase (the French-seemingly had been uncertain of the boundaries of the purchase), and that East Florida should be American because the Spanish government had failed to restrain the Indians as stipulated in Pinckney's Treaty, because Negroes had escaped from the United States to the Floridas, and because of Spanish actions against American commerce during the recent wars in Europe. On the eve of the War of 1812 and during the early months of that conflict, the United States had occupied West Florida between the Mississippi River and the Pearl River, the latter being the eastern boundary of the present-day state of Louisiana below the thirty-first parallel. It was clear that the United States was going to take the Floridas, by hook or crook. With good reason, Onís was worried. General Andrew Jackson, acting under ambiguous instructions, invaded the Floridas in 1818 with a force of 3,000 men, and nearly threw Onís into hysterics. Adams coolly supported the general. Interestingly, the other members of Monroe's cabinet were lukewarm or hostile. Not long after Jackson's convenient expedition the Spanish government gave up most of its arguments, and the secretary set out to ensure title to the Floridas and conclude a steplike Spanish-American boundary running from the present-day western border of the state of Louisiana, the Sabine River, north and west by rivers and parallels to the Pacific coast. The reader will observe Adams's insistence on the western banks of the rivers, even though the custom in drawing international boundaries was to run the line down mid-channel. Source: *Charles Francis Adams* (ed.), Memoirs of John Quincy Adams, Comprising Portions of His Diary from 1795 to 1848 (12 vols., Philadelphia, 1874–77), IV, 264, 266–267, 270, 274–275.

[February] 18th [,1819] Mr. Onis came to the office, and brought me a draft of the treaty in Spanish, as he said, according to the counterprojet offered by me, modified by the discussions which have taken place by the intervention of the French Minister, Mr. Hyde de Neuville. Onis himself has for the last ten days been confined to the house by chilblains, and this was the first time of his coming out. Upon reading over his projet, however, I found he had made some variations from the agreement as settled with De Neuville. He had in particular assumed the middle of the rivers for the boundaries, instead of the western bank of the Sabine and the southern bank of the Arkansas. I told him we should not agree to

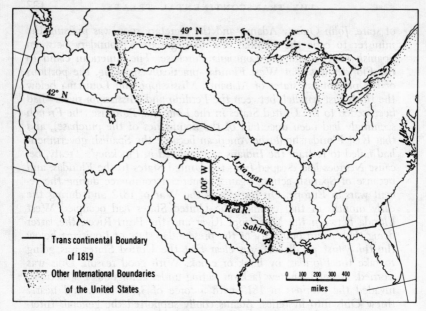

5. The Transcontinental Treaty.

this—when, to my astonishment, he told me that he had spoken of it last evening, at the drawing-room, to the President, who had promised him that we would agree to the middle of the rivers. I made no reply, but merely took it with the rest for reference. He importuned me again very obstately to omit the limitation of five millions of dollars to the sum assumed by the United States to be paid to their citizens for claims upon Spain, and, finding me inflexible, he at last urged that at least we should agree to take six millions for the limitation—which, however, I still resisted. . . .

19th. Cabinet meeting at the President's to consider the amended projet of a treaty with Spain, and the modifications still desired by Mr. Onis. . . .

At the meeting this morning I remarked that Onis still insisted upon having the middle of the rivers; but I did not notice his assertion that the President at the drawing-room had promised him we would agree to it. I proposed that we should adhere to the principle of owning the rivers and all the islands in them ourselves, and of course to having the banks, and not the middle of the rivers, for boundaries. The President thought it was not a point upon which we should endanger the conclusion of the treaty. Mr.

Thompson, Secretary of the Navy, asked if Onis would agree to take the banks of the rivers rather than break off. I said he would—he must; he had substantially agreed to it already. "Then," said Thompson, "insist upon it, by all means." The President acquiesced, as did Calhoun and Wirt. Crawford was not present, being confined to his house and bed by illness. . . .

20th. Mr. Onis came this morning to my house, and told me that he must accept the treaty as now prepared, since we would have it so, though he still thought we ought to give up the limitation of the five millions, and the banks for the middle of the rivers as the boundaries. I observed there was no time left for further discussion, and we had yielded so much that he would have great cause to commend himself to his Court for what he had obtained. He said I was harder to deal with than the President, and he must say, as a suitor once said to Philip IV., "Sire, your Majesty has no influence with the Minister of Grace and Justice, for he refuses me what you have granted." . . .

22d. . . . It was near one in the morning when I closed the day with ejaculations of fervent gratitude to the Giver of all good. It was, perhaps, the most important day of my life. What the consequences may be of the compact this day signed with Spain is known only to the all-wise and all-beneficent Disposer of events, who has brought it about in a manner utterly unexpected and by means the most extraordinary and unforeseen. Its prospects are propitious and flattering in an eminent degree. May they be realized by the same superintending bounty that produced them! May no disappointment embitter the hope which this event warrants us in cherishing, and may its future influence on the destinies of my country be as extensive and as favorable as our warmest anticipations can paint! Let no idle and unfounded exultation take possession of my mind, as if I could ascribe to my own foresight or exertions any portion of the event. It is the work of an intelligent and all-embracing Cause. May it speed as it has begun! for, without a continuation of the blessings already showered down upon it, all that has been done will be worse than useless, and vain.

The acquisition of the Floridas has long been an object of earnest desire to this country. The acknowledgment of a definite line of boundary to the South Sea forms a great epocha in our history. The first proposal of it in this negotiation was my own, and I trust it is now secured beyond the reach of revocation. It was not even among our claims by the Treaty of Independence with Great Britain. It was not among our pretensions under the purchase of Louisiana—for that gave us only the range of the Mississippi and its waters. I first introduced it in the written proposal of 31st October last, after having discussed it verbally both with Onis and De Neuville. It is the only peculiar and appropriate right acquired by this treaty in the event of its ratification. I record the first assertion of this claim for the United States as my own, because it is known to be mine perhaps only to the members of the present Administration, and may perhaps never be known to the public—and, if ever known, will be soon and easily forgotten. The provision, by the acquisition of the Floridas, of a fund for the satisfaction of claims held by citizens of the United States upon the Spanish Government, has been steadily pursued through a negotiation now of fifteen years' standing. It is of the whole treaty that which, in the case of the ratification, will have the most immediate and sensible effects. The change in the relations with Spain, from the highest mutual exasperation and imminent war to a fair prospect of tranquillity and of secure peace, completes the auspicious characters of this transaction in its present aspect, which fills my heart with gratitude unutterable to the First Cause of all. Yet let me not forget that in the midst of this hope there are seeds of fear. The ratification of Spain is yet uncertain, and may, by many possible events, be defeated. If ratified, many difficulties will certainly arise to clog the execution of the treaty. There is some discontent at the acceptance of the Sabine as our boundary from the Gulf of Mexico to the Red River. . . .

23. John Quincy Adams, defender of the New World

No reader of John Quincy Adams's diary can doubt the crotchety nationalism of the man. When he confronted the British minister, Stratford Canning, a cousin of the foreign secretary, Anglo-American rivalries were never more evident. Later he set down dramatically in the diary the discussions in the Monroe cabinet that preceded announcement of the Monroe Doctrine. Source: ibid., IV, 438–439; V, 249–252; VI, 157, 163, 177–179, 185–186, 194–199, 203–205, 208.

[November] 16th [,1819] . . . Great Britain, after vilifying us twenty years as a mean, low-minded, peddling nation, having no generous ambitions and no God but gold, had now changed her tone, and was endeavoring to alarm the world at the gigantic grasp of our ambition. Spain was doing the same, and Europe, who, even since the commencement of our Government under the present Constitution, had seen those nations intriguing with the Indians and negotiating to bound us by the Ohio, had first been startled by our acquisition of Louisiana, and now by our pretension to extend to the South Sea, and readily gave credit to the envious and jealous clamor of Spain and England against our ambition. Nothing that we could say or do would remove this impression until the world shall be familiarized with the idea of considering our proper dominion to be the continent of North America. From the time when we became an independent people it was as much a law of nature that this should become our pretension as that the Mississippi should flow to the sea. Spain had possessions upon our southern and Great Britain upon our northern border. It was impossible that centuries should elapse without finding them annexed to the United States; not that any spirit of encroachment or ambition on our part renders it necessary, but because it is a physical, moral, and political absurdity that such fragments of territory, with sovereigns at fifteen hundred miles [sic] beyond sea, worthless and burdensome to their owners, should exist permanently contiguous to a great, powerful, enterprising, and rapidly-growing nation. Most of the Spanish territory which had been in our neighborhood had already become our own by the most unexceptionable of all acquisitions—fair purchase for a valuable consideration. This rendered it still more unavoidable that the remainder of the continent should ultimately be ours. But it is very lately that we have distinctly seen this ourselves; very lately that we have avowed the pretension of extending to the South Sea; and until Europe shall find it a settled geographical element that the United States and North America are identical, any effort on our part to reason the world out of a belief that we are ambitious will have no other effect than to convince them that we add to our ambition hypocrisy. . . .

[January] 27th [,1821] The messenger of the Department announced Mr. Canning. I told the messenger to say to Mr. Canning that I would receive him in a few minutes. Mr. Eddy remained with me not more than five minutes longer; and Mr. Canning when he came in, as he sat down, took out his watch, and observed that it was forty minutes faster than the clock here. While he was speaking, the clock in the office struck one. I made no answer to his remark, which might be considered either as a complaint that he had been made to wait, or as an apology for having come before the time appointed. He proceeded to say that, conformably to the desire expressed by me yesterday, he had now come to have some further conversation upon the subject of our interview then.

There was in his manner an apparent effort of coolness, but no appearance of cheerfulness or good humor. I saw there was no relaxation from the tone he had yesterday assumed, and felt that none would on my part be suitable. I said he would recollect that our conference of this day was not at my desire. I had yesterday repeatedly expressed to him the opinion that if this discussion was to be further pursued it should be in writing. He had with some earnestness urged another conference, and when he requested me to fix the time I had told him that I was ready and willing to hear then anything that he had to say on the subject; that perhaps, under the excitement which he was then manifesting, he might himself prefer to resume the conversation some other day, and, if so, I would see him whenever it should be most agreeable to himself; he had then asked me to name a time, and I appointed this day at one o'clock.

He said, "Well, then, be it so." He then took from his pocket the National Intelligencer of yesterday, folded down to the column in which the proceedings of the House of Representatives were reported, and, referring to the statement that Mr. Floyd had reported a bill for the occupation of the Columbia River, said that was an indication of intentions in this Government which he presumed would leave no question of the propriety of his application to me.

I told him it was precisely that in which its greatest impropriety consisted. But I could only repeat what I had said to him yesterday, that I saw no use in continuing a discussion upon the propriety of his conduct or of mine.

He said he would most cheerfully consent to be the sacrifice, if that only was necessary to the harmony of the two countries; but that nothing could exceed his astonishment at the manner in which I had received his application of yesterday. He could assure me with the utmost sincerity that since the existence of this country as a nation there never had been a time when the British Government had been so anxiously desirous of preserving and cherishing the most perfect good understanding and harmony with this; but that at the same time they would not, on that account, yield one particle of their rights.

I told him I had no doubt of the correctness of his statement in both its parts, and I was happy to give him the same assurance on the part of this Government. It was the earnest wish of the President to preserve the most friendly relations with Great Britain; but he would maintain all the rights of the United States. And I would add, as my individual opinion, that any chicaning of our right to the mouth of Columbia River would assuredly not tend to promote that harmony between the two countries.

Mr. Canning again repeated his surprise at the tone and temper with which his application yesterday had been received. He said he had examined and re-examined himself, and had in vain enquired what could have been the cause of the asperity with which he had been treated by me.

"Sir," said I, "suppose Mr. Rush should be present at a debate in the House of Commons, and should hear a member in the course of a speech say something about the expediency of sending a regiment of troops to the Shetland Islands, or a new colony to New South Wales; suppose another member of Parliament should publish in a newspaper a letter recommending the same project; and suppose Mr. Rush should then go to Lord Castlereagh and formally allege those two facts as his motives for demanding whether the British Government had any such intentions; and, if answered that very probably they might, he should assume an imperious and tragical tone of surprise and talk about a violation of treaties: how do you think it would be received?"

He said that now he fully understood me, and could account for what had passed; this answer was perfectly explicit. But did I consider the cases as parallel?

"So far as any question of right is concerned," said I, "perfectly parallel."

"Have you," said Mr. Canning, "any *claim* to the Shetland Islands or New South Wales?"

"Have you any *claim*," said I, "to the mouth of Columbia River?"

"Why, do you not *know*," replied he, "that we have a claim?"

"I do not *know*," said I, "what you claim nor what you do not claim. You claim India; you claim Africa; you claim——"

"Perhaps," said he, "a piece of the moon."

"No," said I; "I have not heard that you claim exclusively any part of the moon; but there is not a spot on *this* habitable globe that I could affirm you do not claim; and there is none which you may not claim with as much color of right as you can have to Columbia River or its mouth."

"And how far would you consider," said he, "this exclusion of right to extend?"

"To all the shores of the South Sea," said I. "We know of no right that you have there."

"Suppose," said he, "Great Britain should undertake to make a settlement there, would you object to it?"

"I have no doubt we should," said I.

"But, surely," said Mr. Canning, "proof was made at the negotiation of the Convention of October, 1818, of the claims of Great Britain, and their existence is recognized in it."

"There was no proof," I said, "made of any claim, nor, to my knowledge, any discussion of claim. The boundary to the Stony Mountains was defined; westward of them Great Britain had no settlement whatever. We had one at the mouth of the Columbia, which, having been broken up during the war, was solemnly restored to us by the British Government, in fulfilment of a stipulation in the treaty of peace. We stipulated in the Convention that the ports and places on the Pacific Ocean should be open to both parties for ten years, and, taking all these transactions together, we certainly did suppose that the British Government had come to the conclusion that there would be neither policy nor profit in cavilling with us about territory on this North American continent."

"And in this," said he, "you include our northern provinces on this continent?"

"No," said I; "there the boundary is marked, and we have no disposition to encroach upon it. Keep what is yours, but leave the rest of this continent to us." . . .

[June] 24th [,1823] . . . Mr. Canning . . . is to depart to-morrow. I shall probably see him no more. He is a proud, high-tempered Englishman, of good but not extraordinary parts; stubborn and punctilious, with a disposition to be overbearing, which I have often been compelled to check in its own way. He is, of all the foreign Ministers with whom I have had occasion to treat, the man who has most severely tried my temper. Yet he has been long in the diplomatic career, and treated with Governments of the most opposite characters. He has, however, a great respect for his word, and there is nothing false about him. This is an excellent quality for a negotiator. Mr. Canning is a man of forms, studious of courtesy, and tenacious of private morals. As a diplomatic man, his great want is suppleness, and his great virtue is sincerity. . . .

[July] 17th [,1823] At the office, Baron Tuyl came, and enquired if he might inform his Government that instructions would be forwarded by Mr. Hughes to Mr. Middleton for negotiating on the Northwest Coast question. I said he might. He then manifested a desire to know as much as I was disposed to tell him as to the purport of those instructions. I told him as much as I thought prudent, as he observed that it was personally somewhat important to him to be so far confided in here as to know the general purport of what we intended to propose. I told him specially that we should contest the right of Russia to any territorial establishment on this continent, and that we should assume distinctly the principle that the American continents are no longer subjects for any new European colonial establishments. . . .

Washington, *November* 7th.—Cabinet meeting at the President's from half-past one till four. Mr. Calhoun, Secretary of War, and Mr. Southard, Secretary of the Navy, present. The subject for consideration was, the confidential proposals of the British Secretary of State, George Canning, to R. Rush, and the correspondence between them relating to the projects of the Holy Alliance upon South America. There was much conversation, without coming to any definite point. The object of Canning appears to have been to obtain some public pledge from the Government of the United States, ostensibly against the forcible interference of the Holy Alliance between Spain and South America; but really or especially against the acquisition to the United States themselves of any part of the Spanish-American possessions.

Mr. Calhoun inclined to giving a discretionary power to Mr. Rush to join in a declaration against the interference of the Holy Allies, if necessary, even if it should pledge us not to take Cuba or the province of Texas; because the power of Great Britain being greater than ours to seize upon them, we should get the advantage

of obtaining from her the same declaration we should make ourselves.

I thought the cases not parallel. We have no intention of seizing
either Texas or Cuba. But the inhabitants of either or both may
exercise their primitive rights, and solicit a union with us. They
will certainly do no such thing to Great Britain. By joining with
her, therefore, in her proposed declaration, we give her a substantial and perhaps inconvenient pledge against ourselves, and
really obtain nothing in return. Without entering now into the
enquiry of the expediency of our annexing Texas or Cuba to our
Union, we should at least keep ourselves free to act as emergencies
may arise, and not tie ourselves down to any principle which might
immediately afterwards be brought to bear against ourselves.

Mr. Southard inclined much to the same opinion.

The President was averse to any course which should have the
appearance of taking a position subordinate to that of Great Britain . . .

I remarked that the communications recently received from the
Russian Minister, Baron Tuyl, afforded, as I thought, a very suitable and convenient opportunity for us to take our stand against
the Holy Alliance, and at the same time to decline the overture of
Great Britain. It would be more candid, as well as more dignified,
to avow our principles explicitly to Russia and France, than to come
in as a cock-boat in the wake of the British man-of-war.

This idea was acquiesced in on all sides . . .

I remained with the President, and observed to him that the
answer to be given to Baron Tuyl, the instructions to Mr. Rush
relative to the proposals of Mr. Canning, those to Mr. Middleton at
St. Petersburg, and those to the Minister who must be sent to
France, must all be parts of a combined system of policy and
adapted to each other; in which he fully concurred. . . .

[November] 13th [,1823] Morning occupied in making a draft
of minutes for the message of the President upon subjects under the
direction of the Department of State. I took to the President's my
draft of minutes and copies of the instructions to R. Rush dispatched last summer. I read and left my draft with him. I find him
yet altogether unsettled in his own mind as to the answer to be
given to Mr. Canning's proposals, and alarmed, far beyond anything that I could have conceived possible, with the fear that
the Holy Alliance are about to restore immediately all South

America to Spain. Calhoun stimulates the panic, and the news that Cadiz has surrendered to the French has so affected the President that he appeared entirely to despair of the cause of South America. He will recover from this in a few days; but I never saw more indecision in him. . . .

15th. . . . the President wished to see me at the office at noon. I went, and found him there. He asked for the correspondence relating to the intercourse with the British American Colonies, with a view to the particular notice which he intends to take of it in the message; which I thought should have been only in general terms. He also showed me two letters which he had received—one from Mr. Jefferson, 23d October, and one from Mr. Madison of 30th October, giving their opinions on the proposals of Mr. Canning. The President had sent them the two dispatches from R. Rush of 23d and 28th August, enclosing the correspondence between Canning and him, and requested their opinions on the proposals. Mr. Jefferson thinks them more important than anything that has happened since our Revolution. He is for acceding to the proposals, with a view to pledging Great Britain against the Holy Allies; though he thinks the island of Cuba would be a valuable and important acquisition to our Union. Mr. Madison's opinions are less decisively pronounced, and he thinks, as I do, that this movement on the part of Great Britain is impelled more by her interest than by a principle of general liberty.

At one I attended the Cabinet meeting at the President's. He read a note from Mr. Crawford saying he was not well enough to attend, but hoped to be out on Monday. Mr. Calhoun and Mr. Southard were there; Mr. Wirt absent at Baltimore. The subject of Mr. Canning's proposals was resumed, and I soon found the source of the President's despondency with regard to South American affairs. Calhoun is perfectly moon-struck by the surrender of Cadiz, and says the Holy Allies, with ten thousand men, will restore all Mexico and all South America to the Spanish dominion.

I did not deny that they might make a temporary impression for three, four, or five years, but I no more believe that the Holy Allies will restore the Spanish dominion upon the American continent than that the Chimborazo[1] will sink beneath the ocean. But, I added, if the South Americans were really in a state to be

[1] The highest mountain in Ecuador.

so easily subdued, it would be but a more forcible motive for us to beware of involving ourselves in their fate. I set this down as one of Calhoun's extravaganzas. He is for plunging into a war to prevent that which, if his opinion of it is correct, we are utterly unable to prevent. He is for embarking our lives and fortunes in a ship which he declares the very rats have abandoned. . . .

21st. . . . I mentioned also my wish to prepare a paper to be delivered confidentially to Baron Tuyl, and the substance of which I would in the first instance express to him in a verbal conference. It would refer to the verbal communications recently made by him, and to the sentiments and dispositions manifested in the extract of a dispatch relating to Spanish affairs which he lately put into my hands. My purpose would be in a moderate and conciliatory manner, but with a firm and determined spirit, to declare our dissent from the principles avowed in those communications; to assert those upon which our own Government is founded, and, while disclaiming all intention of attempting to propagate them by force, and all interference with the political affairs of Europe, to declare our expectation and hope that the European powers will equally abstain from the attempt to spread their principles in the American hemisphere, or to subjugate by force any part of these continents to their will.

The President approved of this idea; and then taking up the sketches that he had prepared for his message, read them to us. Its introduction was in a tone of deep solemnity and of high alarm, intimating that this country is menaced by imminent and formidable dangers, such as would probably soon call for their most vigorous energies and the closest union. It then proceeded to speak of the foreign affairs, chiefly according to the sketch I had given him some days since, but with occasional variations. It then alluded to the recent events in Spain and Portugal, speaking in terms of the most pointed reprobation of the late invasion of Spain by France, and of the principles upon which it was undertaken by the open avowal of the King of France. It also contained a broad acknowledgment of the Greeks as an independent nation, and a recommendation to Congress to make an appropriation for sending a Minister to them.

Of all this Mr. Calhoun declared his approbation. I expressed as freely my wish that the President would reconsider the whole subject before he should determine to take that course. I said the tone of the introduction I apprehended would take the nation by surprise and greatly alarm them. It would come upon them like a clap of thunder. There had never been in the history of this nation a period of so deep calm and tranquillity as we now enjoyed. We never were, upon the whole, in a state of peace so profound and secure with all foreign nations as at this time. This message would be a summons to arms—to arms against all Europe, and for objects of policy exclusively European—Greece and Spain. It would be as new, too, in our policy as it would be surprising. For more than thirty years Europe had been in convulsions; every nation almost of which it is composed alternately invading and invaded. Empires, kingdoms, principalities, had been overthrown, revolutionized, and counter-revolutionized, and we had looked on safe in our distance beyond an intervening ocean, and avowing a total forbearance to interfere in any of the combinations of European politics. This message would at once buckle on the harness and throw down the gauntlet. It would have the air of open defiance to all Europe, and I should not be surprised if the first answer to it from Spain and France, and even Russia, should be to break off their diplomatic intercourse with us. I did not expect that the quiet which we had enjoyed for six or seven years would last much longer. The aspect of things was portentous; but if we must come to an issue with Europe, let us keep if off as long as possible. Let us use all possible means to carry the opinion of the nation with us, and the opinion of the world. . . .

22d. . . . I spoke to him again urging him to abstain from everything in his message which the Holy Allies could make a pretext for construing into aggression upon them. I said there were considerations of weight which I could not even easily mention at a Cabinet meeting. If he had determined to retire from the public service at the end of his present term, it was now drawing to a close. It was to be considered now as a whole, and a system of administration for a definite term of years. It would hereafter, I believed, be looked back to as the golden age of this republic, and I felt an extreme solicitude that its end might correspond with the character of its progress; that the Administration might be delivered into the hands of the successor, whoever he might be, at peace and in amity with all the world. . . . Something had been said yesterday, that if the President did not recommend the recognition of the independence of the Greeks it would be pressed in the House of Representatives. What would be Mr. Clay's course in this case I could not foresee. But he (the President) well knew that at the time when Mr. Clay so urgently pushed for the South American independence, his main object was popularity for himself and to embarrass the Administration. It did not appear that this object was now so important to him, and, as he had some prospect of coming to the succession himself, I should not suppose he would wish it encumbered with a quarrel with all Europe. But, be that as it may, it was infinitely better that the impulse should come from Congress than that it should go from the Executive. Congress are responsible for their own acts. Foreign powers are apt to take less notice of them than of Executive measures, and if they put us in attitudes of hostility with the allies, be the blame upon them. The ground that I wish to take is that of earnest remonstrance against the interference of the European powers by force with South America, but to disclaim all interference on our part with Europe; to make an American cause, and adhere inflexibly to that. . . .

24th. Mr. Gallatin was here, and talked much upon the topics to be touched upon in the President's message. His views coincided entirely with those which I have so earnestly urged upon the President, excepting as to the Greeks, to whom he proposes, as if he was serious, that we should send two or three frigates to assist them in destroying the Turkish fleet, and a loan or a subsidy of two millions of dollars. I told Gallatin that I wished he would talk to the President as he had done to me, upon everything except the Greeks . . .

I called at the President's, and found Mr. Gallatin with him. He still adhered to his idea of sending a naval force and a loan of money to the Greeks; and as he is neither an enthusiast nor a fool, and knows perfectly well that no such thing will be done, I look for the motives of this strange proposal, and find them not very deeply laid. Mr. Gallatin still builds castles in the air of popularity, and, being under no responsibility for consequences, patronizes the Greek cause for the sake of raising his own reputation. His measure will not succeed, and, even if it should, all the burden and danger of it will bear not upon him, but upon the Administration, and he will be the great champion of Grecian liberty. 'Tis the part of Mr. Clay towards South America acted over again. After he withdrew, the President read me his paragraphs respecting the Greeks, Spain, Portugal, and South America. I thought them quite unexceptionable, and drawn up altogether in the spirit that I had so urgently pressed on Friday and Saturday. I was highly gratified at the change, and only hope the President will adhere to his present views. . . .

25th. . . . I replied [during a cabinet discussion] that, at all events, nothing that we should now do would commit us to absolute war; that Great Britain was already committed more than we; that the interest of no one of the allied powers would be promoted by the restoration of South America to Spain; that the interest of each one of them was against it, and that if they could possibly agree among themselves upon a partition principle, the only possible bait they could offer to Great Britain for acceding to it was Cuba, which neither they nor Spain would consent to give her; that my reliance upon the co-operation of Great Britain rested not upon her principles, but her interest—this I thought was clear . . . We avowed republicanism, but we disclaimed propagandism; we asserted national independence, to which she was already fully pledged. We disavowed all interference with European affairs . . .

26th. . . . Mr. Wirt then resumed the objection he had taken yesterday, and freely enlarged upon it. He said he did not think this country would support the Government in a war for the independence of South America. There had never been much general excitement in their favor. Some part of the people of the interior had felt warmly for them, but it never had been general, and never had there been a moment when the people thought of supporting them by war. To menace without intending to strike was neither consistent with the honor nor the dignity of the country. It was possible that the proposals of Mr. Canning themselves were traps laid to ensnare us into public declarations against the Holy Allies, without intending even to take part against them; that if we were to be so far committed, all the documents ought to be communicated to Congress, and they ought to manifest their sentiments in the form of resolutions, and that the Executive ought not to pledge the honor of the nation to war without taking the sense of the country with them. . . .

. . . My opinion was, therefore, that . . . the act of the Executive could not, after all, commit the nation to a pledge of war. Nor was war contemplated by the proposals of Mr. Canning. He had explicitly stated to Mr. Rush from the beginning that his object was merely a concerted expression of sentiment, which he supposed would avert the necessity of war; and, as Great Britain was not and would not be pledged, by anything Mr. Canning had said or proposed, to war, so would anything now done by the Executive here leave Congress free hereafter to act or not, according as the circumstances of the emergency may require. . . .

24. The Monroe Doctrine

Monroe's State of the Union Address was sent in to Congress on December 2, 1823. Source: James D. Richardson (ed.), A Compilation of the Messages and Papers of the Presidents: 1789–1897 (10 vols., Washington, D.C., 1896–99), II, 207, 209, 217–220.

Fellow Citizens of the Senate and House of Representatives:

Many important subjects will claim your attention during the present session, of which I shall endeavor to give, in aid of your deliberations, a just idea in this communication. I undertake this duty with diffidence, from the vast extent of the interests on which I have to treat and of their great importance to every portion of our Union. I enter on it with zeal from a thorough conviction that there never was a period since the establishment of our Revolution when, regarding the condition of the civilized world and its bearing on us, there was greater necessity for devotion in the public servants to their respective duties, or for virtue, patriotism, and union in our constituents. . . .

At the proposal of the Russian Imperial Government, made through the minister of the Emperor residing here, a full power and instructions have been transmitted to the minister of the United States at St. Petersburg to arrange by amicable negotiation the respective rights and interests of the two nations on the northwest coast of this continent. A similar proposal had been made by His Imperial Majesty to the Government of Great Britain, which has likewise been acceded to. The Government of the United States has been desirous by this friendly proceeding of manifesting the great value which they have invariably attached to the friendship of the Emperor and their solicitude to cultivate the best understanding with his Government. In the discussions to which this interest has given rise and in the arrangements by which they may terminate the occasion has been judged proper for asserting, as a principle in which the rights and interests of the United States are involved, that the American continents, by the free and independent condition which they have assumed and maintain, are henceforth not to be considered as subjects for future colonization by any European powers. . . .

A strong hope has been long entertained, founded on the heroic struggle of the Greeks, that they would succeed in their contest and resume their equal station among the nations of the earth. It is believed that the whole civilized world take a deep interest in their welfare. Although no power has declared in their favor, yet none, according to our information, has taken part against them. Their cause and their name have protected them from dangers which might ere this have overwhelmed any other people. The ordinary calculations of interest and of acquisition with a view to aggrandizement, which mingles so much in the transactions of nations, seem to have had no effect in regard to them. From the facts which have come to our knowledge there is good cause to believe that their enemy has lost forever all dominion over them; that Greece will become again an independent nation. That she may obtain that rank is the object of our most ardent wishes.

It was stated at the commencement of the last session that a great effort was then making in Spain and Portugal to improve the condition of the people of those countries, and that it appeared to be conducted with extraordinary moderation. It need scarcely be remarked that the result has been so far very different from what was then anticipated. Of events in that quarter of the globe, with which we have so much intercourse and from which we derive our origin, we have always been anxious and interested spectators. The citizens of the United States cherish sentiments the most friendly in favor of the liberty and happiness of their fellow-men on that side of the Atlantic. In the wars of the European powers in matters relating to themselves we have never taken any part, nor does it comport with our policy so to do. It is only when our rights are invaded or seriously menaced that we resent injuries or make preparation for our defense. With the movements in this hemisphere we are of necessity more immediately connected, and by causes which must be obvious to all enlightened and impartial observers.

The political system of the allied powers is essentially different in this respect from that of America. This difference proceeds from that which exists in their respective Governments; and to the defense of our own, which has been achieved by the loss of so much blood and treasure, and matured by the wisdom of their most enlightened citizens, and under which we have enjoyed unexampled felicity, this whole nation is devoted. We owe it, therefore, to candor and to the amicable relations existing between the United States and those powers to declare that we should consider any attempt on their part to extend their system to any portion of this hemisphere as dangerous to our peace and safety. With the existing colonies or dependencies of any European power we have not interfered and shall not interfere. But with the Governments who have declared their independence and maintained it, and whose independence we have, on great consideration and on just principles, acknowledged, we could not view any interposition for the purpose of oppressing them, or controlling in any other manner their destiny, by any European power in any other light than as the manifestation of an unfriendly disposition toward the United States. In the war between those new Governments and Spain we declared our neutrality at the time of their recognition, and to this we have adhered, and shall continue to adhere, provided no change shall occur which, in the judgment of the competent authorities of this Government, shall make a corresponding change on the part of the United States indispensable to their security.

The late events in Spain and Portugal shew that Europe is still unsettled. Of this important fact no stronger proof can be adduced than that the allied powers should have thought it proper, on any principle satisfactory to themselves, to have interposed by force in the internal concerns of Spain. To what extent such interposition may be carried, on the same principle, is a question in which all independent powers whose governments differ from theirs are interested, even those most remote, and surely none more so than the United States. Our policy in regard to Europe, which was adopted at an early stage of the wars which have so long agitated that quarter of the globe, nevertheless remains the same, which is, not to interfere in the internal concerns of any of its powers; to consider the government de facto as the legitimate government for us; to cultivate friendly relations with it, and to preserve those relations by a frank, firm, and manly policy, meeting in all instances the just claims of every power, submitting to injuries from none. But in regard to those continents circumstances are eminently and conspicuously different. It is impossible that the allied powers should extend their political system to any portion of either continent without endangering our peace and happiness; nor can anyone believe that our southern brethren, if left to themselves, would adopt it of their own accord. It is equally impossible, therefore, that we should behold such interposition in any form with indifference. If we look to the comparative strength and resources of Spain and those new Governments, and their distance from each other, it must be obvious that she can never subdue them. It is still the true policy of the United States to leave the parties to themselves, in the hope that other powers will pursue the same course.

If we compare the present condition of our Union with its actual state at the close of our Revolution, the history of the world furnishes no example of a progress in improvement in all the important circumstances which constitute the happiness of a nation which bears any resemblance to it. At the first epoch our population did not exceed 3,000,000. By the last census it amounted to about 10,000,000, and, what is more extraordinary, it is almost altogether native, for the immigration from other countries has been inconsiderable. At the first epoch half the territory within our acknowledged limits was uninhabited and a wilderness. Since then new territory has been acquired of vast extent, comprising within it many rivers, particularly the Mississippi, the navigation of which to the ocean was of the highest importance to the original States. Over this territory our population has expanded in every direction, and new States have been established almost equal in number to those which formed the first bond of our Union. This expansion of our population and accession of new States to our Union have had the happiest effect on all its highest interests. That it has eminently augmented our resources and added to our strength and respectability as a power is admitted by all. But it is not in these important circumstances only that this happy effect is felt. It is manifest that by enlarging the basis of our system and increasing the number of States the system itself has been greatly strengthened in both its branches. Consolidation and disunion have thereby been rendered equally impracticable. Each Government, confiding in its own strength, has less to apprehend from the other, and in consequence each, enjoying a greater freedom of action, is rendered more efficient for all the purposes for which it was instituted. It is unnecessary to treat here of the vast improvement made in the system itself by the adoption of this Constitution and of its happy effect in elevating the character and in protecting the rights of the nation as well as of individuals. To what, then, do we owe these blessings? It is known to all that we derive them from the excellence of our institutions. Ought we not, then, to adopt every measure which may be necessary to perpetuate them?

IX

Texas

When the Democratic Party waged its presidential campaign of 1844 on the issue of the "reannexation" of Texas, it was arguing that the United States had gained this great Mexican province in the Louisiana Purchase and that John Quincy Adams improvidently gave it away in the Transcontinental Treaty of 1819. The claim was more ingenious than accurate. Napoleon in 1802 had instructed General Victor, the general in charge of the expedition that never went to Louisiana, to occupy the lands down to the Rio Grande. When Victor's instructions later became known, the Americans were sure that Texas had come in the Louisiana package. Meanwhile they were claiming that the Floridas also had been part of the purchase; and they did not like to remember that the instructions to Victor did not include the Floridas. Napoleon's instructions were a thin basis for any claim to Texas. It was true that Onís in 1819 was ready to give up Texas, if Adams had pressed him hard enough for it. Adams did not know this. Two years after signature of the treaty of 1819 the American settlers began to move into Texas, and by the mid-1830's were in sufficient numbers to declare and maintain their independence from Mexico. By 1844, over 100,000 Americans were in Texas, and annexation to the United States by joint resolution was irresistible. President John Tyler signed the resolution on March 1, 1845.

25. Cession?

In his diary Adams set down carefully the issue of Texas during the negotiation with Onís in 1819. Source: Adams (ed.), Memoirs of John Quincy Adams, IV, 237–239; V, 67–69.

February 1st [1819]. Called upon the President, and had a conversation with him upon this renewal of negotiations with the Spanish Minister. There are various symptoms that if we do come to an arrangement there will be a large party in the country dissatisfied with our concessions from the Rio del Norte [the Rio Grande] to the Sabine on the Gulf of Mexico. Clay has taken the

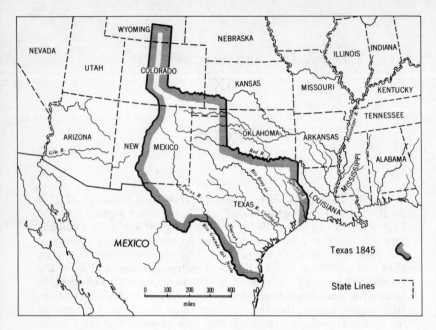

6. Texas in 1845.

alarm at hearing that Onis was again treating with us, and is already taking ground to censure the treaty, if one should be made. He told me last week at Crawford's that he thought we were offering too much for Florida, and and he enclosed me yesterday a letter to himself from a person at Lexington, Kentucky, and hinted at a different opinion from ours respecting the western boundary. I received a long and impertinent letter from Lexington, making many objections to the line which we have proposed; and I mentioned all this to the President for his consideration. He desired me to see and converse with General Jackson upon the subject, and to ask confidentially his opinion.

2d. I called on General Jackson, and mentioned in confidence to him the state of the negotiation with the Spanish Minister, and what we had offered him for the western boundary, and asked his opinion of it. He thought the friends of the Administration would be satisfied . . .

3d. General Jackson came to my house this morning, and I showed him the boundary line which has been offered to the Spanish Minister, and that which we proposed to offer upon

Melish's map. He said there were many individuals who would take exception to our receding so far from the boundary of the Rio del Norte, which we claim, as the Sabine, and the enemies of the Administration would certainly make a handle of it to assail them; but the possession of the Floridas was of so great importance to the southern frontier of the United States, and so essential even to their safety, that the vast majority of the nation would be satisfied with the western boundary as we propose, if we obtain the Floridas. He showed me on the map the operations of the British force during the late war, and remarked that while the mouths of the Florida rivers should be accessible to a foreign naval force there would be no security for the southern part of the United States. . . .

[April] 13th [,1820] . . . Mr. David Trimble, a member of the House from Kentucky, called at the office . . . His ostensible motive was to make up his opinion on the report to be made by the Committee of Ways and Means, of which he is a member. But he came with a long argument to convince me that the only way for me to make myself popular in the Western country was to set the treaty aside and urge the recognition of the South American revolutionists, and insist upon the Rio del Norte as the western boundary.

I told him that I understood the map of the country rather too well to suppose it would ever be possible for me to do anything that could make me popular in the Western country; that as to the treaty, I had never set the value upon it that was supposed, and of all the members of the Administration, I was the last who had consented to take the Sabine for our western boundary. I had no doubt that if the treaty should be set aside we should ultimately obtain more territory than it would secure to us, but we should get the same territory with the treaty sooner than we should want it; and even now I thought the greatest danger of this Union was in the overgrown extent of its territory, combining with the slavery question. I added as my belief, that there would be a majority of the House of Representatives now who would not accept of the province of Texas as a gift unless slavery should be excluded from it. Since the Missouri debate, I considered the continuance of the Union for any length of time as very precarious, and entertained serious doubts whether Louisiana and slavery would not ultimately break us up.

He said he himself considered the slavery question as the greatest that can agitate this Union . . . but if the Union should break up there would be three Confederacies—Eastern, Southern, and Western.

I said, so I had heard Clay say—that within five years we should have three Confederacies . . .

He said he agreed with me in that. But if the Union should break, the country between the Sabine and the Rio del Norte would become indispensably necessary for the Western Confederacy. It would be an excellent country for the cultivation of coffee, and there was an admirable sea-port there which would be necessary to the command of the Gulf of Mexico.

I told him that I did not believe we should ever find either a good sea-port or grounds for cultivating coffee in Texas, nor did I belive there was any article of cultivation that needed slaves. The want of slaves was not in the lands, but in their inhabitants. Slavery had become in the South and Southwestern country a condition of existence. They could not live without them. As to the treaty, we could now very easily disengage ourselves from that. The difficulty would not be in setting it aside, but in obtaining it. He and Mr. Clay were excellent negotiators in theory. They were for obtaining all and granting nothing. They played a game between their own right and left hands, and could allot with admirable management the whole stake to one hand and total discomfiture to the other. In the negotiation with Spain we had a just claim to the Mississippi and its waters, and our citizens had a fair though very precarious claim to indemnities. We had a mere color of claim to the Rio del Norte, no claim to a line beyond the Rocky Mountains, and none to Florida, which we very much wanted. The treaty gives us the Mississippi and all its waters—gives us Florida—gives us an acknowledged line to the South Sea, and seventeen degrees of latitude upon its shores—gives our citizens five millions of dollars of indemnity—and barely gives up to Spain the colorable claim from the Sabine to the Rio del Norte. Now, negotiation implies some concession upon both sides. If after obtaining every object of your pursuit but one, and that one weak in principle and of no present value, what would you have offered to Spain to yield that also?

Trimble had no answer to this question . . .

Trimble is a bustling, talkative, pushing man, professing to be independent of all parties, but in reality a satellite of Clay's. . . .

26. Purchase?

Once the opportunity for cession was lost, presumably by the failures of Jefferson and John Quincy Adams, the Texas issue became one of purchase. Secretary of State Clay, with all the adroitness of a western man, on March 26, 1825 (having by that time been secretary of state under President Adams for nineteen days), broached a proposition for the American minister to Mexico City, Joel R. Poinsett. Source: 25th Cong., 1st Sess., House Document No. 42, p. 6. A check with the original manuscript in the Department of State files shows only variations in styling and punctuation.

. . . The line of the Sabine approaches our great Western mart nearer than could be wished. Perhaps the Mexican Government may not be unwilling to establish that of the Rio Brassos de Dios, or the Rio Colorado, or the Snow mountains, or the Rio del Norte, in lieu of it. By the agreed line, portions of both the Red river and branches of the Arkansas are thrown on the Mexican side, and the navigation of both those rivers, as well as that of the Sabine, is made common to the respective inhabitants of the two countries. When the countries adjacent to those waters shall come to be thickly inhabited, collisions and misunderstandings may arise from the community thus established, in the use of their navigation, which it would be well now to prevent. If the line were so altered as to throw altogether on one side Red river and Arkansas, and their respective tributary streams, and the line on the Sabine were removed further west, all causes of future collision would be prevented. The Government of Mexico may have a motive for such an alteration of the line as is here proposed, in the fact that it would have the effect of placing the city of Mexico nearer the centre of its territories. If the line were so changed, the greater part, if not the whole, of the powerful, warlike, and turbulent Indian nation of the Camanches would be thrown on the side of the United States; and as an equivalent for the proposed cession of territory, they would stipulate to restrain, as far as practicable, the Camanches from committing hostilities and depredations upon the territories and people, whether Indians or otherwise, of Mexico. . . .

Andrew Jackson's secretary of state, Martin Van Buren, made another try for Texas in a letter to Poinsett of August 25, 1829. Source: ibid., pp. 10–14, 16.

It is the wish of the President that you should, without delay, open a negotiation with the Mexican Government for the purchase of so much of the province of Texas as is hereinafter described, or for such a part thereof as they can be induced to cede to us, if the same be conformable to either of the locations with which you are herewith furnished. The President is aware of the difficulties which may be interposed to the accomplishment of the object in view; but he confidently believes that the views of the matter which it will be in your power to submit, and the pecuniary consideration which you will be authorized to propose, will enable you to effect it. He is induced, by a deep conviction of the real necessity of the proposed acquisition, not only as a guard for our Western frontier, and the protection of New Orleans, but also to secure forever to the inhabitants of the valley of the Mississippi, the undisputed and undisturbed posession of the navigation of that river, together with the belief that the present moment is particularly favorable for the purpose, to request your early and unremitting attention to the subject.

The territory of which a cession is desired by the United States is all that part of the province of Texas which lies east of a line beginning at the Gulf of Mexico, in the centre of the desert or Grand prairie, which lies west of the Rio Nueces, and is represented to be nearly two hundred miles in width, and to extend north to the mountains. . . .

The Sabine is a very inconsiderable stream, and only navigable by small crafts. The bay is shallow, and neither it nor the river can ever become the seat of sufficient commerce to authorize the establishment of a custom-house or other public agency in its vicinity. Without such establishment, it is impossible to prevent that frontier from becoming the seat of an extensive system of smuggling, alike injurious to the true interests of both countries. The lands east of the Sabine are, for the most part, and to a great extent, so poor and so effectually cut off from commercial facilities, that they never can receive or sustain a dense or even respectable population. It is mainly to that cause that the objectionable character of its present inhabitants is to be attributed. The frontier, therefore, as long as it remains such, must continue to be what it has heretofore been, a receptable for smugglers and outlaws. In addition to the disadvantage which must result to the United States from their dependance on such a population for the protection, in the first instance, of their border, the present state of things is well calculated to create incessant difficulties and broils with the citizens of the adjacent parts of Mexico, who, owing to the superiority of their soil, and the greater commercial advantages that belong to that side of the river, will naturally be more numerous and of a more respectable character. There may not be cause for much apprehension from this source at the present day, or for a short time to come; but in so grave a matter as the arrangement and establishment of a boundary between independent nations, it becomes us to look into futurity. Thus viewing the matter, it is far from visionary to see in the present condition of things the germ of future discontents, which may grow into national complaints and heartburnings, and perpetually foster and inflame a spirit of jealousy, to which our neighbors are already too much inclined.

We are not left altogether to conjecture and speculation as to the results which are to be expected from a contiguity of settlements under such unfavorable circumstances. The experience of the past affords the means of a safe estimate of the future. A spirit of enterprise, and not unfrequently of encroachment, has been exhibited by our citizens who inhabit that frontier, which has been productive of much uneasiness to the Mexican Government, and not without solicitude to this. Most of the grants that have been made in Texas are already in the hands of Americans and Europeans. Not withstanding the cautious policy evinced by the Mexican Government in the designation of an extensive border territory, within which no grants should be made or settlements permitted, the improvements of the Americans on the Texas side commence from what is regarded as the boundary line, and are scattered over the prohibited territory. . . . The want of confidence and reciprocal attachment between the Government and the present inhabitants of Texas, (not Spanish,) from whatever cause arising, is too notorious to require elucidation. It has, in the short space of five years, displayed itself in not less than four revolts, one of them having, for its avowed object, the independence of the country. . . .

To protect the civilized inhabitants of Texas against Indian aggressions, as well as to keep in check the tumultuous spirit of portions of the inhabitants themselves, the Mexican Government deems it necessary to keep on foot a considerable military establishment in the province. This has been very expensive to the Government, and is, in the present depressed state of their finances, peculiarly burdensome, and will, probably, be of necessary continuance so long as the province belong to Mexico. . . .

Being on the spot, and fully conversant with the feelings of those who constitute the Mexican Government, and with current events, your judgment as to the effect likely to be produced by what is said or proposed upon this subject, is most to be depended upon. The unsettled state of the Mexican Government is too well known to be disguised. The successive revolutions to which it has already been exposed attest the fact; and the dangers which threaten it from the intrigues, if not the open hostilities of Spain, are of a character which cannot be regarded with indifference. This consideration, with many others that might be stated, but which your knowledge of circumstances will readily suggest, expose her extended confederacy to the hazard of dismemberment. It will readily be admitted by her well-informed men that, in such an event, the first successful blow would, most probably, be struck in Texas. . . .

The President does not desire the proposed cession without rendering a just and fair equivalent for it. He, therefore, authorizes you to offer to the Mexican Government for a cession according to the first-mentioned boundary, a sum not exceeding four millions of dollars; and so strong are his convictions of its great value to the United States, that he will not object, if you should find it indispensably necessary, to go as high as five millions. . . .

This despatch will be delivered to you by Colonel Anthony Butler, of the State of Mississippi. . . .

Jackson gave a wide rein to the Texas activities of Colonel Anthony Butler, who succeeded Poinsett as minister to Mexico City. The general came to regret it, and was forced to write Butler on November 27, 1833. Source: John Spencer Bassett (ed.), Correspondence of Andrew Jackson (7 vols., Washington, D.C., 1926–35), V, 228–229. Unless otherwise indicated in the following Jackson-Butler correspondence, italics are translations of ciphers.

Your private and confidential letter of the 28th of October last, with your private letter of previous date have been received—but the dispatches referred to in the latter have not come to hand which we regret as we cannot take any measure on the subject of running the boundery line until these dispatches are received or their duplicates arrive.

I have read your confidential letter with care, and astonishment and duly noted its contents—astonishment that you would entrust such a letter, without being in cypher, to the mail, and that you should state in your letter the reply you made "that you had no money" and give for reason, "recollecting that I had authorised you to apply the amount designated for this object in any way according to (my) your discretion as was best calculated to effect the purpose of your mission"—from this it might be construed that my private letters authorised you to apply to corruption, when nothing could be farther from my intention than to convey such an idea.

. . . my dear Sir, be careful lest these "*shrewd fellows*" may draw you into imputations of attempting to bribe these officers. . . .

Butler to Jackson, February 6, 1834. Source: ibid., 244–246.

. . . What you advise of being cautious of "*these shrewd fellows*" [italics in the original, not in cipher] who may draw me into imputations of attempting to *bribe them* proves how little you know of *mexican character*. I can assure you Sir that *bribery* is not only common and familiar in all ranks and classes, but familiarly and freely spoken of. It is no unusual thing when some Member of Congress is found vehemently opposing a measure in the result of which private interests are involved to hear it said, "*that fellow is calling* [italics in the original, not in cipher] out for his *bribe.*" Nor is it unusual to find the same Member a few days after reversing his vote and opinion, having received conviction (as the phrase goes) that his previous impressions were wrong. Nay Sir, so unblushingly is this thing done, that in many instances you hear the very *sum* stated which the individual *has received.* You may ask, does this work no *disgrace* nor loss of *character* to the *man corrupted?* not a whit. To illustrate what I am saying, let me repeat to you a Conversation I once had with a Senator in Congress on the subject of *Texas.* Speaking on the question of *boundary,* I threw out as a feeler, the advantage which in my opinion the Mexicans would derive from having the *boundary* more west— first in rendering their *territory* more compact, and that it would also interpose a barrier and protection against *Indian hostility,* the

scourge of their *frontiers* for the last Century. Well, said he, suppose we were inclined to extend the *boundary west* conformably
with your views, what should we *receive* as *compensation* for the
territory we might cede *to your government*. I replied, that we
should be prepared to offer a fair *equivalent*. Then Sir, said he let
me tell you, that if you mean to succeed, you must begin with an
Offer of about *two hundred thousand dollars* to the *President* himself. I affected to consider him as jesting with me, and the conversation dropped—the same idea has been more than once advanced
to me by others, and hence the suggestion in my former letters,
that in the event of concluding a *treaty* for *Texas* it might become
necessary to *apply* part of the *sum* designated in securing the co-
operation of certain *persons* whose services would be indispensable,
and this brings me to say a word as to the object disclosed in some
of my former letters to you and your replies to them contrasted
with the observations in your last of Nov. 27th. More than two
years since I wrote informing you that the best if not the only,
mode of attaining our object in relation to *Texas* would be to
interest certain *persons* here through the application of *money* to
lend their *aid* in *negotiating* the *treaty*. You replied that my instructions authorised me to apply a *given sum* in procuring a *cession* of *Texas* and that if I kept myself within the *sum* limited and
procured the *territory* it was a matter of *no consequence to the
Government* [italics in the original, not in cipher] how the *money*
was *disbursed*. Now I beg you Sir to weigh these expressions of
yours, and then say whether they admitted of a different construction than that which I gave to them? Whether I was not justified in
the conclusion that your letter to me authorised the employment
of any part of the *sum* placed under my control, in that way which
in my judgment was best calculated to effect the object we desired
to attain—in short that the *money* was placed completely under
my discretion in regard to the mode of its application? And as the
application of such part as was employed to secure *personal influence* and cooperation would have been provided for in the
treaty, either by *secret article* or under the color of indemnity, you
will recollect that I wrote you at the time when hopes were indulged of consummating the *negociation* to send a vessel for me,
designing to bring home myself the *treaty* in order that I might
make the necessary explanations and secure its *ratification*. And I
now beg leave to repeat to you, that let this *negotiation* be concluded when it may, if it is done in *Mexico* resort must be had to

bribery or by *presents*, if the term is more appropriate. I would here add another remark; that the only hope we have of success is by convincing these people we mean to do ourselves right, and to occupy at least such part of that *country* as justly belongs to us. Depend on it these people are greatly overrating their consequence and influence and are indulging the belief that we dare not occupy any part of *Texas* which they choose to claim, and that whatever may be said to the contrary we will permit them eventually to hold all which they now have in possession. Read the handbill which I now send you in connection with what was published in the "Fenix" of the 4. January last, and the number 4. of the "Indicador" already sent you, and if you can doubt after that, what are the feelings, and intentions of this Government, I have not a word more to say. I repeat then, proceed at once to establish our boundary and take possession. It is the only mode by which you can hope to bring these people to understand their true condition, and lead eventually (if any thing can) to an *amicable* [italics in the original, not in cipher] *transfer* of the *country* to us. sooner or later the *country* must and will become *ours*—the irreversible decree of Nature has decided that all *Texas* as far as the *desert* must form part of the *United States*. But knowing your anxiety to achieve this object in an amicable manner and equally interested myself in the successful result of the *negociation* induces me to press more earnestly upon you the necessity of taking that first and most important step, of occupying immediately that which is ours. Indeed, I cannot see the necessity of even waiting the establishment of *boundary* because as it is well known that the *west* fork of the *Sabine* is nearly 60 miles *west* of the Town of *Nagadoches* it is clear that this Town is within our limits, and might justly be occupied at once. Cantonment Jessup is about 80 miles distant, and General Leavenworth might have his head quarters at *Nagadoches* within a week from the time he received the order. . . .

Butler to Jackson, March 7, 1834. Source: ibid., 249, 251–253.

All late movements, and the expression of all recent opinions, as well by the Members of the Cabinet, as by those who are known to possess intimate knowledge of the policy and views of this Govenmt. indicates most clearly that we need indulge no hope of obtaining *Texas* by amicable arrangement unless we first shew our strength, and at the same time manifest a determination to do ourselves right. In a previous letter you informed me that so soon as it was ascertained this Govern't would not *negotiate* upon the subject of *boundary* that you would then immediately proceed alone to establish that *boundary,* giving *them notice of such* intention. that time has arrived, and I hope very soon to be instructed to give such notice, for rely upon it, that such a movement would have the very best effects in convincing *this administration* that we were *no longer to be postponed* in the enjoyment of a *right so clearly* ours and be assured that without such a *movement* we shall do nothing. . . .

If you will withdraw *me from this place* and make *the movement to possess that part* of Texas which *is ours,* placing me at the head of the country to be occupied, I will pledge *my head* that *we have all we desire in less than six months without a blow* and for *equal the price we are willing to pay for it.*

Why do I recommend this course? It is because I am anxious for your glory: It is because I desire and hope to see that during your Administration every litigated question with foreign powers advantageously and satisfactorily adjusted, to see the National debt paid, the Bank monster crushed, and as the closing scene of so interesting a Drama, to see also once more secured to us that interesting *country Texas,* so unwisely surrendered by the *treaty of* 1819. Rely on me, it requires but that simple movement to assure success; Will you make it? I think I know you too well to doubt that this question will be answered in the Affirmative. . . .

[*Indorsement in Jackson's handwriting:*] "A. Butler: What a scamp. Carefully read. The Secretary of State will reiterate his instructions to ask an extension of the treaty for running boundary line, and then recall him, or if he has recd. his former instructions and the Mexican Govt. has refused, to recal him at once."

27. Annexation

Shortly after the success of the Texas Revolution of 1835–36 the economic and political climate changed in the United States. The panic of 1837 occurred not long after President Van Buren came into office. And the slavery controversy was arising, making Texas annexation a touchy political issue. Secretary of State John Forsyth on August 25, 1837, penned a letter to the Texas representative in Washington, Memucan Hunt. Source: William R. Manning (ed.), Diplomatic Correspondence of the United States: Inter-American Affairs, 1831–1860 (12 vols., Washington, D.C., 1932–39), XII, 12–13.

. . . The question of the annexation of a foreign independent state to the United States has never before been presented to this government. Since the adoption of their Constitution, two large additions have been made to the domain originally claimed by the United States. In acquiring them, this government was not actuated by a mere thirst for sway over a broader space. Paramount interests of many members of the confederacy and the permanent well being of all, imperatively urged upon this government the necessity of an extension of its jurisdiction over Louisiana and Florida. As peace, however, was our cherished policy, never to be departed from unless honor should be perilled by adhering to it, we patiently endured for a time serious inconveniences and privations and sought a transfer of those regions by negotiations and not by conquest. The issue of those negotiations was a conditional cession of those countries to the United States. The circumstance, however, of their being colonial possessions of France and Spain and therefore dependent on the metropolitan governments, renders those transactions materially different from that which would be presented by the question of the annexation of Texas. The latter is a state with an independent government, acknowledged as such by the United States and claiming a territory beyond though bordering on the region ceded by France in the treaty of the 30th of April, 1803. Whether the Constitution of the United States contemplated the annexation of such a state, and if so, in what manner that object is to be effected, are questions in the opinion of the President it would be inexpedient under existing circumstances to agitate.

So long as Texas shall remain at war while the United States are at peace with her adversary, the proposition of the Texian Minister Plenipotentiary necessarily involves the question of war with that adversary. The United States are bound to Mexico by a treaty of amity and commerce which will be scrupulously observed on their part so long as it can be reasonably hoped that Mexico will perform her duties and respect our rights. The United States might justly be suspected of a disregard of the friendly purposes of the compact if the overture of General Hunt were to be even reserved for future consideration, as this would imply a disposition on our part to espouse the quarrel of Texas with Mexico—a disposition wholly at variance with the spirit of the treaty, with the uniform policy and the obvious welfare of the United States.

The inducements mentioned by General Hunt for the United States to annex Texas to their territory are duly appreciated, but powerful and weighty as certainly they are, they are light when opposed in the scale of reason to treaty obligations and respect for that integrity of character by which the United States have sought to distinguish themselves since the establishment of their right to claim a place in the great family of nations, It is presumed, however, that the motives by which Texas has been governed in making this overture will have equal force in impelling her to preserve as an independent power the most liberal commercial relations with the United States. Such a disposition will be cheerfully met in a corresponding spirit by this government. If the answer which the undersigned has been directed to give to the proposition of General Hunt should unfortunately work such a change in the sentiments of that government as to induce an attempt to extend commercial relations elsewhere upon terms prejudicial to the United States, this government will be consoled by a consciousness of the rectitude of its intentions and a certainty that although the hazard of transient losses may be incurred by a rigid adherence to just principles, no lasting prosperity can be secured when they are disregarded.

President Tyler sought to annex Texas by treaty early in 1844, but the treaty failed in the Senate. After James K. Polk's election to the presidency on a pro-annexation platform, Tyler conceived of incorporating Texas through a joint resolution of both houses of Congress, and proposed this stratagem in his annual message of December 3, 1844. Source: Richardson (ed.), A Compilation of the Messages and Papers of the Presidents, IV, 340–345.

. . . In my last annual message I felt it to be my duty to make known to Congress, in terms both plain and emphatic, my opinion in regard to the war which has so long existed between Mexico and Texas, which since the battle of San Jacinto has consisted altogether of predatory incursions, attended by circumstances revolting to humanity. I repeat now what I then said, that after eight years of feeble and ineffectual efforts to reconquer Texas it was time that the war should have ceased. The United States have a direct interest in the question. The contiguity of the two nations to our territory was but too well calculated to involve our peace. Unjust suspicions were engendered in the mind of one or the other of the belligerents against us, and as a necessary consequence American interests were made to suffer and our peace became daily endangered; in addition to which it must have been obvious to all that the exhaustion produced by the war subjected both Mexico and Texas to the interference of other powers, which, without the interposition of this Government, might eventuate in the most serious injury to the United States. This Government from time to time exerted its friendly offices to bring about a termination of hostilities upon terms honorable alike to both the belligerents. Its efforts in this behalf proved unavailing. Mexico seemed almost without an object to persevere in the war, and no other alternative was left the Executive but to take advantage of the well-known dispositions of Texas and to invite her to enter into a treaty for annexing her territory to that of the United States.

Since your last session Mexico has threatened to renew the war, and has either made or proposes to make formidable preparations for invading Texas. She has issued decrees and proclamations, preparatory to the commencement of hostilities, full of threats revolting to humanity, and which if carried into effect would arouse the attention of all Christendom. This new demonstration of feeling, there is too much reason to believe, has been produced in consequence of the negotiation of the late treaty of annexation with Texas. The Executive, therefore, could not be indifferent to such proceedings, and it felt it to be due as well to itself as to the honor of the country that a strong representation should be made to the Mexican Government upon the subject. This was accordingly done, as will be seen by the copy of the accompanying dispatch from the Secretary of State to the United States envoy at Mexico. Mexico has no right to jeopard the peace of the world by urging any longer a useless and fruitless contest. Such a condition of things would not be tolerated on the European continent. Why should it be on this? A war of desolation, such as is now threatened by Mexico, can not be waged without involving our peace and tranquillity. It is idle to believe that such a war could be looked upon with indifference by our own citizens inhabiting adjoining States; and our neutrality would be violated in despite of all efforts on the part of the Government to prevent it. The country is settled by emigrants from the United States under invitations held out to them by Spain and Mexico. Those emigrants have left behind them friends and relatives, who would not fail to sympathize with them in their difficulties, and who would be led by those sympathies to participate in their struggles, however energetic the action of the Government to prevent it. Nor would the numerous and formidable bands of Indians—the most warlike to be found in any land—which occupy the extensive regions contiguous to the States of Arkansas and Missouri, and who are in possession of large tracts of country within the limits of Texas, be likely to remain passive. The inclinations of those numerous tribes lead them invariably to war whenever pretexts exist.

Mexico had no just ground of displeasure against this Government or people for negotiating the treaty. What interest of hers was affected by the treaty? She was despoiled of nothing, since Texas was forever lost to her. The independence of Texas was recognized by several of the leading powers of the earth. She was free to treat, free to adopt her own line of policy, free to take the course which she believed was best calculated to secure her happiness.

Her Government and people decided on annexation to the United States, and the Executive saw in the acquisition of such a territory the means of advancing their permanent happiness and glory. What principle of good faith, then, was violated? What rule of political morals trampled under foot? . . .

Other considerations of a controlling character influenced the course of the Executive. The treaty which had thus been negotiated had failed to receive the ratification of the Senate. One of the chief objections which was urged against it was found to consist in the fact that the question of annexation had not been submitted to the ordeal of public opinion in the United States. However untenable such an objection was esteemed to be, in view of the unquestionable power of the Executive to negotiate the treaty and the great and lasting interests involved in the question, I felt it to be my duty to submit the whole subject to Congress as the best expounders of popular sentiment. No definitive action having been taken on the subject by Congress, the question referred itself directly to the decision of the States and people. The great popular election which has just terminated afforded the best opportunity of ascertaining the will of the States and the people upon it. Pending that issue it became the imperative duty of the Executive to inform Mexico that the question of annexation was still before the American people, and that until their decision was pronounced any serious invasion of Texas would be regarded as an attempt to forestall their judgment and could not be looked upon with indifference. I am most happy to inform you that no such invasion has taken place; and I trust that whatever your action may be upon it Mexico will see the importance of deciding the matter by a resort to peaceful expedients in preference to those of arms. The decision of the people and the States on this great and interesting subject has been decisively manifested. The question of annexation has been presented nakedly to their consideration. By the treaty itself all collateral and incidental issues which were calculated to divide and distract the public councils were carefully avoided. These were left to the wisdom of the future to determine. It presented, I repeat, the isolated question of annexation, and in that form it has been submitted to the ordeal of public sentiment. A controlling majority of the people and a large majority of the States have declared in favor of immediate annexation. Instructions have thus come up to both branches of Congress from their respective constituents in terms the most emphatic. It is the will of both the people and the States that Texas shall be annexed to the Union promptly and immediately. It may be hoped that in carrying into execution the public will thus declared all collateral issues may be avoided. Future Legislatures can best decide as to the number of States which should be formed out of the territory when the time has arrived for deciding that question. So with all others. By the treaty the United States assumed the payment of the debts of Texas to an amount not exceeding $10,000,000, to be paid, with the exception of a sum falling short of $400,000, exclusively out of the proceeds of the sales of her public lands. We could not with honor take the lands without assuming the full payment of all incumbrances upon them.

Nothing has occurred since your last session to induce a doubt that the dispositions of Texas remain unaltered. No intimation of an altered determination on the part of her Government and people has been furnished to the Executive. She still desires to throw herself under the protection of our laws and to partake of the blessings of our federative system, while every American interest would seem to require it. The extension of our coastwise and foreign trade to an amount almost incalculable, the enlargement of the market for our manufactures, a constantly growing market for our agricultural productions, safety to our frontiers, and additional strength and stability to the Union—these are the results which would rapidly develop themselves upon the consummation of the measure of annexation. In such event I will not doubt but that Mexico would find her true interest to consist in meeting the advances of this Government in a spirit of amity. Nor do I apprehend any serious complaint from any other quarter; no sufficient ground exists for such complaint. We should interfere in no respect with the rights of any other nation. There can not be gathered from the act any design on our part to do so with their possessions on this continent. We have interposed no impediments in the way of such acquisitions of territory, large and extensive as many of them are, as the leading powers of Europe have made from time to time in every part of the world. We seek no conquest made by war. No intrigue will have been resorted to or acts of diplomacy essayed to accomplish the annexation of Texas. Free and independent herself, she asks to be received into our Union. It is a question for our own decision whether she shall be received or not.

The two Governments having already agreed through their respective organs on the terms of annexation, I would recommend their adoption by Congress in the form of a joint resolution or act to be perfected and made binding on the two countries when adopted in like manner by the Government of Texas. . . .

X

The Mexican War

Second in importance for American history only to the diary of John Quincy Adams is the diary of President Polk, in which the occupant of the Executive Mansion from 1845 to 1849 set out faithfully, according to his Methodist conscience, the train of events which brought about the war with Mexico and led to a victorious peace. The Treaty of Guadalupe Hidalgo in 1848 awarded the United States a tract of land comparable only to the purchase of 1803. It may well be that Polk's reputation has risen too high since the publication of his diary early in the twentieth century, but then such is the reward of all good diarists and memoirists. One has only to recall the way in which the late Sir Winston Churchill increased his historical reputation by composing masterful histories of his own era.

Polk's diary shows some warts, especially the President's intense partisanship. The President of the Mexican War period believed that members of the opposing Whig Party were not merely politically wrong but probably personally depraved. Polk did discover two Whigs whom he liked. These individuals he admitted to favor only toward the end of his administration.

28. President Polk's war

Source: Milo M. Quaife (ed.), The Diary of James K. Polk (4 vols., Chicago, 1910), I, 86, 129–131, 319, 365, 384–390; II, 185–186, 345, 347–348, 356–358, 364–367; IV, 1–2.

Sunday, 2nd November, 1845.—Attended the Methodist church (called the Foundary church) to-day, in company with my Private Secretary, J. Knox Walker. It was an inclement day, there being rain from an early hour in the morning; & Mrs. Polk and the ladies of my household did not attend church today. Mrs. Polk being a member of the Presbyterian Church I generally attend that Church with her, though my opinions and predilections are in favour of the Methodist Church.

This was my birth-day, being fifty years old, having been born according to the family Register in the family Bible, corroborated by the account given me by my mother, on the 2nd of November, 1795.

The text today was from the Acts of the Apostles, Ch. 15, v. 31 —"Because he hath appointed a day, in the which he will judge the world in righteousness, by the man whom he hath ordained." It was Communion day in the church, and the sermon was solemn and forcible. It awakened the reflection that I had lived fifty years, and that before fifty years more would expire, I would be sleeping with the generations which have gone before me. I thought of the vanity of this world's honours, how little they would profit me half a century hence, and that it was time for me to be "putting my House in Order."

Monday, 22nd December, 1845.— . . . I authorized Mr. [George] Bancroft to intimate to him [John Quincy Adams] my disposition to invite him to dinner, if it should be agreeable to him to accept.

This morning Mr. Bancroft called at my office, and informed me that he had just had a conversation with Mr. Adams, and had intimated to him what I had authorized him to do. Mr. Adams, he informed me, said that a similar communication had been made to him by Genl. Jackson while he was President of the U. S. through a common friend (Col. Richard M. Johnson) and that he had declined it. Mr. Adams, as Mr. Bancroft informed me, said further that his personal relations with me had always been good, and while in Congress together, though we had voted differently on almost every public question, that yet our personal relations had never been disturbed. . . . Mr. Adams, as Mr. B. informed me, then alluded to the controversy which he had had with Gen'l Jackson, Mr. Chas. J. Ingersoll of Penn., and Gov. Brown of Tennessee, in relation to the Boundary fixed by the Florida Treaty of 1819, in which there had been an attempt by these persons to make it appear that he had accepted a less favourable boundary for the U. S. than he could have obtained, and had thereby lost Texas to the U. S. He said that I had written a letter to the same effect, and that I would know what letter it was. He said that he had made a speech in Massachusetts in which he had spoken of that letter, and intimated that some explanation of my statements in that letter would be necessary before he could accept an invitation to dinner.

Mr. Bancroft said he left him in a good humour. I told Mr. Bancroft that it was a matter of no consequence whether he was invited to dinner or not, and that certainly I had no explanations to make. At first I was at some loss to recollect to what letter of mine he alluded. Upon a little reflection I remarked that he must have alluded to my letter to a committee of Citizens of Cincinnati in April, 1844, on the subject of the Annexation of Texas. I told Mr. Bancroft that my statements in that letter were correct, and were sustained by the public records of the country, and that I had no explanations concerning it to make. I told him further that I had never read Mr. Adams' speech in Massachusetts in which Mr. A. had informed him, he had referred to it. I told Mr. B. to let the matter rest where it was, and that I would not think of inviting him to dinner; and that I had only thought of extending that courtesy as President of the U. S. which his age and the stations he had held seemed to make proper. . . .

Tuesday, 7th April, 1846.—The Cabinet held a regular meeting to-day; all the members present except the Secretary of State, who is still absent on a visit to his residence in Pennsylvania. A despatch was received by last night's mail from our consul at Vera Cruz, which renders it probable that Mr. Slidell, our minister to Mexico, will not be received by that Government, & will return to the U. States. The despatch was read & I stated that in the event Mr. Slidell was not accredited, and returned to the U. S., my opinion was that I should make a communication to Congress recommending that Legislative measures be adopted, to take the remedy for the injuries and wrongs we had suffered into our own hands. In this there seemed to be a concurrence on the part of the Cabinet, no one dissenting. . . .

Wednesday, 29th April, 1846.— . . . Despatches were received to-day from the army [of] occupation on the Del Norte [the Rio Grande] in Texas; and a private letter from Mr. McLane in England of the 10th Instant, brought out by the Great Western. Mr. Buchanan called & I had a conversation with him on both subjects. . . .

Saturday, 9th May, 1846.—The Cabinet held a regular meeting to-day; all the members present. I brought up the Mexican question, and the question of what was the duty of the administration in the present state of our relations with that country. The subject was very fully discussed. All agreed that if the Mexican forces at Matamoras committed any act of hostility on Gen'l Taylor's forces I should immediately send a message to Congress recommending an immediate declaration of War. I stated to the Cabinet that up to this time, as they knew, we had heard of no open act of aggression by the Mexican army, but that the danger was imminent that such acts would be committed. I said that in my opinion we had ample cause of war, and that it was impossible that we could stand in *statu quo*, or that I could remain silent much longer; that I thought it was my duty to send a message to Congress very soon & recommend definitive measures. I told them that I thought I ought to make such a message by tuesday next, that the country was excited and impatient on the subject, and if I failed to do so I would not be doing my duty. I then propounded the distinct question to the Cabinet and took their opinions individually, whether I should make a message to Congress on tuesday, and whether in that message I should recommend a declaration of War against Mexico. All except the Secretary of the Navy gave their advice in the affirmative. Mr. Bancroft dissented but said if any act of hostility should be committed by the Mexican forces he was then in favour of immediate war. Mr. Buchanan said he would feel better satisfied in his course if the Mexican forces had or should commit any act of hostility, but that as matters stood we had ample cause of war against Mexico, & he gave his assent to the measure. It was agreed that the message should be prepared and submitted to the Cabinet in their meeting on tuesday. A history of our causes of complaint against Mexico had been at my request previously drawn up by Mr. Buchanan. I stated that what was said in my annual message in December gave that history as succinctly and satisfactorily as Mr. Buchanan's statement, that in truth it was the same history in both, expressed in different language, and that if I repeated that history in [a] message to Congress now I had better employ the precise language used in my message of December last. Without deciding this point the Cabinet passed to the consideration of some other subjects of minor importance. The Cabinet adjourned about 2 O'Clock P.M. Before they separated I directed the Secretary of State to have all the correspondence of Mr. Slidell with the Mexican Government, & such portions of his correspondence with the

Department of State as it was proper to communicate copied; and in like manner I directed the Secretary of War to have all his orders to Gen'l Taylor commanding the army in Texas copied, so as to have these documents ready to be communicated to Congress with my message.

About 6 o'clock P.M. Gen'l R. Jones, the Adjutant General of the army, called and handed to me despatches received from Gen'l Taylor by the Southern mail which had just arrived, giving information that a part of [the] Mexican army had crossed to the Del Norte, [crossed the Del Norte] and attacked and killed and captured two companies of dragoons of Gen'l Taylor's army consisting of 63 officers & men. The despatch also stated that he had on that day (26th April) made a requisition on the Governors of Texas & Louisiana for four Regiments each, to be sent to his relief at the earliest practicable period. Before I had finished reading the despatch, the Secretary of War called. I immediately summoned the Cabinet to meet at 7½ O'Clock this evening. The Cabinet accordingly assembled at that hour; all the members present. The subject of the despatch received this evening from Gen'l Taylor, as well as the state of our relations with Mexico, were fully considered. The Cabinet were unanimously of opinion, and it was so agreed, that a message should be sent to Congress on Monday laying all the information in my possession before them and recommending vigorous & prompt measure[s] to enable the Executive to prosecute the War. The Secretary of War & Secretary of State agreed to put their clerks to work to copy the correspondence between Mr. Slidell & the Mexican Government & Secretary of State and the correspondence between the War Department & Gen'l Taylor, to the end that these documents should be transmitted to Congress with my message on Monday. The other members of the Cabinet tendered the services of their clerks to aid in preparing these copies.

Mr. Senator Houston, Hon. Barkley Martin, & several other members of Congress called in the course of the evening, & were greatly excited at the news brought by the Southern mail from the army. They all approved the steps which had been taken by the administration, and were all of opinion that war with Mexico should now be prosecuted with vigor.

The Cabinet adjourned about 10 O'Clock, & I commenced my

message; Mr. Bancroft and Mr. Buchanan, the latter of whom had prepared a history of our causes of complaint against Mexico, agreed to assist me in preparing the message.

Sunday, 10th May, 1846.—As the public excitement in and out of Congress was very naturally very great, and as there was a great public necessity to have the prompt action of Congress on the Mexican question, and therefore an absolute necessity for sending my message to Congress on tomorrow, I resumed this morning the preparation of my message. About 9½ O'Clock Mr. Bancroft called, and with his assistance I was engaged in preparing it until 11 O'Clock, at which time I suspended my labours in order to attend church. I left the part of the message which had been written to be copied by my Private Secretary, and accompanied Mrs. Polk, my niece, Miss Rucker, & my nephew, Marshall T. Polk, to church. As we were leaving for church the Hon. Mr. Haralson & the Hon. Mr. Baker, members of the Committee of Military affairs, called to see me on the subject of the legislative action proper to be had to provide for the vigorous prosecution of the war with Mexico. I told them I would see them at 5 O'Clock this afternoon.

On my return from church about 1 O'Clock P.M. I resumed the preperation of my message. In the course of half an hour Mr. Bancroft & Mr. Buchanan called and the part of the message which had been written was examined & approved. At 2 O'Clock my family dinner was announced. I invited Mr. Buchanan and Mr. Bancroft to dine with me. Mr. Buchanan declined and Mr. Bancroft dined with me. After dinner Mr. Bancroft and myself returned to the preparation of the message. Two confidential Clerks, viz., H. C. Williams from the War Department an[d] —— ——, from the Navy Department were engaged in assisting my Private Secretary in making two copies of my message, one for the Senate and one for the House.

At 5 O'Clock Mr. Haralson & Mr. Baker called according to the appointment made this morning. They informed me that deeming the present a great emergency they had called the Committee on Military affairs of the Ho. Repts. together this morning and that they had unanimously agreed to support a Bill appropriating ten millions of Dollars, and authorizing the President to raise fifty thousand dollars [men] to prosecute the war with Mexico. They showed to me a copy of the Bill which they proposed to pass. I pointed out some defects in it & advised them to consult with the Secretary and officers connected with the War Department, including Gen'l Scott and Adj't Gen'l Jones. They said they would do so. I discovered in the course of the conversation that both Mr. Haralson and Mr. Baker desired to be appointed to high commands in the army of Volunteers which their Bill proposed to raise. I talked civilly to them but made no promises.

After night and whilst the clerks were still copying my message in my Private Secretary's office, the Secretaries of State, of the Treasury, of the Navy, the P.M. Gen'l, and [the] Atto. Gen'l called, but were not all present at any one time. The Secretary of War was indisposed as I learned, and did not call during the day. Senator Houston & Bartley Martin & Ch. J. Ingersoll called to consult me on the Mexican question, and to learn what I intended to recommend in my message. The two former had retired before Mr. Ingersoll called. I addressed notes to Senator Allen, Ch. of the Comm. of Foreign Affairs of the Senate, & Mr. McKay of N. C., Ch. of the Com. of Ways and Means of the Ho. Repts. requesting them to call at my office to-night. In the course of half an hour they called, and the message being copied, I read it to them and Mr. Ingersoll in presence of some of the members of [the] Cabinet who had remained. They all approved it.

At 10½ O'Clock the company left and I retired to rest. It was a day of great anxiety to me, and I regretted the necessity which had existed to make it necessary for me to spend the Sabbath in the manner I have.

Monday, 11th May, 1846.—I refused to see company generally this morning. I carefully revised my message on the Mexican question, but had no time to read the copies of the correspondence furnished by the War & State Departments which was to accompany it. I had read the original correspondence and presume the copies are correct.

I addressed [notes] to Senators Cass and Benton this morning requesting them to call. Gen'l Cass called first. The message was read to him and he highly approved it. Col. Benton called before Gen'l Cass left, and I gave him the copy of the message and he retired to an adjoining room and read it. After he had read it I had a conversation with him alone. I found he did not approve it in all its parts. He was willing to vote men and money for defence of our territory, but was not prepared to make aggressive war on Mexico. He disapproved the marching of the army from Corpus Christi to the left Bank of the Del Norte, but said he had never said so to the public. I had a full conversation with him, and he left without satisfying me that I could rely upon his support of the measures recommended by the message, further than the mere defence of our territory. I inferred, too, from his conversation that he did not think the territory of the U.S. extended West of the Nueces River.

At 12 O'Clock I sent my message to Congress. . . .

Monday, 4th October, 1847.—I felt much better this morning, but was still feeble. I continued to take some medicine. I rose & dressed myself about 10 O'Clock, and wrapping myself up walked to the office, but was so feeble that I returned to my chamber in a few minutes. I sat up most of the day, and transacted some business with the Secretaries of State, the Treasury, and War, whom I saw in my chamber.

I resolved to-day to recall Mr. Trist as commissioner to Mexico, and requested Mr. Buchanan to prepare the letter of recall.

I directed the Secretary of War to prepare another letter to Gen'l Scott, directing him more stringently than had been done to levy contributions upon the enemy, and make them as far as practicable defray the expenses of the war.

Tuesday, 5th October, 1847.—I continued to feel better this morning. I walked to the office, but after being there but a few minutes I deemed it prudent to return to my chamber.

When the Cabinet assembled in my office at the usual hour, I requested my Private Secretary to invite them to meet me in my chamber. They did so; all the members were present.

Mr. Buchanan read the letter of recal [1], which he had prepared to Mr. Trist. All the Cabinet agreed that it was proper to recall him. The letter was discussed at some length, and by my direction some modifications were made in it.

Gov. Marcy read a draft of the letter to Gen'l Scott which I had requested him to write on yesterday. It was not finished, but he said he would complete it this evening.

The unofficial information received shows that Mexico has refused to treat for peace upon terms which the U. S. can accept; and it is now manifest that the war must be prosecuted with increased forces and increased energy. We must levy contributions and quarter on the enemy. This is part of the object of the letter to Gen'l Scott. Mr. Trist is recalled because his remaining longer with the army could not, probably, accomplish the objects of his mission, and because his remaining longer might, & probably would, impress the Mexican Government with the belief that the U. S. were so anxious for peace that they would ultimate[ly] conclude one upon the Mexican terms. Mexico must now first sue for peace, & when she does we will hear her propositions.

The Cabinet remained upwards of three hours, and when they adjourned I found myself much exhausted & fatigued. . . .

Saturday, 19th February, 1848.— . . . After night a messenger arrived from Mexico bearing despatches from the army, and a Treaty of peace entered into on the 2nd Inst. by Mr. Trist with mexican plenipotentiaries appointed for that purpose. This messenger was Mr. Freanor, who has been with the army for some time in the capacity of a correspondent of the New Orleans *Delta*, over the signature of Mustang. About 9 O'Clock Mr. Buchanan called with the Treaty. He read it. Mr. Trist was recalled in October last, but chose to remain in Mexico and continue the negotiation. The terms of the Treaty are within his instructions which he took out in April last, upon the important question of boundary and limits. There are many provisions in it which will require more careful examination than a single reading will afford. Mr. Trist has acted very badly, as I have heretofore noted in this diary, but notwithstanding this, if on further examination the Treaty is one that can be accepted, it should not be rejected on account of his bad conduct. . . .

Monday, 21st February, 1848.—I saw no company this morning. At 12 O'Clock the Cabinet met; all the members present. I made known my decision upon the Mexican Treaty, which was that under all the circumstances of the case, I would submit it [to] the Senate for ratification. . . . I assigned my reasons for my decision. They were, briefly, that the treaty conformed on the main question of limits & boundary to the instructions given to Mr. Trist in April last; and that though, if the treaty was now to be made, I should demand more territory, perhaps to make the Sierra Madra the line, yet it was doubtful whether this could be ever obtained by the consent of Mexico. I looked, too, to the consequences of its rejection. A majority of one branch of Congress is opposed to my administration; they have falsely charged that the war was brought on and is continued by me with a view to the conquest of Mexico; and if I were now to reject a Treaty made upon my own terms, as authorized in April last, with the unanimous approbation of the Cabinet, the probability is that Congress would not grant either men or money to prosecute the war. Should this be the result, the army now in Mexico would be constantly wasting and diminishing in numbers, and I might at last be compelled to withdraw them, and thus loose the two Provinces of New Mexico & Upper California, which were ceded to the U.S. by this Treaty. Should the opponents of my administration succeed in carrying the next Presidential election, the great probability is that the country would loose all the advantages secured by this Treaty. I adverted to the immense value of Upper California; and concluded by saying that if I were now to reject my own terms, as offered in April last, I did not see how it was possible for my administration to be sustained. . . .

Wednesday, 23rd February, 1848.— . . . I learned from my porter to-night that the Hon. John Quincy Adams died in the Speaker's Room in the Capitol a few minutes past 7 O'Clock this evening. Mr. Adams was struck down with a paralitic affection while in his seat in the House of Representatives on monday, the 21st Instant. He was borne to the Speaker's room, where he remained speechless and in a state of insensibility until his death this evening. The Ho. Repts has met & adjourned each day since he was taken ill, without transacting any business.

Thursday, 24th February, 1848.—In testimony of respect for the memory of the Hon. John Quincy Adams, who died at the Capitol last evening, I issued an order this morning directing all the Executive Offices at Washington to be placed in mourning, & all business to be suspended during this day and tomorrow. Under this order the President's Mansion was placed in mourning by putting black crape over the front door. Orders were also given through the Secretaries of War & the Navy to cause the melancholy event to be observed with appropriate solemnity by the army and navy. Mr. Adams died in the 81st year of his age. He had been more than half a century in the public service, had filled many high stations,

and among them that of President of the U. States. He was the
sixth President under the Constitution. The first seven Presidents
are all now dead. The ninth President is also dead. Mr. Van Buren
who was the eighth President and Mr. Tyler, who succeeded to the
Presidency upon the death of President Harrison, are the only
two of my predecessors who now survive. I am the tenth President
elected by the people. Mr. Tyler was elected Vice President and
became President when Gen'l Harrison died. So that I am the
tenth President elected by the people & the eleventh President who
has administered the Government from 1789 to this time, a period
of Fifty nine years.

The Secretary of War finished his despatch to Maj'r Gen'l Wm.
O. Butler which I directed to be prepared on yesterday. He brought
it over to-day and read it to me. Mr. Buchanan, Mr. Walker, and
Mr. Mason were present. Some modifications were suggested &
made. Mr. Buchanan handed to me two dispatches from Mr. Trist,
one dated Decr. 29th, 1847, and the other Jany. 12th, 1848, which
he stated Mr. Freanor, the bearer of the Treaty from Mexico,
had not delivered to him until this morning. Mr. Freanor's apology
for the delay in delivering them was that they were placed in a
different part of his baggage from that in which he carried the
Treaty, and had been overlooked by him until this morning. After
the members of the Cabinet retired I read these despatches, and
found them to be arrogant, highly exceptionable, & even of an
insulting character. I immediately sent for the Secretary of War and
informed him that I wished him to add a paragraph to his despatch
to Gen'l Butler, directing him, if Trist should attempt to exercise
any official authority in Mexico, to prevent it, and to require him
to leave the Head Quarters of the army as soon as a safe escort could
be furnished to conduct him to Vera Cruz. Trist has proved himself to be an impudent and unqualified scoundrel. The Secretary
of War hesitated about inserting the paragraph, and said if, after
thinking of it to-night I still thought it proper, it could go in a
seperate despatch to-morrow and could overtake the bearer of
despatches at New Orleans. To this I assented with some reluctance. . . .

Monday, 28th February, 1848.— . . . Near 12 O'Clock Senator
Sevier called and informed me that the committee of Foreign affairs
of the Senate, of which he is Chairman, and to which the Mexican

Treaty had been referred, had held a meeting this morning and had resolved to recommend the rejection of the Treaty by the Senate, & to advise the Executive to appoint an imposing commission to be composed of three or five persons belonging to both political parties, to proceed to Mexico to negotiate a Treaty. Mr. Sevier informed me that he stood alone in the committee opposed to this course. The other members of the Committee are Senators Webster, Benton, Mangum, and Hannegan. Mr. Sevier said they did not object to the terms of the Treaty, with the modifications I had recommended in its ratification, but to Mr. Trist's authority to make it after his recall as commissioner. Mr. Sevier informed me that he had waited on me, with the knowledge of the committee, to inform me of what had been done, and to ascertain my views on the subject with a view to communicate them to the committee and to the Senate. He informed me also that both Mr. Webster and Mr. Benton had requested him to say to me that it would be well for me to be casting about for the commissioners, that the commission should be composed of distinguished men of both political parties, who should be appointed immediately after the action of the Senate should take place, and proceed forthwith to Mexico. I remarked to Mr. Sevier that the course proposed was an extraordinary proceeding, and one which I could not approve. I told him that if he deemed it necessary to say anything, as coming from me, to the committee or to the Senate, it would be that upon full deliberation I had submitted the Treaty to the Senate with my recommendation that with certain modifications it should be ratified, and that I had not changed my opinion; but that, if the Senate chose to recommend a different course, I would co-operate with them as far as in my judgment the public interests would permit. I told him I condemned the insubordinate & insolent conduct of Mr. Trist, but that the Treaty itself was the subject for consideration and not his conduct, and that if the provisions of the Treaty were such as could be accepted, it would be worse than an idle ceremony to send out a grand commission to re-negotiate the same Treaty. I told him, also, that if the Senate advised me to send out such a commission, I hoped they would advise me also what terms they would accept. I consider the course of the committe of the Senate weak, if not factious, and cannot doubt that the object of Mr. Webster is to defeat any Treaty, clamorous as the Whig party profess to be for peace, until after the next Presidential election. Indeed, Mr. Sevier informed me that Mr. Webster said he wanted no territory beyond the Rio Grande, and that he said also that if he voted for this Treaty and Mexico should not ratify it, he would be bound to vote for men and money to carry on the War, a position which he did not wish to occupy. I do not wonder at his course, but I am suprised at that of Mr. Hannegan and Mr. Benton. Extremes sometimes meet and act effectively for negative purposes, but never for affirmative purposes. They have done so in this instance. Mr. Webster is for no territory and Mr. Hannegan is for all Mexico, and for opposite reasons both will oppose the Treaty. It is difficult, upon any rational principle, to assign a satisfactory reason for anything Col. Benton may do, especially in his present temper of mind, wholly engrossed as he seems to have been for some months past with the case of his son-in-law, Col. [John C.] Fremont. The truth is the approaching Presidential election absorbs every other consideration, and Senators act as if there was no country and no public interests to take care of. The factions are all at work, and votes are controlled, even upon a vital question of peace or war, by the supposed effect upon the public mind. If the Treaty in its present form is ratified, there will be added to the U.S. an immense empire, the value of which 20 years hence it would be difficult to calculate, & yet Democratic and Whig Senators disregard this, and act solely with the view to the elevation of themselves or their favourites to the Presidential office. In the course of the day I saw Mr. Buchanan, Mr. Walker, Mr. Mason, & Mr. Clifford, and informed them of the information I had received from Senator Sevier. They all disapproved the course of the committee of Foreign affairs of the Senate, & I was happy to learn from the two former, who had opposed my sending the Treaty to the Senate, that they were utterly opposed to its rejection & sending a fresh commission to Mexico to do the same thing. Mr. Walker was excited, and thought the object of Mr. Webster was to defeat the acquisition of any territory. Mr. Buchanan and Mr. Walker left my office after night to visit Senators & urge them to vote against the project of [a] new commission to Mexico.

I received to-night two Resolutions from the Senate, calling for information and for all the correspondence with Mr. Trist. Much of this correspondence, and especially the letters of Mr. Trist after his recall, are impertinent, irrelevant, & highly exceptionable, but

I resolved to send it all in to the Senate, and prepared a message to-night to that effect. . . .

Tuesday, 4th July, 1848.—This being the day appointed for laying the co[r]ner Stone of the Washington monument in Washington, and having been invited by the committee of arrangements to attend the ceremonies of the occasion, and having determined, though in feeble health, to do so, I had invited my Cabinet to meet & accompany me at 10 O'Clock this morning. Before that hour the Rev. Mr. Smith of the Presbyterian church called with the children composing the sunday school of his church. There were between two and three Hundred children, who were invited into the East Room where I met them. It was [an] interesting interview. Mr. Smith made a short address in which he reminded me that three years ago, being the first 4th of July after my election to the Presidency, he had visited me with his sunday school, and now that I had voluntarily determined to retire to private life on the 4th of March next, they had called again to pay their respects. I responded in a few words of reply, in which I stated that I remembered their visit three years ago; that I was then gratified but not more than I was upon this occasion. There were a number of persons present who witnessed the ceremony. At 10 O'Clock, the Cabinet assembled; all the members present. Accompanied by the Cabinet and escorted by Gen'l Walton, the U. S. marshall of the D. C., and his Deputies, and by a troop of horse commanded by Col. May of the U. S. Army, we were conducted in carriages to the City Hall where the procession was formed and moved to the site of the Washington monument on the Banks of the Potomac and South of the President's mansion. I witnessed the ceremony of laying the corner stone, and heard an address delivered by Mr. Speaker Winthrop of the Ho. Repts. I returned to the President's House and in about an hour, at the request of Gen'l Quitman, I received the military on horseback. They were drawn up to receive me in Pennsylvania Avenue. This afternoon Dr. Rayburn arrived, bearing despatches & the ratified Treaty with Mexico. He stated that Mr. Sevier was sick at New Orleans & had requested him to bring on the Treaty. Mr. Sevier would ascend the Mississippi River. I immediately saw the Secretary of State and caused a proclamation to be prepared announcing officially the definitive conclusion of peace with Mexico. At about 11 O'Clock at night I signed the Proclamation. I desired to sign it on the anniversary of Independance. . . .

29. Treaty of Guadalupe Hidalgo

The treaty was signed near Mexico City on February 2, 1848. Source: Miller (ed.), Treaties and Other International Acts . . ., V, 207–208, 213–214, 219–220, 222–223, 230–231.

In the name of Almighty God:

The United States of America, and the United Mexican States, animated by a sincere desire to put an end to the calamities of the war which unhappily exists between the two Republics, and to establish upon a solid basis relations of peace and friendship, which shall confer reciprocal benefits upon the citizens of both, and assure the concord, harmony and mutual confidence, wherein the two peoples should live, as good neighbours, have for that purpose appointed their respective Plenipotentiaries: that is to say, the President of the United States has appointed Nicholas P. Trist, a citizen of the United States, and the President of the Mexican Republic has appointed Don Luis Gonzaga Cuevas, Don Bernardo Couto, and Don Miguel Atristain, citizens of the said Republic; who, after a reciprocal communication of their respective full powers, have, under the protection of Almighty God, the author of Peace, arranged, agreed upon, and signed the following

Treaty of Peace, Friendship, Limits and Settlement between the United States of America and the Mexican Republic.

Article I

There shall be firm and universal peace between the United States of America and the Mexican Republic, and between their respective countries, territories, cities, towns and people, without exception of places or persons. . . .

Article V

The Boundary line between the two Republics shall commence in the Gulf of Mexico, three leagues from land, opposite the mouth of the Rio Grande, otherwise called Rio Bravo del Norte, or opposite the mouth of it's deepest branch, if it should have more than one branch emptying directly into the sea; from thence, up the middle of that river, following the deepest channel, where it has more than one, to the point where it strikes the southern boundary

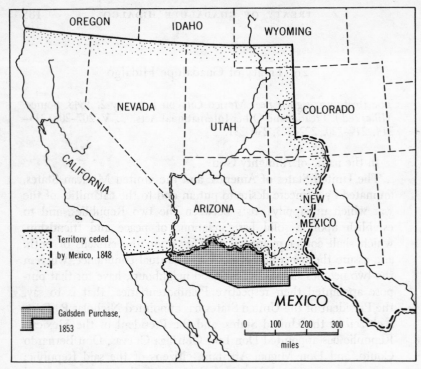

7. The Mexican Cession and Gadsden Purchase.

of New Mexico; thence, westwardly, along the whole southern boundary of New Mexico (which runs north of the town called Paso) to it's western termination; thence, northward, along the western line of New Mexico, until it intersects the first branch of the river Gila; (or if it should not intersect any branch of that river, then, to the point on the said line nearest to such branch, and thence in a direct line to the same;) thence down the middle of the said branch and of the said river, until it empties into the Rio Colorado; thence, across the Rio Colorado, following the division line between Upper and Lower California, to the Pacific Ocean. . . .

Article XI

Considering that a great part of the territories which, by the present Treaty, are to be comprehended for the future within the limits of the United States, is now occupied by savage tribes, who will hereafter be under the exclusive controul of the Government of the United States, and whose incursions within the territory of

Mexico would be prejudicial in the extreme; it is solemnly agreed that all such incursions shall be forcibly restrained by the Government of the United States, whensoever this may be necessary; and that when they cannot be prevented, they shall be punished by the said Government, and satisfaction for the same shall be exacted: all in the same way, and with equal diligence and energy, as if the same incursions were meditated or committed within it's own territory against it's own citizens. . . .

Article XII

In consideration of the extension acquired by the boundaries of the United States, as defined in the fifth Article of the present Treaty, the Government of the United States engages to pay to that of the Mexican Republic the sum of fifteen Millions of Dollars.

Immediately after this treaty shall have been duly ratified by the Government of the Mexican Republic, the sum of three millions of dollars shall be paid to the said Government by that of the United States at the city of Mexico, in the gold or silver coin of Mexico. . . .

Article XIII

The United States engage moreover, to assume and pay to the claimants all the amounts now due them, and those hereafter to become due, by reason of the claims already liquidated and decided against the Mexican Republic, under the conventions between the two Republics severally concluded on the eleventh day of April eighteen hundred and thirty-nine, and on the thirtieth day of January eighteen hundred and forty three: so that the Mexican Republic shall be absolutely exempt for the future, from all expense whatever on account of the said claims. . . .

Article XXI

If unhappily any disagreement should hereafter arise between the Governments of the two Republics, whether with respect to the interpretation of any stipulation in this treaty, or with respect to any other particular concerning the political or commercial relations of the two Nations, the said Governments, in the name of those Nations, do promise to each other, that they will endeavour in the most sincere and earnest manner, to settle the differences so arising, and to preserve the state of peace and friendship, in which the two countries are now placing themselves: using, for this end, mutual representations and pacific negotiations. And, if by these means, they should not be enabled to come to an agreement, a resort shall not, on this account, be had to reprisals, aggression or hostility of any kind, by the one Republic against the other, until the Government of that which deems itself aggrieved, shall have maturely considered, in the spirit of peace and good neighbourship, whether it would not be better that such difference . should be settled by the arbitration of Commissioners appointed on each side, or by that of a friendly nation. And should such course be proposed by either party, it shall be acceded to by the other, unless deemed by it altogether incompatible with the nature of the difference, or the circumstances of the case. . . .

XI

The Northeast and Northwest
Boundaries

The decade of the 1840's marked the settlement of two large boundary controversies with Great Britain. They were technical controversies, both of them, involving disputes over many years. Their solution was a part of the general accommodation of issues with Britain between the end of the War of 1812 and the Geneva arbitration of 1872. In the northeast boundary treaty the United States lost some territory, although not an enormous amount. The northwest boundary treaty gained almost an empire, if one may so describe the middle and western thirds of the present-day state of Washington. In addition to their contribution to Anglo-American amity, the boundary treaties taken together constituted another proof of manifest destiny.

30. The northeast boundary

Here the problem was mostly the boundary between Maine and Canada, which the negotiators of 1782 had drawn as best they could according to Mitchell's Map of North America of 1755, perhaps the best map of its day but inaccurate, especially in its extremities. In the Treaty of Paris the Americans failed to mention specifically that they had used a Mitchell, nor did they append a map to their own copy of the treaty. Article 5 of Jay's Treaty of 1794 sought to mend this oversight. Source: Miller (ed.), Treaties and Other International Acts . . . , II, 249.

Whereas doubts have arisen what River was truly intended under the name of the River St Croix mentioned in the said Treaty of Peace and forming a part of the boundary therein described, that question shall be referred to the final Decision of Commissioners to be appointed in the following Manner—Viz—

One Commissioner shall be named by His Majesty, and one by the President of the United States, by and with the advice and Con-

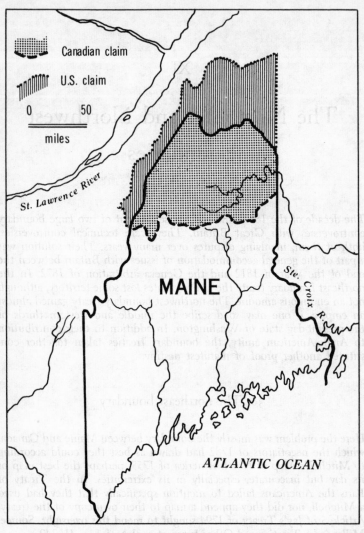

8. The Webster-Ashburton boundary.

sent of the Senate thereof, and the said two Commissioners shall agree on the choice of a third, or, if they cannot so agree, They shall each propose one Person, and of the two names so proposed one shall be drawn by Lot, in the presence of the two original Commissioners. And the three Commissioners so appointed shall be Sworn impartially to examine and decide the said question according to such Evidence as shall respectively be laid before Them on the part of the British Government and of the United States. The said Commissioners shall meet at Halifax and shall have power to adjourn to such other place or places as they shall think fit. They shall have power to appoint a Secretary, and to employ such Surveyors or other Persons as they shall judge necessary. The said Commissioners shall by a Declaration under their Hands and Seals, decide what River is the River St Croix intended by the Treaty. The said Declaration shall contain a description of the said River, and shall particularize the Latitude and Longitude of its mouth and of its Source. Duplicates of this Declaration and of the Statements of their Accounts, and of the Journal of their proceedings, shall be delivered by them to the Agent of His Majesty, and to the Agent of the United States, who may be respectively appointed and authorized to manage the business on behalf of the respective Governments. And both parties agree to consider such decision as final and conclusive, so as that the same shall never thereafter be called into question, or made the subject of dispute or difference between them.

The commission appointed under Jay's Treaty failed to do anything more than identify the St. Croix River as being what then was called the Schoodiac. A marker was affixed at its source, and from that point north and west the boundary remained in dispute. Article 5 of the Treaty of Ghent of 1814 sought to end the controversy. Source: ibid., 577–578.

Whereas neither that point of the Highlands lying due North from the source of the River St Croix, and designated in the former Treaty of Peace between the two Powers as the North West Angle of Nova Scotia, nor the North Westernmost head of Connecticut River has yet been ascertained; and whereas that part of the boundary line between the Dominions of the two Powers which extends from the source of the River St Croix directly North to the above-mentioned North West Angle of Nova Scotia, thence along the said Highlands which divide those Rivers that empty themselves into the River St Lawrence from those which fall into the Atlantic Ocean to the North Westernmost head of Connecticut River, thence down along the middle of that River to the forty fifth degree of North Latitude, thence by a line due West on said latitude until it strikes the River Iroquois or Cataraquy, has not yet been surveyed: it is agreed that for these several purposes two Commissioners shall be appointed, sworn, and authorized to act exactly in the manner directed with respect to those mentioned in the next preceding Article unless otherwise specified in the present Article. The said Commissioners shall meet at St Andrews in the Province of New Brunswick, and shall have power to adjourn to such other place or places as they shall think fit. The said Commissioners shall have power to ascertain and determine the points above mentioned in conformity with the provisions of the said Treaty of Peace of one thousand seven hundred and eighty three, and shall cause the boundary aforesaid from the source of the River St Croix to the River Iroquois or Cataraquy to be surveyed and marked according to the said provisions. The said Commissioners shall make a map of the said boundary, and annex to it a declaration under their hands and seals certifying it to be the true Map of the said boundary, and particularizing the latitude and longitude of the North West Angle of Nova Scotia, of the North Westernmost head of Connecticut River, and of such other points of the said boundary as they may deem proper. And both parties agree to consider such map and declaration as finally and conclusively fixing the said boundary. And in the event of the said two Commissioners differing, or both, or either of them refusing, declining, or wilfully omitting to act, such reports, declarations, or statements shall be made by them or either of them, and such reference to a friendly Sovereign or State shall be made in all respects as in the latter part of the fourth Article is contained, and in as full a manner as if the same was herein repeated.

The Maine boundary dispute wore on and on, until its settlement in 1842. Under Article 5 of the Treaty of Ghent the problem passed eventually to the king of the Netherlands, and that monarch split the difference in an award of 1830. The Jackson administration refused to accept this award, on the technicality that an arbitrator must choose between the contentions and cannot make an arrangement of his own. Meanwhile the British government became more interested in the disputed area, wishing to ensure enough territory for a military road from Halifax via St. John and Fredericton to Quebec and Montreal, such a passage being desirable in winter when the St. Lawrence froze over. The Americans on their part became more insistent in their claims because of discovery by the inhabitants of Maine of the rich Aroostook Valley. A rebellion against British rule in Canada broke out in 1837, and received help from across the American border, greatly agitating the boundary dispute. Then, at last, a change in the British cabinet in 1841 brought in Sir Robert Peel as prime minister and the peace-loving Lord

Aberdeen as foreign secretary. They hoped to solve all issues outstanding with the United States. Alexander Baring, Lord Ashburton, journeyed to the United States, and he and Secretary of State Daniel Webster got down to business. What happened at this juncture in regard to the Maine boundary was curious in its details—and Webster's solution of those details. Webster's special problem was convincing the legislatures of Maine and Massachusetts to consent to an unfavorable boundary settlement, for when Maine split off from Massachusetts as a state in 1820 the arrangement was for the public lands of Maine to be jointly owned, with any proceeds therefrom to be shared jointly. Professor Jared Sparks of Harvard obliged Webster with a map which seemed to support the British claim. Sparks sent Webster a nineteenth-century map of Maine on which he had marked, from memory and notes, a line he recalled seeing some years before on a map in the French archives; the French map, Sparks presumed, was the map used by Franklin in the negotiations of 1782. The outlines of Webster's maneuvering with his own country's boundary claim are in Samuel Flagg Bemis's John Quincy Adams and the Foundations of American Foreign Policy (Alfred A. Knopf: New York, 1949), pp. 585–588, wherein Professor Bemis has printed some private letters which Ashburton wrote from Washington in the summer of 1842 to Aberdeen in London.

[Ashburton to Aberdeen, Washington, June 14] . . . Our great question the Maine Boundary up to this day looks well. It has been ably conducted through Webster during his visit to New England where he defeated the schemes of the Democratic Governor of Maine. Our only serious difficulty here will be with [William Pitt] Preble, a very obstinate, but I believe honest, man, who thinks & dreams of nothing but this boundary and who was appointed to the Commission by the Governor to defeat a settlement. I believe he will ultimately be satisfied.—I have some reason to suspect that Webster has discovered some evidence, known at present to nobody, but favorable to our claim, and that he is using it with the Commissioners. I have some clue to this fact and hope to get at it. . . .

[Aberdeen to Ashburton, July 2] The postscript to your private letter of the 14th of last month [missing from the above document in the British Museum] has only been communicated by me to Peel, under injunctions of the strictest secrecy, and you may rely on our desire to observe the utmost caution with respect to the matter contained in it. But this incident has, I confess, quite taken me by surprise, and opens a new view of measures which perhaps may be followed up with advantage, should there yet be time for you to do so. In order to insure success, you need not be afraid of employing the same means to a greater extent in any quarter where it may be necessary. In what you have done you have been perfectly right; and indeed I look upon the proposal made to you from such a quarter, as the most certain indication we could receive of a determination to bring the negotiation to a happy issue. In any further transactions of the same kind, I have only to desire that it may be made the means of leading to success, as the condition of having recourse to it. If you can command success you need not hesitate. . . .

[Ashburton to Aberdeen, Washington, July 28] I am well pleased to see by your private letter of the 2d that you were satisfied with what I communicated to you the 14th of last month. I had no doubt & did not hesitate but I do not think it likely that I shall have more to say to you on the same subject.—

You will see that I have at last made my important move, and that my Boundary is on the high road to the Senate. The men of Maine were most difficult to deal with, and I was obliged somewhat irregularly to undertake them, for the Secy of State had no influence with them; and for a day or two I was in doubt whether I might not fail altogether, but at last Preble yielded and after Signing he went off to his wilds in Maine as sulky as a Bear.—You may rely that no better terms were obtainable, and that if obtained would be decidedly in danger in the Senate. For my own part you are aware that I have been fighting for details to which I do not attach the same importance as my masters. My great wish was that there should be a settlement, because I was sure that if this failed we should come very soon to collision, but I am well pleased that we end by driving the enmy off that crest of Highlands so much coveted at the war office.

There has been no demand of money by anybody during the whole discussion, & I need not add that on this subject I have been cautiously silent.—. . .

[Ashburton to Aberdeen, Washington, August 9] Since I communicated to you the very extraordinary information about the Boundary, I have seen Sparkes's letter and the map to which he refers. I made immediately a memorandum of the facts from which I now copy. The letter from Dr. Franklin to the Count de Vergennes is dated 6 December 1782, and is in the following words: "I have the honor to return to Your Excellency the map you sent me yesterday and I have marked according to your desire with strong red ink the limits of the United States as decided by the preliminaries of peace signed by the British and American Plenipotentiaries." These preliminaries were signed six days before.—On reading this letter Sparkes went to the topographical department where there were 60000 maps & charts but so well indexed & catalogued that he had no difficulty of finding the map. It is by D'Anville dated 1746—and of the size of about 18 inches—and has the red ink mark referred to by Dr. Franklin of the exact boundaries of the United States, marked apparently by a hair pencil or a blunt pen.—

The line marked gives Great Britain more than what is claimed by our line, for beginning at the St. Croix it runs carefully round all the tributaries of the St John so as to throw even the country about Houlton into New Brunswick. It is evident that the division intended was by rivers and that, as we always maintained, the waters of the St John throughout were intended to belong to G Britain.—

This extraordinary evidence places this case beyond all possible doubt, and if I had known it before I agreed to sign I should have asked your orders, notwithstanding the manner of my becoming acquainted with it. At the same time the communication to me was strictly confidential and then communicated because I had agreed to sign, so that taking all things into consideration I could not and did not hesitate. I should certainly, if I had known the secret earlier, have made my stand on the upper St Johns & probably at the Madawaska settlements. But these speculations come now too late. The money I wrote about went to compensate Sparkes & to send him, on my first arrival, to the Governors of Maine & Massachusetts. My informant thinks that without this stimulant Maine would never have yielded, and here it has removed many objections in other quarters.—The secret now is with the President & his Cabinet the Governors of Maine & Massachusetts, seven Commissioners, four Senators, and it has this day been communicated to two more who are leading members of the Senates Committee for foreign affairs. In my house it is known only by Mildmay. This is a large number for keeping so singular a Secret but I must beg it may be strictly kept on your side, as my source of information would be betrayed. I am assured that it is not known by Everett.—There is one consolation to be derived from our tardy acquaintance with this fact. If I had known it before treating, in any way which would have permitted me to use it, we could not well have refrained from maintaining our undoubted right and yet we never should have got the Aroostook without fighting for it. All the evidence of angels would not have moved the Maine lumberers. This is my scrap of consolation. I have drawn on you a bill for £2998–1–[c. $14,000] 30 days sight for the purpose mentioned in my former private letter and you will find this put into proper form. I am not likely to want anything more. The President is at open war with his Congress & Webster's Whig friends press him strongly to retire when he has finished our treaty. I think he will do so and he has a hankering to go to London & send Everett to Paris in Cass's place. I think this will be so arranged & Cass can now do no mischief here. I think you may now confidently reckon on peace with this country for some time barring very extraordinary accidents & with common care. I now relieve you my dear Ld Aberdeen from a tiresome correspondent.

ps. It is very singular that among the number of persons who have been busy with this Boundary question nobody should have thought of so very natural an Enquiry at Paris excepting Sparkes.

Webster and Ashburton signed the treaty on August 9, 1842. Source: Miller (ed.), Treaties and Other International Acts . . . , IV, 363–365.

Whereas certain portions of the line of boundary between the United States of America and the British Dominions in North America, described in the second article of the Treaty of Peace of 1783, have not yet been ascertained and determined, notwithstanding the repeated attempts which have been heretofore made for that purpose, and whereas it is now thought to be for the interest of both Parties, that, avoiding further discussion of their respective rights, arising in this respect under the said Treaty, they should agree on a conventional line in said portions of the said boundary, such as may be convenient to both Parties, with such equivalents and compensations, as are deemed just and reasonable: . . . The United States of America and Her Britannic Majesty, having resolved to treat on these several subjects, have for that purpose appointed their respective Plenipotentiaries to negotiate and conclude a Treaty, that is to say: the President of the United States has, on his part, furnished with full powers, Daniel Webster, Secretary of State of the United States; and Her Majesty the Queen of the United Kingdom of Great Britain and Ireland, has, on her part, appointed the Right honorable Alexander Lord Ashburton, a peer of the said United Kingdom, a member of Her Majesty's most honorable Privy Council, and Her Majesty's Minister Plenipotentiary on a Special Mission to the United States; who, after a reciprocal communication of their respective full powers, have agreed to and signed the following articles:

Article I

It is hereby agreed and declared that the line of boundary shall be as follows: Beginning at the monument at the source of the river St Croix, as designated and agreed to by the Commissioners under the fifth article of the Treaty of 1794, between the Governments of the United States and Great Britain; thence, north, following the exploring line run and marked by the Surveyors of the two Governments in the years 1817 and 1818, under the fifth article of the Treaty of Ghent, to its intersection with the river St John, and to the middle of the channel thereof: thence, up the middle of the main channel of the said river St John, to the mouth of the river St Francis; thence up the middle of the channel of the said river St Francis, and of the lakes through which it flows, to the outlet of the Lake Pohenagamook; thence, southwesterly, in a straight line to a point on the northwest branch of the river St John, which point shall be ten miles distant from the mainbranch of the St John, in a straight line, and in the nearest direction; but if the said point shall be found to be less than seven miles from the nearest point of the summit or crest of the highlands that divide those rivers which empty themselves into the river Saint Lawrence from those which fall into the river Saint John, then the said point shall be made to recede down the said northwest branch of the river St John, to a point seven miles in a straight line from the said summit or crest; thence, in a straight line, in a course about south eight degrees west, to the point where the parallel of latitude of 46°25′ north, intersects the southwest branch of the St John's; thence, southerly, by the said branch, to the source thereof in the highlands at the Metjarmette Portage; thence, down along the said highlands which divide the waters which empty themselves into the river Saint Lawrence from those which fall into the Atlantic Ocean, to the head of Hall's Stream; thence, down the middle of said Stream, till the line thus run intersects the old line of boundary surveyed and marked by Valentine and Collins previously to the year 1774, as the 45th degree of north latitude, and which has been known and understood to be the line of actual division between the States of New York and Vermont on one side, and the British Province of Canada on the other; and, from said point of intersection, west along the said dividing line as heretofore known and understood, to the Iroquois or St Lawrence river. . . .

Shortly after conclusion of the Webster-Ashburton Treaty it became evident that a Mitchell map fully supporting the American claim in Maine had been among the papers left by George III to the British Museum, and that after a reference to this map in a debate in Parliament in 1839 the then foreign secretary, Lord Palmerston, had secreted the map at the foreign office. He apparently did not tell Aberdeen about it. A similar map was in the papers of Lord Lansdowne, from the correspondence of Lord Shelburne, prime minister in 1782. Moreover, in 1843 a map was found in the United States in the papers of John Jay, again proving the American claim. Samuel Flagg Bemis in 1933 discovered a fourth map in the Spanish archives, among the papers of the Spanish ambassador to Paris in 1782, the Count of Aranda. Webster in 1842 had directed the American minister in London, Edward Everett, not to look for maps.

31. The northwest boundary

An Anglo-American treaty in 1818 drew the boundary between Canada and the United States along the forty-ninth parallel from the Lake of the Woods to the crest of the Rocky Mountains, and declared the area westward to the Pacific to be free and open. The area in dispute, then known as "the Oregon country," comprised the entire Pacific Northwest from California north to Alaska. The Transcontinental Treaty of 1819 set a northern boundary of the forty-second parallel for Spanish possessions, and the Russian-American and Russian-British treaties of 1824 and 1825 respectively set the parallel of 54° 40′ as the southernmost extension of Russian possessions (the parties chose this odd line so that the Alaska panhandle might include Prince of Wales Island). The Oregon territory in dispute, broadly speaking, thereupon ran from the forty-second parallel north to 54° 40′. Practically, the Americans by settlement of the Willamette Valley soon established a good claim to the lands between the forty-second parallel and the Columbia River. The British through exploration and fur trading likewise established a respectable claim to the lands from 54° 40′ south to the forty-ninth parallel. Hence the area in dispute really lay between the Columbia and the forty-ninth parallel, that is, the middle and western thirds of the present-day state of Washington. In several negotiations the American government showed itself willing to take the forty-ninth parallel to the Pacific (presumably taking also the southern tip of Vancouver Island). The British stuck for the line of the Columbia, because the Hudson's Bay Company seemed to need the river. When the Company in 1845 moved its trading post from Fort Vancouver on the Columbia to Fort Victoria on Vancouver Island the British government at last was able to settle for the forty-ninth parallel, excluding the tip of Vancouver Island. But by this time the boundary had become a highly charged political issue in the United States. It was an almost incredibly complicated piece of politics. Before his election in 1844, Polk had made a pronouncement for All Oregon, and the Democratic convention in Baltimore had chosen him to run on a platform demanding "the reannexation of Texas and the reoccupation of Oregon." He judiciously offered the forty-ninth parallel to the British government in 1845. The minister in Washington, Richard Pakenham, turned the offer down without referring it to London. Polk withdrew the offer and encouraged the All Oregon enthusiasts. He asked Congress for permission to give notice canceling with Britain the free and open arrangement of 1818 (which a treaty of 1827 had continued on a yearly basis, subject to notice). In December 1845, a grand debate on "notice" began in Congress which raged almost to the outbreak of the Mexican War in May 1846. In the middle of the debate Polk seems to have felt that the talk was getting out of control. Far from becoming a threat to the British, as he may have intended, it was becoming a platform upon which worthy solons were puffing themselves, not for 49° or 54° 40′ but for 48° (Polk had foresworn a second term). The President undoubtedly divined the British government's wish to settle the issue at 49°. Having encouraged his supporters, Polk had to let them down easily, the more so because all the 54° 40′ men were Democrats. If he did not retreat with care, he ran the danger of splitting the party. He envisaged the horrible prospect of a split similar to what had happened to the Whigs when Tyler acceded to the presidency upon the death of Harrison in 1841. So, Polk had to let the All Oregon men down easily, and seems to have chosen for this task his old college roommate and close friend, Senator William H. Haywood, Jr., of North Carolina, who on March 4–5, 1846, made what appeared to be an authorized speech. Senator Edward Hannegan of Indiana questioned Haywood closely on March 5. Source: 29th Cong., 1st Sess., Congressional Globe, p. 460.

. . . Who, then, defines the limits of Oregon? Has not the President himself defined them in his Message?

Mr. H. [Senator Hannegan] then quoted from the President's Message the following paragraph:

"The extraordinary and wholly inadmissible demands of the British Government, and the rejection of the proposition made in deference alone to what had been done my predecessors, and the implied obligation which their acts seemed to impose, afford satisfactory evidence that no compromise which the United States ought to accept can be effected. With this conviction, the proposition of compromise which had been made and rejected was, by my direction, subsequently withdrawn, and our title to the whole Oregon territory asserted, and, as is believed, maintained by irrefragable facts and arguments."

What does the President here claim? Up to 54° 40′—every inch of it. He has asserted that claim, and is, as he says, sustained by "irrefragable facts and arguments." But this is not all: I hold that the language of the Secretary of State is the language of the President of the United States; and has not Mr. Buchanan, in his last communication to Mr. Pakenham, named 54° 40′ in so many words? He has. The President adopts this language as his own. He plants himself on 54° 40′. I well remember that the President was the choice neither of myself nor—I beg his pardon, I should have named the Senator first—neither of the Senator from North Carolina nor of myself. Neither of us preferred him. Both of us had another choice. And I must confess I am most happy to see that, since his election, he has grown so much in favor with my friend from North Carolina as to induce him to come here with a valorous defence against attacks never made—never made, sir. But this I will say—and make it attack, if you please—if the President has betrayed that standard which the Baltimore convention put into his hands, and whereby he committed himself to the country, into the hands of the enemy, I will not do, as the Senator from North Carolina threatens, turn my back upon him—I suppose he cares little whether both of us do that—but I shall hold him recreant to the principles which he professed, recreant to the trust which he accepted, recreant to the generous confidence which a majority of the people reposed in him. I shall not abandon the principles of the democratic party. I shall not abate one jot or tittle of the principles we gave to the country then; I shall sustain them; but I shall hold and exercise the privilege of speaking of him in the language of truth and fearlessness. The Senator from North Carolina attempted to speak of the resolution of the Baltimore convention. I ask him if he seriously meant his statement of it as a fair exhibition of its substance? If so, it was unworthy of the Senator to—

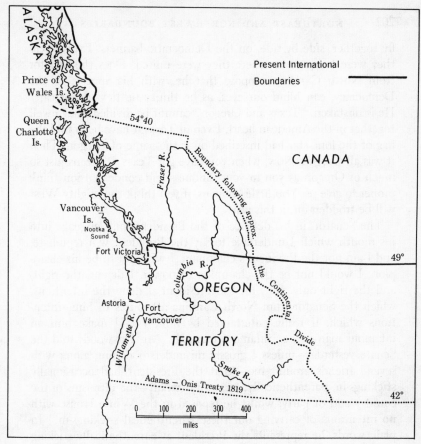

9. The Oregon Treaty.

Mr. HAYWOOD. I took the resolution from Mr. Breese's speech—the only place I believe I ever saw it. Here it is:

"*Resolved*, That our title to the whole of the territory of Oregon is clear and unquestionable; that no portion of the same ought to be ceded to England or any other Power; and that the reoccupation of Oregon, and the reannexation of Texas at the earliest practicable period, are great American measures, which the convention recommends to the cordial support of the democracy of the Union."

Mr. HANNEGAN. There is a great deal of difference between that and the statement of it given by the Senator. The Democratic party is thus bound to the whole of Oregon—every foot of it; and let the Senator rise in his place who will tell me in what quarter of this Union—in what assembly of Democrats in this Union, pending the Presidential election, the names of Texas and Oregon did not fly together, side by side, on the Democratic banners. Everywhere they were twins—everywhere they were united. Does the Senator from North Carolina suppose that he, with his appeals to the Democracy, can blind our eyes, as he thinks he tickled our ears? He is mistaken. "Texas and Oregon" cannot be divided; they dwell together in the American heart. Even in Texas, I have been told the flag of the lone star had inscribed on it the name of Oregon. Then it was all Oregon. Now, when you have got Texas, it means just so much of Oregon as you in your kindness and condescension think proper to give us. You little know us, if you think the mighty West will be trodden on in this way. . . .

The Senator, in his defence of the President, put language into his mouth which I undertake to say the President will repudiate, and I am not the President's champion. I wish not to be his champion. I would not be the champion of power. I defend the right, and the right only. But, for the President, I deny the intentions, which the Senator from North Carolina attributes to him—intentions which, if really entertained by him, would make him an infamous man—ay, an infamous man. He [Mr. Haywood] told the Senate yesterday—unless I grossly misunderstood him, along with several friends around me—"that the President had occasionally stickings-in, parenthetically, to gratify—what?—the ultraisms of the country and of party; whilst he reposed in the White House with no intentions of carrying out these parenthetical stickings-in." In plain words, he represents the President as parenthetically sticking in a few hollow and false words to cajole the "ultraisms of the country?" What is this, need I ask, but charging upon the President conduct the most vile and infamous? If this allegation be true, these intentions of the President must sooner or later come to light, and when brought to light what must follow but irretrievable disgrace? So long as one human eye remains to linger on the page of history, the story of his abasement will be read, sending him and his name together to an infamy so profound, a damnation so deep, that the hand of resurrection will never be able to drag him forth. He who is the traitor to his country can never have forgiveness of God, and cannot ask mercy of man. I asked the Senator whether he came here charged with missives from the President, or whether he assumed the dogmatic style on his own responsibility, and——

Mr. MANGUM. I call the Senator to order. I protest against these remarks.

Mr. HAYWOOD. Let him proceed.

Mr. MANGUM. I withdraw my objection.

Mr. HANNEGAN. Let me say one thing to the Senator from North Carolina over the way, [Mr. Mangum] that if I have uttered one syllable disrespectful to the Senator, it has not been my intention. If he apprehended that I was in danger of saying anything disrespectful, I thank him for his kind hint. I shall not forget the place where I am, and the respect which I owe myself. I reply in the same spirit in which the Senator spoke. I have no personal motives; I am speaking to principles, and using, as he did, plain language. We were told that this question was agitated in the country for the purpose of putting small men into large offices. I have seen small men in large offices before to-day. "Small men in large offices!" "The country agitated to put small men in large offices!" Those who live in glass houses should not throw stones. The proverb is somewhat stale, but it is a salutary one; and even some great men may occasionally be reminded of it to their profit. Let me tell the Senator from North Carolina, that, for my own part, I would much sooner be found a small man seeking a high place, than the subservient, pliant, supple tool—the cringing flatterer, the fawning sycophant, who crouches before power, and hurries from its back stairs to bring before the Senate its becks, and nods, and wreathed smiles. . . . I have only to add, that so far as the whole tone, spirit, and meaning of the remarks of the Senator from North Carolina are concerned, if they speak the language of James K. Polk, James K. Polk has spoken words of falsehood, and with the tongue of a serpent.

Mr. ALLEN rose, but

Mr. EVANS obtaining the floor, moved that the Senate adjourn. The motion was carried, and the Senate accordingly adjourned.

Buchanan and Pakenham signed the Oregon treaty on June 15, 1846. Source: Miller (ed.), Treaties and Other International Acts . . . , V, 3–4.

Article I

From the point on the forty-ninth parallel of north latitude where the boundary laid down in existing treaties and conventions between the United States and Great Britain terminates, the line of boundary beween the territories of the United States and those of Her Britannic Majesty shall be continued westward along the said forty-ninth parallel of north latitude to the middle of the channel which separates the continent from Vancouver's Island; and thence southerly through the middle of the said channel, and of Fuca's Straits to the Pacific Ocean; provided, however, that the navigation of the whole of the said channel and Straits south of the forty ninth parallel of north latitude remain free and open to both Parties.

Article II

From the point at which the forty-ninth parallel of north latitude shall be found to intersect the great northern branch of the Columbia River, the navigation of the said branch shall be free and open to the Hudson's Bay Company and to all British subjects trading with the same, to the point where the said branch meets the main stream of the Columbia, and thence down the said main stream to the Ocean, with free access into and through the said River or Rivers, it being understood that all the usual portages along the line thus described shall in like manner be free and open. . . .

Article III

In the future appropriation of the territory, south of the forty-ninth parallel of north latitude, as provided in the first article of this Treaty, the possessory rights of the Hudson's Bay Company and of all British subjects who may be already in the occupation of land or other property, lawfully acquired within the said Territory, shall be respected.

Article IV

The farms, lands, and other property of every description belonging to the Puget's Sound Agricultural Company on the north side of the Columbia River, shall be confirmed to the said Company. . . .

The treaty contained some loose ends, and the Treaty of Washington of 1871 (below, pp. 276–278) considered the principal one, in its Article 34. Source: Statutes at Large, XVII, 874–875.

Whereas it was stipulated by Article I of the treaty concluded at Washington on the 15th of June, 1846, between the United States and her Britannic Majesty, that the line of boundary between the territories of the United States and those of her Britannic Majesty, from the point on the forty-ninth parallel of north latitude up to which it had already been ascertained, should be continued westward along the said parallel of north latitude "to the middle of the channel which separates the continent from Vancouver's Island, and thence southerly, through the middle of the said channel and of Fuca Straits, to the Pacific Ocean;" and whereas the commissioners appointed by the two high contracting parties to determine that portion of the boundary which runs southerly through the middle of the channel aforesaid, were unable to agree upon the same; and whereas the government of her Britannic Majesty claims that such boundary line should, under the terms of the treaty above recited, be run through the Rosario Straits, and the government of the United States claims that it should be run through the Canal de Haro, it is agreed that the respective claims of the government of the United States and of the government of her Britannic Majesty shall be submitted to the arbitration and award of his Majesty the Emperor of Germany, who, having regard to the above-mentioned article of the said treaty, shall decide thereupon, finally and without appeal, which of those claims is most in accordance with the true interpretation of the treaty of June 15, 1846.

The German emperor recognized the American claim in an award of 1872.

XII

Expansive Projects

In a book written some years ago, Empire on the Pacific (1955), Norman A. Graebner contended that President Polk's war with Mexico was for ports on the Pacific—for San Diego and San Francisco—and not for so ethereal an idea as manifest destiny. Graebner was supporting the contention of an earlier book by Albert K. Weinberg, Manifest Destiny (1935), which wrote off as logically stupid the whole theory announced by John L. O'Sullivan in 1845. But is it not true that nations, like individuals, will refuse to fight for mundane matters, physical objects, territory, but must have an idea, a driving intellectual force? And if manifest destiny was nonsense, how does one explain the extra-continental projects of the era, by which the government of the United States arranged its rights for construction of a future isthmian canal, and opened diplomatic relations with the empires of China and Japan? If the acts of the 1840's and 1850's in Central America and the Far East were not in the spirit of manifest destiny they were episodes in the national history, and the whole course of American history in the nineteenth century runs against such an interpretation. It is of interest that the distinguished scholar Frederick Merk recently has published three volumes in favor of manifest destiny: Manifest Destiny and Mission in American History (1963); The Monroe Doctrine and American Expansionism, 1843–1849 (1966); and The Oregon Question (1967).

32. A few words to Europe

In the 1840's and 1850's the mood of the people of the United States was high indeed, as the hand of destiny seemed to be guiding the nation. Americans liked to think of themselves as a great people in a great land. And they enjoyed nothing so much as to inform Europeans of their successes. The Hungarian revolution of 1848 proved an opportunity for instructing Europe, and Secretary of State Daniel Webster on December 21, 1850, serving at that time under President Millard Fillmore, made the most of the occasion. He fastened his attention upon the poor Chevalier J. G. Huelsemann, chargé d'affaires of Austria. Source: Writings and Speeches of Daniel Webster (18 vols., Boston, 1903), XII, 168–170, 177–178. After Webster had chastised Huelsemann, he received a letter from a Mr. McGaw, dated February 6, 1851, which noted his triumph (Writings and Speeches . . . , XVIII, 418): "Now for poor Huelsemann one word. I certainly should pity him, if you had left a remnant of him of sufficient size to affix any thing like compassion upon. But he is consumed, entirely consumed."

. . . The undersigned will first observe, that the President is persuaded his Majesty the Emperor of Austria does not think that the government of the United States ought to view with unconcern the extraordinary events which have occurred, not only in his dominions, but in many other parts of Europe, since February, 1848. . . .

But the undersigned goes further, and freely admits that, in proportion as these extraordinary events appeared to have their origin in those great ideas of responsible and popular government, on which the American constitutions themselves are wholly founded, they could not but command the warm sympathy of the people of this country. Well-known circumstances in their history, indeed their whole history, have made them the representatives of purely popular principles of government. In this light they now stand before the world. They could not, if they would, conceal their character, their condition, or their destiny. They could not, if they so desired, shut out from the view of mankind the causes which have placed them, in so short a national career, in the station which they now hold among the civilized states of the world. They could not, if they desired it, suppress either the thoughts or the hopes which arise in men's minds, in other countries, from contemplating their successful example of free government. That very intelligent and distinguished personage, the Emperor Joseph the Second, was among the first to discern this necessary consequence of the American Revolution on the sentiments and opinions of the people of Europe. In a letter to his minister in the Netherlands in 1787, he observes, that "it is remarkable that France, by the assistance which she afforded to the Americans, gave birth to reflections on freedom." This fact, which the sagacity of that monarch perceived at so early a day is now known and admitted by intelligent powers all over the world. True, indeed, it is, that the prevalence on the other continent of sentiments favorable to republican liberty is the result of the reaction of America upon Europe; and the source and centre of this reaction has doubtless been, and now is, in these United States. . . .

The power of this republic, at the present moment, is spread over a region one of the richest and most fertile on the globe, and of an extent in comparison with which the possessions of the house of Hapsburg are but as a patch on the earth's surface. Its population, already twenty-five millions, will exceed that of the Austrian empire within the period during which it may be hoped that Mr. Hülsemann may yet remain in the honorable discharge of his duties to his government. Its navigation and commerce are hardly exceeded by the oldest and most commercial nations; its maritime means and its maritime power may be seen by Austria herself, in all seas where she has ports, as well as they may be seen, also, in all other quarters of the globe. Life, liberty, property, and all personal rights, are amply secured to all citizens, and protected by just and stable laws; and credit, public and private, is as well established as in any government of Continental Europe; and the country, in all its interests and concerns, partakes most largely in all the improvements and progress which distinguish the age. Certainly, the United States may be pardoned, even by those who profess adherence to the principles of absolute government, if they entertain an ardent affection for those popular forms of political organization which have so rapidly advanced their own prosperity and happiness, and enabled them, in so short a period, to bring their country, and the hemisphere to which it belongs, to the notice and respectful regard, not to say the admiration, of the civilized world. . . .

Toward the conclusion of his note [of September 30, 1850] Mr. Hülsemann remarks, that "if the government of the United States were to think it proper to take an indirect part in the political movements of Europe, American policy would be exposed to acts of retaliation, and to certain inconveniences which would not fail to affect the commerce and industry of the two hemispheres." As to this possible fortune, this hypothetical retaliation, the government and people of the United States are quite willing to take their chances and abide their destiny. Taking neither a direct nor an indirect part in the domestic or intestine movements of Europe, they have no fear of events of the nature alluded to by Mr. Hülsemann. It would be idle now to discuss with Mr. Hülsemann those acts of retaliation which he imagines may possibly take place at some indefinite time hereafter. Those questions will be discussed when they arise; and Mr. Hülsemann and the Cabinet at Vienna may rest assured, that, in the mean time, while performing with strict and exact fidelity all their neutral duties, nothing will deter either the government or the people of the United States from exercising, at their own discretion, the right belonging to them as an independent nation, and of forming and expressing their own opinions, freely and at all times, upon the great political events which may transpire among the civilized nations of the earth. Their own institutions stand upon the broadest principles of civil liberty; and believing those principles and the fundamental laws in which they are embodied to be eminently favorable to the prosperity of states, to be, in fact, the only principles of government which meet the demands of the present enlightened age, the President has perceived, with great satisfaction, that, in the constitution recently introduced into the Austrian empire, many of these great principles are recognized and applied, and he cherishes a sincere wish that they may produce the same happy effects throughout his Austrian Majesty's extensive dominions that they have done in the United States.

Undoubtedly the most bumptious American diplomatic pronouncement in many a year was the so–called Ostend Manifesto, composed in 1854 by three American ministers to Europe—James Buchanan (Great Britain), John Y. Mason (France), and Pierre Soulé (Spain). It was dated from Aix–la–Chapelle, October 18, and sent in secret to Secretary of State William L. Marcy, who had asked for a "conference" of the three ministers. Rumor arose of the document's sensational contents. President Franklin Pierce then released the "manifesto" to a curious Congress and public. The pronouncement by the three ministers was not so much a declaration of the United States against Europe as an assertion that the United States ought to take Cuba. But the sense of manifest destiny was there for everyone to read. Source: William R. Manning (ed.), Diplomatic Correspondence of the United States: Inter-American Affairs, 1831–1860, VII, 580–581, 583–584.

. . . We have arrived at the conclusion and are thoroughly convinced that an immediate and earnest effort ought to be made by the Government of the United States to purchase Cuba from Spain, at any price for which it can be obtained, not exceeding the sum of one hundred and twenty millions of dollars.

The proposal should, in our opinion, be made in such a manner as to be presented, through the necessary diplomatic forms, to the supreme Constitutent Cortes about to assemble.

On this momentous question, in which the people both of Spain and the United States are so deeply interested, all our proceedings ought to be open, frank, and public. They should be of such a character as to challenge the approbation of the World.

We firmly believe that, in the progress of human events, the time has arrived when the vital interests of Spain are as seriously involved in the sale as those of the United States in the purchase of the Island, and that the transaction will prove equally honorable to both nations.

Under these circumstances, we cannot anticipate a failure, unless, possibly, through the malign influence of foreign Powers who possess no right whatever to interfere in the matter. . . .

It must be clear to every reflecting mind, that from the peculiarity of its geographical position and the considerations attendant on it, Cuba is as necessary to the North American Republic as any of its present members, and that it belongs naturally to that great family of States of which the Union is the Providential Nursery.

From its locality it commands the mouth of the Mississippi and the immense and annually increasing trade which must seek this avenue to the ocean.

On the numerous navigable streams, measuring an aggregate course of some thirty thousand miles, which disembogue themselves through this magnificent river into the Gulf of Mexico, the increase of the population, within the last ten years, amounts to more than that of the entire Union, at the time Louisiana was annexed to it.

The natural and main outlet to the products of this entire population, the highway of their direct intercourse with the Atlantic and the Pacific States can never be secure, but must ever be endangered whilst Cuba is a dependency of a distant Power, in whose possession it has proved to be a source of constant annoyance and embarassment to their interests.

Indeed, the Union can never enjoy repose, nor possess reliable security, as long as Cuba is not embraced within its boundaries.

Its immediate acquisition by our Government is of paramount importance, and we cannot doubt but that it is a consummation devoutly wished for by its inhabitants.

The intercourse which its proximity to our coasts begets and encourages between them and the citizens of the United States, has, in the progress of time, so united their interests and blended their fortunes, that they now look upon each other as if they were one people and had but one destiny. . . .

We know that the President is justly inflexible in his determination to execute the neutrality laws, but such the Cubans themselves rise in revolt against the oppressions which they suffer, no human power could prevent citizens of the United States and liberal minded men of other countries from rushing to their assistance.

Besides the present is an age of adventure in which restless and daring spirits abound in every portion of the world.

It is not improbable, therefore, that Cuba may be wrested from Spain by a successful revolution and, in that event, she will lose both the Island and the price which we are now willing to pay for it—a price far beyond what was ever paid by one people to another for any province.

It may also be remarked that the settlement of this vexed question, by the cession of Cuba to the United States, would forever prevent the dangerous complications between nations to which it may otherwise give birth.

It is certain that, should the Cubans themselves organize an insurrection against the Spanish Government, and should other independent nations come to the aid of Spain in the contest, no human power could, in our opinion, prevent the people and Government of the United States from taking part in such a civil war in support of their neighbors and friends.

But, if Spain, deaf to the voice of her own interest, and actuated, by stubborn pride and a false sense of honor, should refuse to sell Cuba to the United States, then the question will arise what ought to be the course of the American Government under such circumstances.

Self-preservation is the first law of nature, with States as well as with individuals. All nations have, at different periods, acted upon this maxim. Although it has been made the pretext for committing flagrant injustice, as in the partition of Poland and other similiar cases which history records, yet the principle itself, though often abused, has always been recognised.

The United States have never acquired a foot of territory, except by fair purchase, or, as in the case of Texas, upon the free and voluntary application of the people of that independent State, who desired to blend their destinies with our own.

Even our acquisitions from Mexico are no exception to this rule, because, although we might have claimed them by the right of conquest in a just war, yet we purchased them for what was then considered by both parties a full and ample equivalent.

Our past history forbids that we should acquire the Island of Cuba without the consent of Spain, unless justified by the great law of self-preservation. We must in any event preserve our own conscious rectitude and our own self-respect.

Whilst pursuing this course, we can afford to disregard the censures of the world to which we have been so often and so unjustly exposed.

After we shall have offered Spain a price for Cuba, far beyond its present value, and this shall have been refused, it will then be time to consider the question, does Cuba in the possession of Spain seriously endanger our internal peace and the existence of our cherished Union.

Should this question be answered in the affirmative, then, by every law human and Divine, we shall be justified in wresting it from Spain, if we possess the power; and this, upon the very same principle that would justify an individual in tearing down the burning house of his neighbor, if there were no other means of preventing the flames from destroying his own house.

Under such circumstances, we ought neither to count the cost, nor regard the odds which Spain might enlist against us. We forbear to enter into the question, whether the present condition of the Island would justify such a measure. We should however be recreant to our duty, be unworthy of our gallant forefathers and commit base treason against our posterity, should we permit Cuba to be Africanized and become a second St. Domingo with all its attendant horrors to the white race, and suffer the flames to extend to our own neighboring shores, seriously to endanger or actually to consume the fair fabric of our Union.

We fear that the course and current of events are rapidly tending towards such a catastrophe. We however hope for the best, though we ought certainly to be prepared for the worst. . . .

33. An isthmian canal

The American minister to New Granada (Colombia), Benjamin A. Bidlack concluded a treaty of commerce on December 12, 1846, which contained a prescient guarantee. Bidlack signed his treaty well before the

10. Filibuster territory.

idea of a canal gained popularity during the California gold rush. Source: Miller (ed.), *Treaties and Other International Acts . . . ,* V, 138–140. Many years later when the Panama Revolution of 1903 was imminent, the distinguished international lawyer John Bassett Moore advised President Theodore Roosevelt that the Bidlack Treaty gave the United States the right to construct an isthmian canal.

Article 35

The United States of America and the Republic of New Granada desiring to make as durable as possible, the relations which are to be established between the two parties by virtue of this treaty, have declared solemnly, and do agree to the following points.

1st For the better understanding of the preceding articles, it is, and has been stipulated, between the high contracting parties, that the citizens, vessels and merchandize of the United States shall enjoy in the ports of New Granada, including those of the part of the granadian territory generally denominated *Isthmus of Panamá* from its southernmost extremity until the boundary of Costa Rica, all the exemptions, privileges and immunities, concerning commerce and navigation, which are now, or may hereafter be enjoyed by Granadian citizens, their vessels and merchandize; and that this equality of favours shall be made to extend to the passengers, correspondence and merchandize of the United States in their transit across the said territory, from one sea to the other. The Government of New Granada guarantees to the Government of the United States, that the right of way or transit across the *Isthmus of Panamá*, upon any modes of communication that now exist, or that may be, hereafter, constructed, shall be open and free to the Government and citizens of the United States, and for the transportation of any articles of produce, manufactures or merchandize, of lawful commerce, belonging to the citizens of the United States; that no other tolls or charges shall be levied or collected upon the citizens of the United States, or their said merchandize thus passing over any road or canal that may be made by the Government of New Granada, or by the authority of the same, than is under like circumstances levied upon and collected from the granadian citizens: that any lawful produce, manufactures or merchandize belonging to citizens of the United States thus passing from one sea to the other, in either direction, for the purpose of exportation to any other foreign country, shall not be liable to any import duties whatever; or having paid such duties, they shall be entitled to drawback, upon their exportation: nor shall the citizens of the United States be liable to any duties, tolls, or charges of any kind to which native citizens are not subjected for thus passing the said Isthmus. And, in order to secure to themselves the tranquil and constant enjoyment of these advantages, and as an especial compensation for the said advantages and for the favours they have acquired by the 4ᵗʰ, 5ᵗʰ and 6ᵗʰ articles of this Treaty, the United States guarantee positively and efficaciously to New Granada, by the present stipulation, the perfect neutrality of the before mentioned Isthmus, with the view that the free transit from the one to the other sea, may not be interrupted or embarassed in any future time while this Treaty exists; and in consequence, the United States also guarantee, in the same manner, the rights of sovereignty and property which New Granada has and possesses over the said territory. . . .

The Bidlack Treaty of 1846 was an unexpected result from an unlikely envoy. President Polk in his diary (I, 220–221) relates a conversation with Senator Simon Cameron of Pennsylvania who claimed that Bidlack had been appointed to Colombia when, according to Cameron, the minister "would have been satisfied with an $800 clerkship. I told him it was true Mr. Buchanan had urged his appointment, and I had yielded to it." As for the treaty, the Polk cabinet was not sure what to do with it. According to Polk's diary for January 30, 1847 (II, 363):

> Mr. Buchanan brought before the Cabinet a Treaty recently signed by the U.S. chargé de affairs [sic] to New Granada and the Secretary of Foreign affairs of that Republic. As a commercial Treaty it was liberal & in all respects satisfactory, but in addition to its commercial provisions it contained an article giving the guaranty of the U.S. for the neutrality of the Isthmus of Panama and the sovereignty of New Granada over that territory. Serious doubts were entertained whether this stipulation was consistent with our long-settled policy to "cultivate friendship with all nations, entangling alliances with none." The subject was discussed at some length, and was finally postponed to enable the Secretary of State to give to it a further examination and Report upon the subject.

The Treaty at last was ratified in June 1848.

After discovery of gold in California, this diplomatic gingerliness disappeared. The United States government now espied a sinister British purpose in Central America. Partly by muddling, partly by design, the British were acquiring all the narrow places of world commerce: they had begun thoughtfully with the Channel, of course; and eventually obtained Gibraltar, Singapore, and the Falklands; later would come Suez and the Cape of Good Hope. The Americans by 1849–50 suspected the British of conniving for control of a future canal across Central America. British Honduras seemed an expansive colony, constantly trying to extend its boundaries. The British exercised a hazy protectorate over the Mosquito Islands, off the coast of what is now Nicaragua, and in 1841 took the port of San Juan, at the mouth of the river of that name, thus dominating one of the principal communication routes across Central America. By going up the San Juan River and crossing Lakes Nicaragua and Managua, a mid-nineteenth-century traveler could cross easily to the Pacific coast. Nicaragua seemed an ideal location for a canal, with a good deal of the construction work already done by nature. Its climate was salubrious, unlike fever-ridden Panama. For Americans a future canal across Nicaragua held the special attraction of being closer than Panama to the east and west coasts, shortening transit time by several days. Secretary of State John M. Clayton on April 19, 1850, signed a treaty with the British minister, Sir H. L. Bulwer, which however covered the entire area of Central America, not merely Nicaragua. Source: Miller (ed.), Treaties and Other International Acts . . . , V, 671–673, 675, 681–682.

Article I

The Governments of the United States and Great Britain hereby declare, that neither the one nor the other will ever obtain or maintain for itself any exclusive control over the said Ship Canal; agreeing, that neither will ever erect or maintain any fortifications commanding the same, or in the vicinity thereof, or occupy, or fortify, or colonize, or assume, or exercise any dominion over Nicaragua, Costa Rica, the Mosquito Coast, or any part of Central America; nor will either make use of any protection which either affords or may afford, or any alliance which either has or may have, to or with any State or People for the purpose of erecting or maintaining any such fortifications, or of occupying, fortifying, or colonizing Nicarague, Costa Rica, the Mosquito Coast or any part of Central America, or of assuming or exercising dominion over the same; nor will the United States or Great Britain take advantage of any intimacy, or use any alliance, connection or influence that either may possess with any State or Government through whose territory the said Canal may pass, for the purpose of acquiring or holding, directly or indirectly, for the citizens or subjects of the one, any rights or advantages in regard to commerce or navigation through the said Canal, which shall not be offered on the same terms to the citizens or subjects of the other. . . .

Article IV

The contracting parties will use whatever influence they respectively exercise, with any State, States or Governments possessing, or claiming to possess, any jurisdiction or right over the territory which the said Canal shall traverse, or which shall be near the waters applicable thereto; in order to induce such States, or Governments, to facilitate the construction of the said Canal by every means in their Power: and furthermore, the United States and Great Britain agree to use their good offices, wherever or however it may be most expedient, in order to procure the establishment of two free Ports,—one at each end of the said Canal.

Article V

The contracting parties further engage that, when the said Canal shall have been completed, they will protect it from interruption, seizure or unjust confiscation, and that they will guarantee the neutrality thereof, so that the said Canal may forever be open and free, and the capital invested therein, secure. Nevertheless, the Governments of the United States and Great Britain, in according their protection to the construction of the said Canal, and guaranteeing its neutrality and security when completed, always understand that, this protection and guarantee are granted conditionally, and may be withdrawn by both Governments, or either Government, if both Governments, or either Government, should deem that the persons, or company, undertaking or managing the same, adopt or establish such regulations concerning the traffic thereupon, as are contrary to the spirit and intention of this Convention,—either by making unfair discriminations in favor of the commerce of one of the contracting parties over the commerce of the other, or by imposing oppressive exactions or unreasonable tolls upon passengers, vessels, goods, wares, merchandize or other articles. Neither party, however, shall withdraw the aforesaid protection and guarantee, without first giving six months notice to the other. . . .

Article VIII

The Governments of the United States and Great Britain having not only desired in entering into this Convention, to accomplish a particular object, but, also, to establish a general principle, they hereby agree to extend their protection, by Treaty stipulations, to any other practicable communications, whether by Canal or railway, across the Isthmus which connects North and South America; and, especially, to the interoceanic communications,—should the same prove to be practicable, whether by Canal or rail-way,—which are now proposed to be established by the way of Tehuantepec, or Panama. In granting, however, their joint protection to any such Canals, or rail-ways, as are by this Article specified, it is always understood by the United States and Great Britain, that the parties constructing or owning the same, shall impose no other charges or conditions of traffic thereupon, than the aforesaid Governments shall approve of, as just and equitable; and, that the same Canals, or rail-ways, being open to the citizens and subjects of the United States and Great Britain on equal terms, shall, also, be open on like terms to the citizens and subjects of every other State which is willing to grant thereto, such protection as the United States and Great Britain engage to afford. . . .

Declaration

In proceeding to the exchange of the Ratifications of the Convention signed at Washington on the 19th of April 1850 between Her Britannick Majesty and the United States of America, relative to the establishment of a communication by ship canal between the Atlantic and Pacific Oceans, The undersigned, Her Britannick Majesty's Plenipotentiary, has received Her Majesty's instructions to declare, that Her Majesty does not understand the engagements of that Convention to apply to Her Majesty's settlement at Honduras or to its Dependencies.

Her Majesty's Ratification of the said convention is exchanged under the explicit Declaration abovementioned.

Memorandum

DEPARTMENT OF STATE
Washington July 5. 1850

The within declaration of Sir H. L. Bulwer was received by me on the 29th day of June 1850. In reply I wrote him my note of the 4th of July acknowledging that I understood British Honduras was not embraced in the treaty of the 19th day of April last, but at the same time carefully declining to affirm or deny the British title in their settlement or its alleged dependencies. After signing my note last night I delivered it to Sir Henry & we immediately proceeded without any further or other action to exchange the ratifications of said treaty. . . . The consent of the Senate to the declaration was not required and the treaty was ratified as it stood when it was made

N.B. The rights of no Central American state have been compromised by the treaty or by any part of the negotiations

34. China

Until Tyler's presidency, American merchants trading to the Chinese empire (and indeed the merchants of all nations) could use only the single port of Canton, under close supervision of designated Chinese intermediaries, the so-called hong merchants. In the Opium War of

1839–42 the British and French governments forced the Chinese to open additional ports. The American government thereupon sent out a plenipotentiary, Caleb Cushing, a distinguished citizen of Massachusetts, who carried as an introduction a presidential letter dated July 12, 1843. Source: ibid., IV, 660–661.

I, John Tyler, President of the United States of America, which States are—Maine, New-Hampshire, Massachusetts, Rhode-Island, Connecticut, Vermont, New-York, New-Jersey, Pennsylvania, Delaware, Maryland, Virginia, North Carolina, South Carolina, Georgia, Kentucky, Tennessee, Ohio, Louisiana, Indiana, Mississippi, Illinois, Alabama, Missouri, Arkansas and Michigan—send you this letter of Peace and Friendship, signed by my own hand.

I hope your health is good. China is a Great Empire, extending over a great part of the World. The Chinese are numerous. You have millions and millions of subjects. The Twenty-six United States are as large as China, though our People are not so numerous. The rising Sun looks upon the great mountains and great rivers of China. When he sets, he looks upon rivers and mountains equally large, in the United States. Our Territories extend from one great ocean to the other,—and on the West we are divided from your Dominions only by the Sea. Leaving the mouth of one of our great rivers, and going constantly towards the setting Sun, we sail to Japan, and to the Yellow Sea.

Now, my words are, that the Governments of two such Great Countries, should be at Peace. It is proper, and according to the will of Heaven, that they should respect each other, and act wisely. I, therefore, send to your Court, Caleb Cushing, one of the wise and learned men of this Country. On his first arrival in China, he will inquire for your health. He has then strict orders to go to Your Great City of Pekin, and there to deliver this letter. He will have with him, Secretaries and Interpreters.

The Chinese love to trade with our People, and to sell them Tea and Silk—for which our People pay Silver, and sometimes other articles. But if the Chinese and the Americans will trade, there should be rules, so that they shall not break your laws, nor our laws. Our Minister, Caleb Cushing, is authorised to make a Treaty, to regulate trade. Let it be just. Let there be no unfair advantage on either side. Let the People trade, not only at Canton, but also at Amoy, Ning-po, Shang-hai, Foo-Choo-foo, and all such other places as may offer profitable exchanges, both to China and the

United States; provided they do not break your laws, nor our laws. We shall not take the part of evil-doers. We shall not uphold them that break your laws. Therefore, we doubt not, that you will be pleased that our Messenger of Peace, with this letter in his hand, shall come to Pekin, and there deliver it,—and that Your great officers will, by Your order, make a Treaty with him to regulate affairs of Trade,—so that nothing may happen to disturb the Peace, between China and America. Let the Treaty be signed by Your own Imperial hand. It shall be signed by mine,—by the authority of our Great Council, the Senate.

And so may your health be good, and may Peace reign.

Written at Washington, this twelfth day of July, in the year of Our Lord, one thousand eight hundred and forty-three.

Your Good Friend!

JOHN TYLER

Cushing signed a treaty at the little town of Wanghia, near Macao, on July 3, 1844. Source: ibid., 559–561, 564–567, 569–570.

The United States of America, and The Ta Tsing Empire, Desiring to establish firm, lasting, and sincere friendship between the two Nations, have resolved to fix, in a manner clear and positive, by means of a treaty or general convention of peace, amity, and commerce, the rules which shall in future be mutually observed in the intercourse of their respective countries:—For which most desirable object, the President of the United States has conferred full powers on their Commissioner Caleb Cushing, Envoy Extraordinary and Minister Plenipotentiary of the United States to China; and the August Sovereign of the Ta Tsing Empire on his Minister and Commissioner Extraordinary Tsiyeng, of the Imperial House, a vice Guardian of the Heir Apparent, Governor-general of the Two Kwang, and Superintendant General of the trade and foreign intercourse of the five ports.

And the said Commissioners, after having exchanged their said full powers, and duly considered the premises, have agreed to the following articles.

Article I

There shall be a perfect, permanent, universal peace, and a sincere and cordial amity, between the United States of America on the one part, and the Ta Tsing Empire on the other part, and between their people respectively, without exception of persons or places.

Article II

Citizens of the United States resorting to China for the purposes of commerce will pay the duties of import and export prescribed in the Tariff, which is fixed by and made a part of this Treaty. They shall, in no case, be subject to other or higher duties than are or shall be required of the people of any other nation whatever. Fees and charges of every sort are wholly abolished, and officers of the revenue, who may be guilty of exaction, shall be punished according to the laws of China. If the Chinese Government desire to modify, in any respect, the said Tariff, such modifications shall be made only in consultation with consuls or other functionaries thereto duly authorized in behalf of the United States, and with consent thereof. And if additional advantages or privileges, of whatever description, be conceded hereafter by China to any other nation, the United States, and the citizens thereof, shall be entitled thereupon, to a complete, equal, and impartial participation in the same.

Article III

The citizens of the United States are permitted to frequent the five ports of Kwangchow, Amoy, Fuchow, Ningpo and Shanghai, and to reside with their families and trade there, and to proceed at pleasure with their vessels and merchandize to and from any foreign port and either of the said five ports, and from either of the said five ports to any other of them. But said vessels shall not unlawfully enter the other ports of China, nor carry on a clandestine and fraudulent trade along the coasts thereof. And any vessel belonging to a citizen of the United States, which violates this provision, shall, with her cargo, be subject to confiscation to the Chinese government.

Article IV

For the superintendence and regulation of of [sic] the concerns of the citizens of the United States doing business at the said five ports, the government of the United States may appoint Consuls, or other officers, at the same, who shall be duly recognized as such by the officers of the Chinese government, and shall hold official intercourse and correspondence with the latter, either personal or in writing, as occasions may require, on terms of equality and reciprocal respect. If disrespectfully treated or aggrieved in any way by the local authorities, said officers on the one hand shall have the right to make representation of the same to the superior officers of the Chinese Government, who will see that full inquiry and strict justice be had in the premises; and on the other hand, the said Consuls will carefully avoid all acts of unnecessary offence to, or collision with, the officers and people of China.

Article V

At each of the said five ports, citizens of the United States lawfully engaged in commerce, shall be permitted to import from their own or any other ports into China, and sell there, and purchase therein, and export to their own or any other ports, all manner of merchandize, of which the importation or exportation is not prohibited by this Treaty, paying the duties which are prescribed by the Tariff hereinbefore established, and no other charges whatsoever. . . .

Article XV

The former limitation of the trade of foreign nations to certain persons appointed at Canton by the government, and commonly called hong-merchants, having been abolished, citizens of the United States engaged in the purchase or sale of goods of import or export, are admitted to trade with any and all subjects of China without distinction; they shall not be subject to any new limitations, nor impeded in their business by monopolies or other injurious restrictions. . . .

Article XVII

Citizens of the United States residing or sojourning at any of the ports open to foreign commerce, shall enjoy all proper accommodation in obtaining houses and places of business, or in hiring sites from the inhabitants on which to construct houses and places of business, and also hospitals, churches and cemeteries. The local authorities of the two Governments shall select in concert the sites for the foregoing objects, having due regard to the feelings of the people in the location thereof: and the parties interested will fix the rent by mutual agreement, the proprietors on the one hand not demanding any exorbitant price, nor the merchants on the other unreasonably insisting on particular spots, but each conducting with justice and moderation. And any desecration of said cemeteries by subjects of China shall be severely punished according to law.

At the places of anchorage of the vessels of the United States, the citizens of the United States, merchants, seamen, or others sojourning there, may pass and repass in the immediate neighborhood; but they shall not at their pleasure make excursions into the country among the villages at large, nor shall they repair to public marts for the purpose of disposing of goods unlawfully and in fraud of the revenue.

And, in order to the preservation of the public peace, the local officers of government at each of the five ports, shall, in concert with the Consuls, define the limits beyond which it shall not be lawful for citizens of the United States to go. . . .

Article XXI

Subjects of China who may be guilty of any criminal act towards citizens of the United States, shall be arrested and punished by the Chinese authorities according to the laws of China: and citizens of the United States, who may commit any crime in China, shall be subject to be tried and punished only by the Consul, or other public functionary of the United States, thereto authorized according to the laws of the United States. And in order to the prevention of all controversy and disaffection, justice shall be equitably and impartially administered on both sides. . . .

Article XXV

All questions in regard to rights, whether of property or person, arising between citizens of the United States in China shall be subject to the jurisdiction, and regulated by the authorities of their own Government. And all controversies occurring in China between citizens of the United States and the subjects of any other government, shall be regulated by the treaties existing between the United States and such governments respectively, without interference on the part of China.

Article XXVI

Merchant vessels of the United States lying in the waters of the five ports of China open to foreign commerce, will be under the jurisdiction of the officers of their own government, who, with the masters and owners thereof, will manage the same without control on the part of China. . . .

Article XXX

The superior authorities of the United States and of China, in corresponding together, shall do so in terms of equality, and in the form of mutual communication (*cháu hwui*). The Consuls, and the local officers civil and military, in corresponding together, shall likewise employ the style and form of mutual communication (*cháu hwui*). When inferior officers of the one government address superior officers of the other, they shall do so in the style and form of memorial (*shin chin*). Private individuals, in addressing superior officers, shall employ the style of petition (*pin ching*). In no case shall any terms or style be suffered which shall be offensive or disrespectful to either party. And it is agreed that no presents, under any pretext or form whatever, shall ever be demanded of the United States by China, or of China by the United States. . . .

Article XXXIII

Citizens of the United States, who shall attempt to trade clandestinely with such of the ports of China as are not open to foreign commerce, or who shall trade in opium or any other contraband article of merchandize, shall be subject to be dealt with by the Chinese Government, without being entitled to any countenance or protection from that of the United States; and the United States will take measures to prevent their flag from being abused by the subjects of other nations, as a cover for the violation of the laws of the Empire. . . .

The emperor of China on December 16, 1844, replied to President Tyler's letter with a scroll of heavy yellow silk and brocade, backed with linen, mounted on two wooden rods, and contained in a case of yellow silk. The contemporaneous translation by Cushing's assistant, the missionary Peter Parker, read as follows (the words underscored once being here printed in italics, and those underscored twice, in capitals and small capitals). Source: ibid., 661–662. The Department of State's treaty expert, David Hunter Miller, has published from the department records the following gloss on the emperor's letter, written by Raymond Parker Tenney: "The characters for 'President' are used without honorifics, while those for 'Emperor' are preceded by the character 'Great.' The importance of the Emperor is emphasized by the position of the three characters for 'The Great Emperor (His Imperial Highness)' at the beginning of the letter. The opening sentence is in colloquial Chinese, as if addressed to an illiterate person. The second sentence requires no comment."

The GREAT EMPEROR presents his regards to the PRESIDENT and trusts HE is well.

I the EMPEROR having looked up and received the manifest Will of HEAVEN, hold the reins of Government over, and sooth and tranquilize, the Central Flowery Kingdom, regarding all within & beyond the border seas as one and the same Family.

Early in the Spring the Ambassador of Your Honorable Nation, Caleb Cushing, having received Your Letter, arrived from afar at my Province of Yuè. He having passed over the vast oceans with unspeakable toil and fatigue, I the EMPEROR not bearing to cause him further inconvenience of travelling by land and water, to dispense with his coming to Peking to be presented at Court, specially appointed Ke Ying, of the IMPERIAL HOUSE, Minister and Commissioner Extraordinary to repair thither and to treat Him with courteous attentions.

Moreover, they having negotiated and settled all things proper, the said Minister took the Letter and presented it for MY INSPECTION, and YOUR sincerity and friendship being in the highest degree real, & the thoughts and sentiments being with the utmost sincerity & truth kind, at the time of opening & perusing it, my pleasure and delight were exceedingly profound.

All, and every thing, they had settled regarding the Regulations of Commerce, I the EMPEROR further examined with utmost scrutiny, and found they are all perspicuous, and entirely and perfectly judicious, and forever worthy of adherence.

To Kwang Chow, Heu Mūn, Fūh Chow, Ning-Po, and Shang Hae, it is alike permitted the Citizens of the United States to proceed, and according to the articles of Treaty, at their convenience to carry on Commerce.

Now bound by perpetual Amity and Concord advantage will accrue to the Citizens of both Nations, which I trust must certainly cause the PRESIDENT also to be extremely well satisfied and delighted.

After another Anglo-French military action, four treaties were signed at Tientsin in 1858, by representatives of Britain, France, Russia, and the United States. The American treaty was concluded on June 18. Source: ibid., VII, 793–796, 799, 803–804.

The United States of America and the Ta Tsing Empire, desiring to maintain firm, lasting, and sincere friendship, have resolved to renew, in a manner clear and positive, by means of a Treaty or general convention of peace, amity and commerce, the rules which shall in future be mutually observed in the intercourse of their respective countries; for which most desirable object, the President of the United States and the August Sovereign of the Ta Tsing Empire, have named for their Plenipotentiaries to wit: The President of the United States of America, William B. Reed, Envoy Extraordinary and Minister Plenipotentiary to China and His Majesty the Emperor of China, Kweiliang, a member of the Privy Council and Superintendant of the Board of Punishments; and Hwashana, President of the Board of Civil Office and Major General of the Bordered Blue Banner Division of the Chinese Bannermen, both of them being Imperial Commissioners and Plenipotentiaries: And the said Ministers, in virtue of the respective full powers they have received from their Governments, have agreed upon the following articles. . . .

Article IV

In order further to perpetuate friendship, the Minister or Commissioner or the highest diplomatic representative of the United States of America in China, shall at all times have the right to correspond on terms of perfect equality and confidence with the Officers of the Privy Council at the capital, or with the Governors General of the Two Kwangs, the Provinces of Fuhkien and Chehkiang or of the Two Kiangs, and whenever he desires to have such correspondence with the Privy Council at the Capital, he shall have the right to send it through either of the said Governors General or by the General Post, and all such communications shall be sent under seal which shall be most carefully respected. The Privy Council and Governors General, as the case may be, shall in all cases consider and acknowledge such communications promptly and respectfully.

Article V

The Minister of the United States of America in China, whenever he has business, shall have the right to visit and sojourn at the Capital of His Majesty the Emperor of China, and there confer with a member of the Privy Council, or any other high officer of equal rank deputed for that purpose, on matters of common interest and advantage. His visits shall not exceed one in each year, and he shall complete his business without unnecessary delay. He shall be allowed to go by land or come to the mouth of the Peiho, into which he shall not bring ships of war and he shall inform the authorities at that place in order that boats may be provided for him to go on his journey. He is not to take advantage of this stipulation to request visits to the capital on trivial occasions. Whenever he means to proceed to the capital he shall communicate in writing his intention to the Board of Rites at the capital, and thereupon the said Board shall give the necessary directions to facilitate his journey and give him necessary protection and respect on his way. On his arrival at the capital, he shall be furnished with a suitable residence prepared for him and he shall defray his own expenses and his entire suite shall not exceed twenty persons, exclusive of his Chiense attendants, none of whom shall be engaged in trade.

Article VI

If at any time His Majesty the Emperor of China shall by Treaty voluntarily made, or for any other reason, permit the Representative of any friendly nation to reside at his Capital for a long or short time, then without any further consultation or express permission, the Representative of the United States in China shall have the same privilege.

Article VII

The superior authorities of the United States and of China in corresponding together, shall do so on terms of equality, and in form of mutual communication (chau hwui). The consuls and the local officers, civil and military, in corresponding together, shall likewise enmploy the style and form of mutual communication (chau-hwui). When inferior officers of the one government address superior officers of the other, they shall do so in the style and form of memorial (shin chin). Private individuals in addressing superior officers, shall employ the style of petition (pin ching). In no case shall any terms or style be used or suffered which shall be offensive or disrespectful to either party. And it is agreed that no presents, under any pretext or form whatever shall ever be demanded of the United States by China, or of China by the United States.

Article VIII

In all future personal intercourse between the Representative of the United States of America and the Governors General or Governors the interviews shall be had at the official residence of the said officers or at their temporary residence or at the residence of the Representative of the United States of America, whichever may be agreed upon between them nor shall they make any pretext for declining these interviews. Current matters shall be discussed by correspondence so as not to give the trouble of a personal meeting. . . .

Article XV

At each of the ports open to Commerce, citizens of the United States shall be permitted to import from abroad and sell, purchase, and export, all merchandize of which the importation or exportation is not prohibited by the laws of the Empire. The Tariff of duties to be paid by citizens of the United States on the export and import of goods from and into China shall be the same as was agreed upon at the Treaty of Wanghia, except so far as it may be modified by treaties with other nations; it being expressly agreed that citizens of the United States shall never pay higher duties than those paid by the most favoured nation. . . .

Article XXVI

Relations of peace and amity between the United States and China being established by this treaty, and the vessels of the United States being admitted to trade, freely to and from the ports of China open to foreign commerce, it is further agreed, that in case at any time hereafter China should be at war with any foreign nation whatever, and should for that cause exclude such nation from entering her ports, still the vessels of the United States shall not the less continue to pursue their commerce in freedom and security, and to transport goods to and from the ports of the belligerent powers, full respect being paid to the neutrality of the flag of the United States: provided that the said flag shall not protect vessels engaged in the transportation of officers or soldiers in the enemy's service, nor shall said flag be fraudulently used to enable the enemy's ships with their cargoes to enter the ports of China: but all such vessels so offending shall be subject to forfeiture and confiscation to the Chinese Government. . . .

Article XXIX

The principles of the Christian religion as professed by the Protestant and Roman Catholic churches, are recognised as teaching men to do good, and to do to others as they would have others do to them. Hereafter, those who quietly profess and teach these doctrines shall not be harassed or persecuted on account of their faith. Any person, whether citizen of the United States or Chinese convert, who according to these tenets peaceably teach and practise the principles of Christianity, shall in no case be interfered with or molested.

Article XXX

The contracting parties hereby agree that should at any time the Ta Tsing Empire, grant to any nation or the merchants or citizens of any nation, any right, privilege or favour, connected either with navigation, commerce, political or other intercourse which is not conferred by this treaty, such right, privilege and favour shall at once freely enure to the benefit of the United States, its public officers, merchants and citizens. . . .

35. Japan

Commodore Matthew C. Perry was one of three brothers who were naval officers. Matthew Calbraith spent some time on the African coast in the mid-1840's in command of a squadron stationed there to prevent American-flag ships from engaging in the slave trade (in accord with

Article 8 of the *Webster-Ashburton Treaty; see Miller (ed.), Treaties and Other International Acts . . . , IV, 369)*. He there gained experience in over-awing native tribes who acted in unfriendly fashion toward American missionaries and merchants, and his was a natural appointment to command the squadron designed to open Japan. He set out his Japanese experiences in a letter to the secretary of the navy, August 3, 1853. Source: 33d Cong., 2d Sess., Senate Document No. 34, pp. 45, 47, 49–51, 53–54.

The squadron, consisting of the steamers Susquehanna and Mississippi, and the sloops of war Plymouth and Saratoga, commanded respectively by Commanders Buchanan, Lee, Kelly, and Walker, left Napa Keang, island of Lew-Chew [the Ryukyus], on Saturday the 2d, and anchored off the city of Uraga, bay of Yedo, Japan, on the afternoon of Friday the 8th of July.

I had, before reaching the coast, fully considered and determined upon the course I should pertinaciously pursue in conducting the delicate and responsible duties which had been entrusted to my charge.

It was to adopt an entirely contrary plan of proceedings from that of all others who had hitherto visited Japan on the same errand —to demand as a right, and not to solicit as a favor, those acts of courtesy which are due from one civilized nation to another; to allow of none of those petty annoyances which have been unsparingly visited upon those who had preceded me, and to disregard the acts as well as the threats of the authorities, if they in the least conflicted with my own sense of what was due to the dignity of the American flag.

The question of landing by force was left to be decided by the development of succeeding events.

In pursuance of these intentions. I caused the crews to be thoroughly drilled, and the ships kept in perfect readiness as in time of active war, and being thus prepared for any contingency, I determined to practice upon them a little of their own diplomacy, by forbidding the admission of a single individual on board any of the ships, excepting those officers who might have business with me, and the visits of these were to be confined to the flag ship on board of which they were not allowed to enter until they had declared their rank and the business upon which they came.

I had also made up my mind to confer personally with no one but a functionary of the highest rank in the empire, and consequently refused to see the lieutenant governor and governor of Uraga, referring them to Commanders Buchanan and Adams, and Lieutenant Contee, who had orders from me to receive them, and to reply under my instructions to their inquiries and verbal communications.

I was well aware that the more exclusive I should make myself, and the more exacting I might be, the more respect these people of forms and ceremonies would be disposed to award me; hence my object, and the sequel will show the correctness of these conclusions. . . .

On the following morning, the 9th, the governor of Uraga, "Kayama Yezaïmon," came on board . . .

The governor, after a long discussion, in which he more than once declared that the Japanese laws made it impossible that the letter should be received at Uraga, that the squadron must go to Nagasaki, and even if the letter of the President were to be received at this place, a reply would be sent to Nagasaki. In answer to this he was told that I would never consent to such arrangement, and would persist in delivering it where I then was; that if the Japanese government did not appoint a suitable person to receive the documents addressed to the emperor, I would go on shore with a sufficient force and deliver them, whatever the consequences might be.

On this being communicated to him, he said he would return to the city and send a communication to Yedo asking for further instructions; that it would require four days to obtain a reply; upon which he was told that I would wait until Tuesday, the 12th, three days, when I should certainly expect a definite answer. . . .

Wednesday, July 13.—The governor came on board in the afternoon of this day, apologizing for not being earlier, by saying that the high officer from Yedo had only just arrived; he brought with him the original order of the emperor addressed to the functionary who had to receive me, as also a copy and translation of the same in Dutch, and a certificate of his own verifying the authenticity of the appointment; he also said that the person appointed by the emperor had no power to enter into discussion with me, but was empowered merely to receive the papers and carry them to his sovereign. . . .

Here follow translations of the papers referred to . . .

The governor remarked that he had made inquiry as to the practibility of changing the place of meeting, and said that a suitable building had already been constructed, and it would be inconvenient to make a change. This reply I had expected and was prepared for, and not knowing whether any treachery was intended, had ordered the surveying party to examine the little bay at the head of which the building had been erected for my reception. They promptly performed the service, and reported that the ships could be brought within gun shot of the position where they observed great numbers of people employed in the completion of the building, transporting furniture, &c. Accordingly I directed the squadron to be removed in the morning to an anchorage in line covering the whole bay, being determined to prepare against the well-known duplicity of the people with whom I had to deal, the object of selecting the place of meeting not being clearly explained to my mind.

Thursday, July 14th.—This being the day appointed for my reception on shore, and every preparation having been made for landing a formidable escort, composed of officers, seamen, and marines, from the respective ships, about 400 in number, all well armed and equipped, and being ready for disembarcation, the two steamers moved to a position commanding the proposed landing-place, (the sloops-of-war not being able to move for want of wind,) and shortly after the detachments forming the escort were in the boats, and on their way to the shore, where they landed and formed, and were immediately followed by me.

The whole shore of the bay, extending more than a mile, was crowded with Japanese troops—from five to seven thousand—drawn up under arms. These troops were composed of cavalry, artillery, infantry, and archers; some of the infantry with flint muskets, others with match-locks.

On landing, I proceeded at once to the building erected for the purpose, and was there received by the prince of Idzu, first counsellor of the emperor, and his coadjutor, the prince of Iwami. To the former of these I presented the President's letter, my letter of credence, and three communications from myself, together with transcripts of the same in the English, Dutch, and Chinese languages, for which the prince of Idzu gave me a receipt.

The princes were attended by the governor of Uraga, the chief interpreter, and a secretary.

As it was understood that there was to be no discussion at this meeting, I remained but a short time, taking my departure and embarking with the same ceremony with which I had landed. . . .

Having completed the survey of the west side of this magnificent bay from Uraga to a point about 14 miles below Yedo, and sounded with the Mississippi and boats six miles nearer to that city, and acquiring a sufficient knowledge of the bay to conduct the Vermont to the American anchorage, and higher if necessary, I thought it advisable to return to Lew-Chew, intending to dispatch the Saratoga, after we cleared the coast of Japan, to Shanghai, and employ the other vessels on the way in the further examination of the island Oho-sima, but, unfortunately, before reaching that island we encountered a severe gale, which in part defeated the object.

It has already been observed that, in adherence to my previous determination, I had no personal communication with the governor of Uraga, the officer employed by the Japanese government to visit the ship and conduct the preliminary arrangements for my reception; the only persons with whom I had an an interview were the princes of Idzu and Iwami; consequently the conferences with the governor were conducted on my part by Commanders Buchanan and Adams, and Lieutenant Contee, assisted by the Chinese interpreter, Mr. S. Wells Williams, and by the Dutch interpreter, Mr. Portman. Although these officers acted under my immediate instructions and were in constant communication with me, much credit is due to them for managing the discussion with great judgment and skill.

I take pleasure, also, in commending the coolness and industry with which the surveying officers under Lieutenant Silas Bent, conducted their laborious duties.

It is proper that I should add, in conclusion, that the governor, in the several conferences on shipboard, evinced great anxiety to learn how long I intended to remain upon the coast, remarking repeatedly that it was the custom of the Japanese government to be very slow in deciding upon matters having reference to foreign countries. Upon these representations, and knowing that the propositions contained in the President's letter were of such importance as to require time for deliberation, overturning as they would, if acceded to, many of the fundamental laws of the empire, I deemed it advisable not to wait for a reply, and for the following reasons:

I had not provisions or water sufficient to allow of my remaining on the coast more than a month longer. I well knew that they could easily and very reasonably defer for a long time any satis-factory reply, for reason of the alleged necessity of calling together and consulting the princes of the empire, as also to consult the dairi or ecclesiastical emperor. Thus I should be put off from day to day, and ultimately be obliged to sail without any satisfaction whatever. This would be construed into a triumph by them and cause a serious injury to the success of my mission.

Taking into view, also, the present disturbed state of China, and the need of one or more ships of the squadron in that quarter, and considering that not a single vessel which had been promised by the department should immediately follow me had yet joined my force, and being without the presents sent from the United States, and those expected in the Vermont, I was glad to have a good excuse for consenting to wait until the ensuing spring for the final answer of the Japanese government.

In the spring I shall have concentrated my whole force, and be prepared with store and coal vessels, and all other conveniences for remaining, if it be necessary, an indefinite time, to secure such con-cessions as I believe they will be constrained to make.

The exhibition of so large a force, and a continuation of the policy so far successfully pursued, and having given them full time for the consideration of the propositions of the President, I shall be prepared to act very decidedly . . .

Perry signed his treaty on March 31, 1854. Source: Miller (ed.), Treaties and Other International Acts . . . , VI, 440–441.

. . . The United States of America, and the Empire of Japan, desiring to establish firm, lasting and sincere friendship between the two Nations, have resolved to fix in a manner clear and positive, by means of a Treaty or general convention of peace and Amity, the rules which shall in future be mutually observed in the intercourse of their respective Countries; for which most desirable object, the President of the United States has conferred full powers on his Commissioner, Matthew Calbraith Perry, Special Ambassador of the United States to Japan: And the August Sovereign of Japan, has given similar full powers to his Commissioners, Hayashi, Dai-gaku no-kami; Ido, Prince of Tsus-Sima; Izawa, Prince of Mima-saki; and Udono, Member of the Board of Revenue. And the said Commissioners after having exchanged their said full powers, and duly considered the premises, have agreed to the following Articles.

Article I

There shall be a perfect, permanent, and universal peace, and a sincere and cordial amity between the United States of America, on the one part, and the Empire of Japan on the other part; and between their people respectively, without exception of persons or places.

Article II

The Port of Simoda in the principality of Idzu, and the Port of Hakodade, in the principality of Matsmai, are granted by the Japanese as ports for the reception of American Ships, where they can be supplied with Wood, Water, provisions, and Coal, and other articles their necessities may require as far as the Japanese have them. . . .

Article III

Whenever Ships of the United States are thrown or wrecked on the Coast of Japan, the Japanese vessels will assist them, and carry their crews to Simoda, or Hakodade, and hand them over to their Countrymen appointed to receive them; whatever articles the Shipwrecked men may have preserved shall likewise be restored, and the expenses incurred in the rescue and support of Americans and Japanese who may thus be thrown upon the shores of either nation are not to be refunded. . . .

Article VII

It is agreed that Ships of the United States resorting to the ports open to them, shall be permitted to exchange gold and Silver Coin and articles of goods for other articles of goods, under such regulations as shall be temporarily established by the Japanese Government for that purpose. It is stipulated however that the Ships of the United States shall be permitted to carry away whatever articles they are unwilling to exchange.

Article VIII

Wood, water, provisions, Coal and goods required shall only be procured through the agency of Japanese Officers appointed for that purpose, and in no other manner.

Article IX

It is agreed, that if at any future day the government of Japan shall grant to any other Nation or Nations privileges and advantages which are not herein granted to the United States, and the Citizens thereof, that these same privileges and advantages shall be granted likewise to the United States, and to the Citizens thereof, without any consultation or delay. . . .

President Franklin Pierce's secretary of state, William L. Marcy, was a personal friend of a New York merchant with experience in the China trade, Townsend Harris, and when the time arrived to improve Perry's "shipwreck convention" Marcy called upon Harris, whom he appointed consul general to Japan in 1855. Harris concluded a treaty during the subsequent presidency of James Buchanan, on July 29, 1858. Source: ibid., VII, 947–948, 950–953, 955, 957–958.

The President of the United States of America, and His Majesty the Ty-coon of Japan, desiring to establish on firm and lasting foundations, the relations of peace and friendship now happily existing between the two Countries, and to secure the best interests of Their respective Citizens and Subjects, by encouraging, facilitating and regulating their industry and trade, have resolved to conclude a Treaty of amity and commerce, for this purpose . . .

Article Third

In addition to the Ports of Simoda and Hakodade, the following Ports and Towns, shall be opened on the dates respectively appended to them, that is to say:

Kanagawa on the (4th of July 1859) fourth day of July, one thousand, eight hundred and fifty nine.

Nagasaki, on the (4th of July 1859) fourth day of July, one thousand eight hundred and fifty nine.

Nee-e-gata, on the (1st of January 1860) first day of January, one thousand, eight hundred and sixty.

Hiogo; on the (1st of January 1863) first day of January, one thousand, eight hundred and sixty three.

If Nee-e-gata is found to be unsuitable as a Harbour, another Port, on the West coast of Nipon, shall be selected by the two Governments, in lieu thereof.

Six Months after the opening of Kanagawa, the Port of Simoda shall be closed, as a place of residence and trade, for American Citizens.

In all the foregoing Ports and Towns, American Citizens may permanently reside, they shall have the right to lease ground, and purchase the buildings thereon, and may erect dwelling and warehouses. But no fortification or place of military strength, shall be erected under pretence of building dwelling or warehouses, and to see that this Article is observed, the Japanese Authorities shall have the right, to inspect from time to time any buildings, which are being erected, altered or repaired.

The place, which the Americans shall occupy for their buildings, and the Harbour Regulations, shall be arranged by the American Consul, and the Authorities of each place, and if they cannot agree, the matter shall be referred to, and settled by the American Diplomatic Agent and the Japanese Government.

No wall, fence, or gate shall be erected by the Japanese, around the place of residence of the Americans, or anything done, which may prevent a free egress and ingress to the same.

From the (1st of January 1862) first day of January, one thousand, eight hundred and Sixty two, Americans shall be allowed, to reside in the City of Yedo, and from the (1 of January 1863) first day of January one thousand, eight hundred and sixty three, in the City of Osaca, for the purposes of trade only. In each of these two Cities, a suitable place, within which they may hire houses, and the distance they may go, shall be arranged by the American Diplomatic Agent, and the Government of Japan.

Americans may freely buy from Japanese and sell to them, any articles, that either may have for sale, without the intervention of any Japanese Officers, in such purchase or sale or in making or receiving payment for the same, and all classes of Japanese, may purchase, sell, keep or use, any Articles sold to them, by the Americans.

The Japanese Government will cause this clause, to be made public, in every part of the Empire, as soon as the Ratifications of this Treaty, shall be exchanged.

Munitions of war shall only be sold to the Japanese Government and Foreigners.

No rice or wheat shall be exported from Japan, as cargo, but all

Americans resident in Japan, and ships for their crews and passengers, shall be furnished with sufficient supplies of the same.

The Japanese Government will sell from time to time, at public auction, any surplus quantity of copper, that may be produced.

Americans, residing in Japan, shall have the right to employ Japanese as servants, or in any other capacity. . . .

Article Sixth

Americans, committing offences against Japanese, shall be tried in American Consular Courts, and when guilty, shall be punished according to American Law.

Japanese, committing offences against Americans, shall be tried by the Japanese Authorities, and punished according to Japanese Law.

The Consular Courts shall be open to Japanese Creditors, to enable them, to recover their just claims, against American Citizens, and the Japanese Courts shall in like manner be open to American Citizens, for the recovery of their just claims, against Japanese. . . .

Article Eighth

Americans in Japan, shall be allowed the free exercise of their Religion, and for this purpose shall have the right to erect suitable places of worship. No injury shall be done to such buildings, nor any insult be offered to the religious worship of the Americans.

American Citizens shall not injure, any Japanese temple or mia, or offer any insult or injury, to Japanese religious ceremonies, or to the objects of their worship.

The Americans and Japanese shall not do anything, that may be calculated to excite religious animosity. The Government of Japan has already abolished, the practice of trampling on religious emblems. . . .

XIII

Civil War

During the war between North and South of 1861 to 1865—the greatest domestic catastrophe in American history, the largest and most prolonged war in the western world between the years 1815 and 1914 (which era one might define as the historical nineteenth century)—the United States government under President Abraham Lincoln worried incessantly over the attitude of the government of Great Britain. Many members of the leading classes in England admired what they considered the aristocratic traditions of the South as opposed to the grasping traditions of northern Yankee merchants and the bragging traditions of western men. Sentiment disposed the British government to favor the South. In addition there was a problem of economics: manufacture of cotton cloth was the leading British industry, one fifth of the population directly depending on it; if the southern boast should prove true, and cotton indeed be king, the necessity to ensure a supply of raw cotton would force the British to break the North's blockade of southern ports. Then there were the inadequate regulations of British neutrality, a special source of worry because of the prospect, the horrible prospect, that the Confederacy might be able to build a navy in British shipyards which would be so technologically advanced that it might sweep the large but architecturally obsolete Union navy from the seas.

36. Seward's April Fool's Day proposition

Secretary of State William H. Seward on April Fool's Day, 1861, offered the President some advice. Source: Roy P. Basler (ed.), The Collected Works of Abraham Lincoln (8 vols. plus index, New Brunswick, N.J., 1953–55), IV, 317–318.

1st. We are at the end of a month's administration and yet without a policy either domestic or foreign.

2d This, however, is not culpable, and it has been unavoidable. The presence of the Senate, with the need to meet applications for patronage have prevented attention to other and more grave matters.

3d. But further delay to adopt and prosecute our policies for both domestic and foreign affairs would not only bring scandal on the Administration, but danger upon the country.

4th. To do this we must dismiss the applicants for office. But how? I suggest that we make the local appointments forthwith, leaving foreign or general ones for ulterior and occasional action.

5th. The policy—at home. I am aware that my views are singular, and perhaps not sufficiently explained. My system is built upon this *idea* as a ruling one, namely that we must

Change the question before the Public from one upon Slavery, or about Slavery

for a question upon *Union* or *Disunion*.

In other words, from what would be regarded as a Party question to one of *Patriotism* or *Union*

The occupation or evacuation of Fort Sumter, although not in fact a slavery, or a party question is so *regarded*. Witness, the temper manifested by the Republicans in the Free States, and even by Union men in the South.

I would therefore terminate it as a safe means for changing the issue. I deem it fortunate that the last Administration created the necessity.

For the rest. I would simultaneously defend and reinforce all the Forts in the Gulf, and have the Navy recalled from foreign stations to be prepared for a blockade. Put the Island of Key West under Martial Law

This will raise distinctly the question of *Union* or *Disunion*. I would maintain every fort and possession in the South.

For *Foreign Nations*

I would demand explanations from *Spain* and France, categorically, at once.

I would seek explanations from Great Britain and Russia, and send agents into *Canada*, *Mexico* and *Central America*, to rouse a vigorous continental *spirit of independence* on this continent against European intervention.

And if satisfactory explanations are not received from Spain and France,

Would convene Congress and declare war against them

But whatever policy we adopt, there must be an energetic prosecution of it.

For this purpose it must be somebody's business to pursue and direct it incessantly.

Either the President must do it himself, and be all the while active in it; or

Devolve it on some member of his Cabinet. Once adopted, debates on it must end, and all agree and abide.

It is not in my especial province.

But I neither seek to evade nor assume responsibility.

It is not at all certain that Lincoln sent Seward the following answer, also dated April 1, but the President certainly composed it. Source: ibid., 316–317.

Since parting with you I have been considering your paper dated this day, and entitled "Some thoughts for the President's consideration." The first proposition in it is, "1st. We are at the end of a month's administration, and yet without a policy, either domestic or foreign."

At the *beginning* of that month, in the inaugeral, I said "The power confided to me will be used to hold, occupy and possess the property and places belonging to the government, and to collect the duties, and imposts." This had your distinct approval at the time; and, taken in connection with the order I immediately gave General Scott, directing him to employ every means in his power to strengthen and hold the forts, comprises the exact domestic policy you now urge, with the single exception, that it does not propose to abandon Fort Sumpter.

Again, I do not perceive how the re-inforcement of Fort Sumpter would be done on a slavery, or party issue, while that of Fort Pickens would be on a more national, and patriotic one.

The news received yesterday in regard to St. Domingo, certainly brings a new item within the range of our foreign policy; but up to that time we have been preparing circulars, and instructions to ministers, and the like, all in perfect harmony, without even a suggestion that we had no foreign policy.

Upon your closing propositions, that "whatever policy we adopt, there must be an energetic prossecution of it."

"For this purpose it must be somebody's business to pursue and direct it incessantly"

"Either the President must do it himself, and be all the while active in it, or"

"Devolve it on some member of his cabinet"

"Once adopted, debates on it must end, and all agree and abide"
I remark that if this must be done, I must do it. When a general
line of policy is adopted, I apprehend there is no danger of its being changed without good reason, or continuing to be a subject of
unnecessary debate; still, upon points arising in its progress, I wish,
and suppose I am entitled to have the advice of all the cabinet.

37. The Trent affair

The first major crisis with Britain was not of Seward's devising, but arose
out of the capture—on November 8, 1861—from the British mail steamer
Trent in the Bahama Channel of two Confederate commissioners bound
for Europe, John Slidell and James M. Mason (not to be confused with
the John Y. Mason of Ostend Manifesto fame). The captor of the
Confederates, Captain Charles Wilkes of U.S.S. San Jacinto, reasoned
from some law books in his cabin that Mason and Slidell were embodied dispatches from a belligerent power. He failed to notice the
similarity of his action to British impressment of American sailors before
the War of 1812. Because the transatlantic cable which Cyrus Field
had laid in 1858 had gone dead soon thereafter, it took some time for
news of Wilkes's exploit to reach England. There followed an explosion
of sentiment, and a serious threat of war. Palmerston, the old foe of the
Ashburton capitulation (he had so described the Webster–Ashburton
Treaty), was prime minister. Lincoln came to see that Wilkes's victory,
vastly admired in the United States, had given him two "white ele-
phants." After allowing the storm of domestic enthusiasm to blow itself
out, the President and Seward released the men, who went off to Europe.
In England, Mason eventually proved unable to advance the Confederacy's cause, and one of his personal habits may well have harmed it. So
wrote the secretary of the American legation, an individual named Benjamin Moran whose piquant diary was published almost a century after
the events it described. Source: Sarah Agnes Wallace and Frances Elma
Gillespie (eds.), The Journal of Benjamin Moran: 1856–1865 (by permission of the University of Chicago Press: 2 vols., Chicago, 1948–49),
II, 913–917, 921–930, 939–940, 1040–1041, 1212.

Wed. 27 Nov. '61. . . . At about ½ past 12 this morning we received
a telegram from Capt. Britton at Southampton announcing that
the West India steamer at that port brought news in there this
morning that Capt. Wilkes, of the U.S. Ship of War San Jacinto,

had stopped the British mail steamer Trent in the Bahama Channel, not far from St. Thomas, on the 9th Inst, & had forcibly taken Mason, Slidell, Eustis, & Macfarlane [J. E. McFarland, secretary to Mason] out of her: and at 1 o'clk a telegram from Reuter confirmed the statement. That the capture of these arch-rebeles gave us great satisfaction at the first blush, was natural: & we gave free vent to our exultation. But on reflection I am satisfied that the act will do more for the Southerners than ten victories, for it touches John Bull's honor, and the honor of his flag. At present the people have hardly receovered from the paralysing effect of the news; but they are beginning to see that their flag has been insulted, and if that devil The Times, feeds their ire to-morrow, as it assuredly will, nothing but a miracle can prevent their sympathies running to the South, and Palmerston getting up a war. We have no particulars, but from what we hear, it would seem that Capt. Wilkes acted on his own responsibility, and not on that of the Govt. . . .

Thursday, 28 Nov. '61. . . . I was addressed by a number of the Diplomatic Corps & asked if we were going to have war with England about Mason & Slidell; but I thought it prudent to be quiet. On leaving, I drove to the Legation in my uniform, where I found Mr. Bright, M. P. deploring Capt. Wilkes act. There was a note from Earl Russell, asking an interview of Mr. Adams at 2 o'ck to-day . . . The newspapers are violent in the extreme, and yet seem in a mist. In all this there is still an ugly look of war. We have had a great deal to do to-day, and many American visitors in a great state of excitement. [Charles L.] Wilson and Henry Adams seem to me very indiscreet in some of their remarks about the business to strangers.

Friday, 29 Nov. 61. Mr. Adams returned to town last night. It appears he got my telegram promptly. He regards the Trent affair as serious, and is very grave about it. To-day he has been writing home concerning it, and I have had a vast deal of hard work. Earl Russell fixed quarter to two for an interview, but beyond asking a few questions about the orders of the Capt. of the James Adger, his Lordship said nothing. It is quite evident that Ministers consider the question as serious, and many of them feel very sore and hostile about it. As I was detained late, I remained to dinner. Mr. Adams expressed apprehensions that we would not be here a month . . .

Monday, 2 Dec. '61. This state of feeling was not improved on finding this morning that no despatches had arrived. All the evil spirits are at work against us, and the Despatch bag is shuffling about somewhere between this and Cork. . . . Mr. Adams continues to entertain very gloomy apprehensions of the future, but I don't know what he founds his fears upon. He probably has private advices of which I know nothing.

Tuesday, 3 Dec. '61. I stayed here at work until 7.30 last evening, and had to go away without hearing of the arrival of the bag. On my return this morning, I was sick at heart to hear there was nothing from Washington on this trouble. . . . At present the excitement in England is truly terrific. The Europa was detained at Cork or Queenstown, until last night, or this morning, to carry out an Ultimatum, and the purport of that is indicated by the London papers of yesterday and to-day. It is alleged that the Law Officers of the Crown have decided that Wilkes did not insult England enough, and the result is a demand for an apology, and the restoration of the men. By harping on this, and asserting that Capt. Wilkes' act was an authorized and deliberate insult of our Gov't, the journals have lashed the nation into a most indecent rage, and the consequence is that mob rule reign supreme, and the natural English hatred of the American people, which is ordinarily concealed, has been allowed to gush up in its full bitterness from all hearts, high and low. . . . That pink of modesty and refinement, *The Times,* is filled with such slatternly abuse of us and ours, that it is fair to conclude that all the Fishwifes of Billingsgate have been transferred to Printing House Square to fill the ears of the writers there with their choicest phraseology. . . .

Tuesday, 10 Dec. 1861. Several Despatches were received late last evening from Washington, and one of them rather indicates a disposition to argue this Trent business, as it instructs Mr. Adams to obtain, if possible, from the records here, the facts respecting the capture and nationality of the Mercury, on board of which Mr. Henry Laurens, then on his way to Holland as a Minister, was taken in Sept. 1780. George Sumner, a brother of the Massachusetts Senator, has been writing on the subject, and has declared the Mercury was a Dutch vessel bound from the Island of St. Eustace to Rotterdam. But as this is not clear, Mr. Seward wants the facts. By Mr. Adams' direction I went down to Doctor's Commons to see Sir John D. Harding and ask him where the facts could be had.

He received me very kindly, but was evidently anxious, and his manner was grave. I briefly informed him what I came for, when he frankly told me the Admiralty had all the available facts in the case on this side of the water, and he had already examined them. They were the log book of the capturing ship and original report of Condemnation at St. John's Newfoundland, and were at the office in Whitehall. I told him I had no acquaintance there and felt some hesitation about going to ask the privilege of inspecting the records without being assured that such a proceeding would not be regarded as impertinent. He said "Oh, no," and on my asking permission to use his name, authorized me to do so to Mr. Romaine, the Secretary. Before my leaving, Sir John conversed with me on the subject of the arrest of Slidell & Mason, and convinced me by his manner that he was extremely apprehensive of a war from it. I hoped not. The case of the Mercury was remarked upon, and he said there was no doubt she was an American vessel from Philadelphia, and therefore the case was not a parallel one. But, when I asked him what this Government would do if it could be shewn that she was a Dutch vessel going from one neutral port to another, and Mr. Laurens was on just such an errand as Mason & Slidell, he declared they could have nothing to say. I instanced the Russian officers of the Diana seized on a Bremen vessel going from one neutral port to another, after shipwreck in the late war, and he defended that on the ground that the vessel and men were carried into an Admiralty Court, and duly condemned. What the British Gov't objected to was the failure of Capt. Wilkes to take the vessel in. It would not do for Naval officers to constitute themselves captors & judges at the same time. I might have replied, but I did not, that his declaration on this point was agreeable news, for heretofore British Naval officers had oftener acted as judges in such cases than otherwise. But I did put the case directly to him that if Wilkes had taken his prize in for adjudication, the British people would have been even more violent than now, and he acknowledged that he did not know but that I was correct about that. I inferred from his manner, and a few remarks that fell from him, that the Gov't would be satisfied with nothing short of the restoration of the men & an apology. I drove by St. Paul's down Ludgate Hill, Fleet St., and the Strand to the Admiralty. On my way I for the first time saw the rebel flag. It was flying at the top of the Adelphi Theatre, west side, and the Stars and Stripes were at the east. The sight of this base emblem of slavery, treason and piracy made me ill with rage, flaunted as it is daily in the faces of loyal Americans over a London theatre, by Bourcicalt [Boucicault], a naturalized American citizen. . . .

Wednesday, 11 Dec. '61. . . . There have been a great many people here to-day, asking all kinds of questions about this Trent business. It is provoking to know that men are such fools as to think we would, if we could, tell them our secrets. . . .

Sat. 14 Dec. '61. This morning's papers announce the serious illness of Prince Albert. This is so unexpected as to create much alarm. In fact The Times of this morning evidently regards his life in danger, and has a notice almost amounting to an obituary. He has been ill for several days, but no intimation of anything like the possibility of his death has been whispered until now. From his appearance, I shall not be astonished at his death, in case his disease should prove to be a violent fever. This morning's Times contains a letter from Thurlow Weed defending Mr. Seward against the charge, so prevalent in England, of enmity to this country, in which there is an attempted explanation of Mr. Seward's alleged statement last fall a year ago at Albany to the Duke of Newcastle that he would be either President or Sec. of State, & then he would insult England. The letter is strong in some things, but weak in others, and The Times assails its vulnerable points with its usual malignity. . . . We are told that the Queen is opposed to a war with the United States, and that she and Prince Albert greatly modified the demands, and the tone of the despatch to our Gov't. on the Trent affair. . . .

Monday, 16 Dec. '61. Being weary I remained at home on Saturday evening and did not get any special news. Yesterday I left the house for the Legation, and was rather shocked to read on a bulletin board as I passed a newsman's near Paddington Green about 12 o'clock that the Prince Consort was dead. He expired at Windsor Castle at 10 minutes to 11 on Saturday night of typhoid fever. The news was generally known and a gloom pervaded all London. . . . I returned to the Legation and found a telegram from Reuter giving a summary of the Prest's message [on the state of the Union]. As there was no mention of the Trent, I took it for granted that that was for a reason, & meant peace. . . . We are to go into mourning until some time in March, and London will wear a gloomy air until then. The shops at the West End were generally half closed, almost every window having two or more shutters up.

Tuesday, 17 Dec. '61. Late last evening we received what I consider a very important despatch. It is dated the 30th of November, and is numbered 136. After complimenting Mr. Adams on his speech at the Lord Mayor's dinner, it states distinctly that the arrest of Mason & Slidell on the Trent is an unforseen & unknown event, altogether unauthorized by the Gov't, and solely the act of Capt Wilkes. This, it is remarked, leaves the subject free from those embarrassments which would attach to it, had the act been directed by the President, and Mr. Seward says he will wait for the demands of the Brit. Govt. and if they should be, as he hopes they will, in the same spirit of good will as is his despatch, they will be complied with. He directs Mr. Adams to read his note to Ld. Russell as he sees fit. This Mr. Adams hesitates to do; but both Mr. Wilson and myself think he should waste no time in delay. He will consider the matter to night. . . .

Wed. 18 Dec. '61. . . . Mr. Adams has determined to read 136 to Ld. R., & has written for an interview.

Thursday, 19 Dec. '61. Lord Russell fixed 3 o'clock to-day to see Mr. Adams, & he has gone down for the purpose. It is understood that all our notes to the British Gov't are to be on black edged paper during the mourning for the Prince, and to be enclosed in envelopes with black borders, sealed with black. All other official notes from the Legation need only the black seal, but private letters should be in full mourning. . . .

Friday, 21 Dec. '61. . . . Mr. Adams read the Despatch to Lord Russell yesterday, but did not leave a copy. It was very satisfactory to his Lordship. During the interview Mr. Adams said he couldn't compliment England on her consistency on the search question, and remarked that the Brit. Navy had done some very bad things in that way 50 years ago. His Lordship replied that there were many things in British policy 50 years ago that he would be very sorry to defend. . . .

Monday, 23 Dec. '61. Prince Albert was buried this morning, and a gloomier day I never passed. All the shops were closed in London, the sky was dull, the people were in black, and an unusual stillness prevailed in the great city. . . .

Tuesday, 24 Dec. '61. The gloomy pall thrown over London by Prince Albert's death still continues, and Xmas bids fair to be as funereal as the grave. Mr. Adams has gone to spend a few days at Russell Sturgis' house at Walton-on-Thames, and he certainly needs some relaxation from the cares of office. He is gratified with the better state of feeling now evident in England towards the U. States, and thinks our Gov't will release Mason & Slidell.

Thursday, 26 Dec. '61. Wilson and I spent the morning of yesterday here, and then loafed about town for some hours, & finally brought up at Ward's, where we dined. By common consent dullness has hung its pall over everybody and everything. We have had a good many visitors to-day to gossip, and to ask about the probability of a war, but there was nothing said worth remembering. Mr. Adams has come back to town & has been very chatty this morning. It is clear that he does not entertain a very high opinion of President Lincoln, for he said in so many words this morning that he considered him unfit for his place.

Friday, 27 Dec. '61. I walked here this morning through a sharp chilly atmosphere, and have been busy all day. There has been the usual anxious discussion between us about the impending war, & when we can have the reply to the English demands for reparation in the Trent affair. Mr. Adams is apprehensive that he may have to leave here by the middle of January. A change has come over his views since his visit to Mr. Sturgis; but I don't sympathise with his present opinions. I cannot think we art to have a war, after Mr. Seward's despatch of the 30th heretofore described. . . .

Wednesday, 8 Jany. 1862. . . . A telegram came about half-past four that the Washington was in, & Mason & Slidell would be given up to Lord Lyons when and where he pleased. This lifted a load of lead from our hearts, and Mr. & Mrs. Adams heartily congratulated each other. I was full of the news, & drove to Morley's to see Wilson but he was out. I then went to the Club, where I found the news was unknown. Count Conti, the Italian Sec.y came into the Drawing Room to see me & asked with rather a gloomy countenace where there would be war. I laughed . . . He was delighted, and went into the next Room to communicate the tidings to some twenty other Secretaries there assembled. They all sprng to their feet as if electrified, and several came to me for confirmatory news. In a few minutes messages were flashing over the wires to all the Courts of Europe, and I was congratulated on our escape from war by many. . . .

Thursday, 9 Jany. '62. It seems the peace news yesterday was received everywhere but at *The Times* office with unfeigned joy. It was announced at the most of the London theatres between the acts, and the audiences arose like one & cheered tremendously. The wires carried it far & wide over the Kingdom . . .

Sat. 19 July, '62. Last evening being the time fixed for the discussion of Lindsay's motion for the recognition of the Rebels, I was sent down to the House by Mr. Adam's direction to observe the feeling and report the proceedings. . . . At this time the rebel Mason came up attended by Williams, our late Minister at Constantinople, Geo. McHenry and two or three vulgar looking confederates, whose appearance and manners were not favorable to their modest pretensions to be considered as specimens of the only gentlemen in America. Mason and Williams are both coarse, gross, ponderous, vulgar looking men, and on this occasion they did not show to the best advantage. They were badly dressed. William always was a sloven. Last night his shirt front was crumpled and stained with tobacco spit and his trousers were unbuttoned. . . . An ineffectual attempt having been made to induce Lindsay to withdraw his motion, that gentleman rose and began his speech. He opened by striking off every offer of *recognition* and fell back on simple mediation, without referring to hostilities. He is a wretched speaker and soon drove half the members of a very full House away. . . . After an hour's abuse of us, and his reasons therefore, he wound up by saying that independently of all these, he desired the disruption of the American Union, as every honest Englishman did, because it was too great a Power and England sh'd not let such a power exist on the American continent. Old Mason spat tobacco more furiously at this than ever, and covered the carpet. . . .

Tuesday, 22 Sept. '63. . . . Mr. Mason was the unfittest man they [the rebels] could have sent here, and has proved an ignominious failure. His antecedents were bad, his associates were questionable, and his manners vulgar. Even Bear Ellice [Edward Ellice, called "Bear" by Lord Brougham because of his large holdings in the Hudson's Bay Company] couldn't endorse his coarseness, much as he supported his cause, and had to rebuke him hypothetically for spitting tobacco on his drawing room carpets in Scotland. Mr. Mason spirted his tobacco juice about there liberally, and Mr. Ellice stopped him by telling an anecdote in his presence one evening to the ladies about a vulgar Virginian who had done the same thing in the same place. The shot told, and the Commissioner never chewed tobacco more while in that house.

38. The Laird rams

In the latter nineteenth century the navies of the world progressed from wood and sails and smoothbore guns toward a vastly improved archi-tecture of steel and steam and huge shell-firing rifles (more about this in Vol. II of the present series). The naval revolution was proceeding so rapidly by the 1860's that it was nearly impossible to know what new type of ship might prove successful. For a while, naval architects believed that a wrought-iron "piercer" at the prow of a small steam vessel, a ram of about seven feet in length, three feet under the surface, would permit the sinking of any opposing wooden ship. The firm of William Laird and Sons in 1863 had two rams under construction, on consignment for His Serene Highness the Pasha of Egypt. Minister Adams was certain they were for the Confederacy, and importuned the British government to seize them. He believed that his British opposite, Foreign Secretary Russell, was moving too slowly, and the rams might escape. The crisis came in the first days of September 1863. Source: Diary of Charles Francis Adams. Quotations from the Adams Papers are from the micro-film edition, reel 77, by permission of the Massachusetts Historical Society.

[London,] Thursday [September] 3d [,1863]. At six o'clock of the morning of this, the thirty-fourth anniversary of my Wedding day I was in London and at my own door soon afterwards. On the whole it was lucky I came. In though there was no extraordinary pressure of business, the question of the outfit of Mr Lai[r]ds Iron Clads had come to a point requiring measures to be taken by me at once. After long waiting and hesitation there are signs that the ministry will not adopt any prevention policy. Their moral petti-ness [?] culminates in cowardice which acts like the greatest daring. It precipitates a conflict. My duty is therefore a difficult one. With-out indulging in menace I must be faithful to my country in giving warning of its sense of injury. Nothing must be left undone that shall appear likely to avert the danger. To that end I addressed a note to Lord Russell at once. The remainder of my time was de-voted to the drafting of the ordinary Despatches of the week, and

to reading up the arrears of news from America. On the whole, it
is very encouraging. The attack on Charleston is going on with
great vigour, and the cries of the Richmond press indicate success.
Barring the conduct of foreign powers, I should say that the rebellion would collapse before New Year's. But the pestilent malignity of the English and the insidious craft of Napoleon are not yet
exhausted. . . .

Friday 4th   A large part of the morning was spent in my
customary way of writing to my son. A notice from Mr Dudley,
however, that the war vessel was about to depart impelled me to
adress another and a stronger note of solemn protest against the
permission of this proceeding by the government. I feared however
that it would be of little avail. And my prognostication proved but
too true; for I received at four o'clock a note announcing that the
Government could find no evidence upon which to proceed in
stopping the vessel. This affected me deeply. I clearly foresee that
a collision must now come out of it. I must not however do any
thing to accelerate it, and yet must maintain the honor of my
country with proper spirit. The issue must be properly made up
before the world on its merits. The prospect is dark for poor
America. Her trials are not yet over. Luckily the difficulties do not
all come together. A telegram receivid tonight announces the destruction of Fort Sumter, and the shelling of that pestilent nest of
heresy, Charleston. This will produce a great effect in Europe. It
may go so far as to save us from imminent danger pressing both
here and in France. I trust in a higher power which is working out
its ends by ways that I cannot fathom. . . .

Saturday 5th   My thoughts turned strongly upon the present
evils and the difficulty of my task. My conclusion was that another
note must be addressed to Lord Russell today. So I drew one which
I intended only to gain time previous to the inevitable result. I
have not disclosed to Lord Russell those portions of my instructions
which describe the policy to be adopted by the government at
home in the case, because that course seemed to me likely to cut
off all prospect of escape. Contenting myself with intimating the
existence of them I decide upon awaiting farther directions. This
will give a month. After I had sent the note I receiv'd one from
His Lordship, in answer to my two previous ones of Thursday and
Friday, saying that the subject of them was receiving the earnest
and anxious consideration of the government. There is then one

chance left and but one. . . . if the Iron Clad goes out, it will take
a month or more for her to go over and get her armament and be
ready for an attack. So that the excitement in America will not
react here for six weeks. In that interval, something may happen
to save us from this fearful addition to the public calamities. I
cannot help thinking that the ministry here were not quite prepared for the direct issue which has thus been made. The very
fact that it comes at a moment when they are all dispersed, and
nothing but ordinary business is transacted shows it. This is perhaps the most unlucky part of it. For Lord Palmerston may, if he
chooses, take advantage of the circumstance to precipitate the
object he may have in view. I do not believe he wants a war, but
if he should find himself cornered, he will not scruple at it to save
himself by an appeal to the pride of the British people. Of his bad
disposition towards America I have no doubt. Considering all these
various chances, I confess my hope of tiding over this difficulty is
not bright. . . . Mr Dudley came in from Liverpool to consult me
about further measures in regard to those war vessels. He suggested
the expediency of getting an opinion from Mr. . . . [?] on a case
presented with the same evidence that has been sent to the foreign
office. I explained to him the precise situation of the question with
the government here. Such a step as he suggested might be well
enough to put into the record which must be ultimately made up
between the countries, but I had no idea it could in the least avail
to affect the immediate result. I should counsel the measure as a
part of a policy in advance of the rupture which now looked more
than probable. He remarked that as it was late he must wait until
tomorrow to show me the papers he had, before deciding what
course to take. . . .

Sunday 6th   Fine but cooler. I went with my son Brooks on
a pilgrimate to church in the city. This time, it was to St. Peter's
Cornhill. On entering, I perceived at once that the interior was
unmistakably Sir Christopher's. The distribution much in his
usual manner with rather awkard columns supporting a series of
arches without any galleries, excepting over the door of entrance.
There was much less ornament than usual. Some carving on wood
along the top of the panel behind the altar. Between the chancel
and the nave was a woodscreen, made of dark wood, supporting in
the centre, images of the Lion and the Unicorn, the royal arms
which never look to me the right thing inside of a church. The

services were read by the Incumbent who preached a sermon with much more substance in it than is common. His topic was the Roman Catholic doctrine of transubstantiation. With the customary self complacency of this church he assumed that it was the right mean between one extreme in the Romans and the other in the Dissenters. Unfortunately that mean is a compromise which carries the seed of its own destruction. . . .

Monday 7th   Clear with a high wind. The Times has a leader this morning which rather shows a disposition to stop these vessels. It may be inferred that there is a pause of deliberation at the possible consequences of raising such an issue as this before the world. I was engaged in answering several letters which have been on my table for some time. I had visits from several Americans desirous to see me and all more or less anxious about the difficulty. . . .

Tuesday 8th   In the Morning Post there was a short article announcing that the government had decided on detaining the vessels, in order to give them an opportunity to try the merits in Court. It had an official aspect, and yet I could scarcely put faith in it while I had no notice myself. Later in the day however, a brief notification came from Lord Russell to the effect that orders had been given to prevent their departure. I knew not that even in the Trent case I felt a greater relief. After the very unequivocal character of the announcement made on the 5th I had scarcely expected so sudden a revolution. The government had very singularly interpolated my two notes between theirs in a way to raise an inevitable conjecture that they were the actual course. I shall not venture to claim any such victory. Non nobis will be my motto. I am profoundly thankful to the Divine Being who turned the hearts of the rulers at the cricial moment. I do hope it will be the last occasion upon which the harmony of the two nations will be in danger; at least whilst I remain on duty. . . .

The British navy bought the Laird rams and named them the Wivern and the Scorpion. Several years after the Civil War, Adams saw one of the vessels during a grand naval review at Portsmouth, and it did not seem formidable: "as I looked on the little mean thing. I could not help a doubt whether she was really worthy of all the anxiety she had cost us." Two scholars recently have questioned the fighting qualities of the rams, and also their seaworthiness; see Thomas W. Green and Frank J. Merli, "Could the Laird Rams Have Lifted the Union Blockade?", Civil War Times, II (April 1963), 14–17.

39. The assassination

Movements of public sentiment often are difficult to trace, but no one could doubt the depth of the reaction in London to Lincoln's assassination. The Times (London) published two notable editorials.

[April 27, 1865] . . . The critical condition of affairs in America, the position of the Southern States at the feet of their victorious antagonists, the gigantic task of reconstruction which must be undertaken by the political leaders of the North, and, above all, the unpromising character of the man whom an accident has made the ruler of the Union for the next four years, tend to exalt our estimate of the loss which the States have suffered in the murder of their PRESIDENT; but it would be unjust not to acknowledge that Mr. LINCOLN was a man who could not under any circumstances have been easily replaced. Starting from a humble position to one of the greatest eminence, and adopted by the Republican party as a make-shift, simply because Mr. SEWARD and their other prominent leaders were obnoxious to different sections of the party, it was natural that his career should be watched with jealous suspicion. The office cast upon him was great, its duties most onerous, and the obscurity of his past career afforded no guarantee of his ability to discharge them. His shortcomings, moreover, were on the surface. The education of a man whose early years had been spent in earning bread by manual labour had necessarily been defective, and faults of manner and errors of taste repelled the observer at the outset. In spite of these drawbacks, Mr. LINCOLN slowly won for himself the respect and confidence of all. His perfect honesty speedily became apparent, and, what is, perhaps, more to his credit, amid the many unstudied speeches which he was called upon from time to time to deliver, imbued though they were with the rough humour of his early associates, he was in none of them betrayed into any intemperance of language towards his opponents or towards neutrals. His utterances were apparently careless, but his tongue was always under command. The quality of Mr. LINCOLN's administration which served, however, more than any other to enlist the sympathy of bystanders was its conservative progress. He felt his way gradually to his conclusions, and those who will compare the different stages of his career one with another will find that his mind was growing throughout the course of it. The naïveté with which he once suggested to the negroes that they should take themselves off to Central America, because their presence in the States was inconvenient to the white population, soon disappeared. The gradual change of his language and of his policy was most re- markable. Englishmen learnt to respect a man who showed the best characteristics of their race in his respect for what is good in the past, acting in unison with a recognition of what was made necessary by the events of passing history. But the growth of Mr. LINCOLN's mind was subject to a singular modification. It would seem that he felt himself of late a mere instrument engaged in working out a great cause, which he could partly recognize, but which he was powerless to control. In the mixed strength and weak- ness of his character he presented a remarkable contrast to Mr. SEWARD, who was his coadjutor for more than four years, and who must, we fear, be reckoned his fellow victim. The SECRETARY of STATE long before his elevation to office was a prominent citizen of New York. More than a quarter of a century ago he was the Governor of that State, and for twelve years he represented it in the Senate. In the Empire City and at Washington he had attained a culture which the Illinois lawyer never acquired. But the ex- perience of the politician had, perhaps, weakened the independence of Mr. SEWARD's character, and he never inspired the same con- fidence as his chief, because it was not known by what influences his course might not be modified.

What may be the actual destiny of the United States deprived of the guiding hand of Mr. LINCOLN and of the experience of Mr. SEWARD no one would venture to foretell. In compliance with the provision of the Constitution, Mr. ANDREW JOHNSON has assumed the Presidency for the rest of Mr. LINCOLN's term. At the time when the last mail left New York the States had not recovered from the feeling of horror and astonishment which had been created by the news of Mr. LINCOLN's assassination, but the possibility of Mr. JOHNSON's succeeding to the Presidency had been discussed when such an event was thought highly improbable, and it was earnestly deprecated by all parties. The indecorous exhibition upon the occa- sion of the inauguration of Mr. JOHNSON as Vice-President was of a piece with his previous career, and, indeed, the memory of his conduct as Governor of Tennessee must fill every American with the gloomiest forebodings. On the other hand, anything like a violent interruption of the succession is a thing which an American citizen with his almost idolatrous veneration for the Constitution would shrink from instinctively. The best solution of the difficulty would be a voluntary resignation by Mr. JOHNSON of an office which no one ever seriously intended him to fill, and if his own sense of decency does not suggest this course to him it may be hoped that such a pressure of public opinion will be brought to bear upon him that he may be led to adopt it. . . .

[April 29] If anything could mitigate the distress of the American people in their present affliction, it might surely be the sympathy which is expressed by the people of this country. We are not using the language of hyperbole in describing the manifestation of feeling as unexampled. Nothing like it has been witnessed in our generation, for we except of course those domestic visitations in which the affliction of a Sovereign is naturally the affliction of the nation. But President LINCOLN was only the chief of a foreign State, and of a State with which we were not unfrequently in diplomatic or political collision. He might have been regarded as not much more to us than the head of any friendly Government, and yet his end has already stirred the feelings of the public to their uttermost depths. It has been said that the Papal Aggression created a more universal excitement among us than had been produced by any political event for a whole generation, but that excitement was of gradual and tardy growth. At first the news fell flat upon the public mind, and was treated with unconcern. It was not till later in the day that the resentment of the nation found a voice. But now a space of twenty-four hours has sufficed not only to fill the country with grief and indignation, but to evoke almost unprecedented expressions of feeling from constituted bodies. It was but on Wednesday that the intelligence of the murder reached us, and on Thursday the Houses of Lords and Commons, the Corporation of the city of London, and the people of our chief manufacturing towns in public meeting assembled had recorded their sentiments or expressed their views. In the House of Lords the absence of precedent for such a manifestation was actually made the subject of remark.

That much of this extraordinary feeling is due to the tragical character of the event and the horror with which the crime is regarded is doubtless true, nor need we dissemble the fact that the loss which the Americans have sustained is also thought our own loss in so far as one valuable guarantee for the amity of the two nations may have been thus removed. But, upon the whole, it is neither the possible embarrassment of international relations nor the infamous wickedness of the act itself which has determined public feeling. The preponderating sentiment is sincere and genuine sympathy—sorrow for the chief of a great people struck down by an assassin, and sympathy for that people in the trouble which at a crisis of their destinies such a catastrophe must bring. ABRAHAM LINCOLN was as little of a tyrant as any man who ever lived. He could have been a tyrant had he pleased, but he never uttered so much as an ill-natured speech. The Civil War was attended by all war's own horrors in too many instances, but there was no cruelty at Washington or New York—hardly any prolonged or unaccountable severity. In the whole of this sanguinary strife, notwithstanding the exasperation of popular feeling, there has been no political bloodthirstiness. Fanatical speakers have given vent to their passions on the platform, but violence never went beyond words. If the people of the Seceding States were rebels, as the people of the North chose to consider them, never was rebellion, except on the field of battle, more gently handled. The North put forth its whole strength and exerted its whole energies to conquer the insurrection and subdue the insurgents, but, on the single condition of reunion, it would promptly have made peace with them again. At first, the South might have had almost its will even in the matter of slavery, and to the very last, even up to the meeting of President LINCOLN with the Southern Commissioners in Hampton Roads, he was ready with amnesty, oblivion, and liberal consideration for incidental difficulties. At any moment the rebellion itself and all its terrible cost would have been forgiven, and the South might have had its venture for independence at no charge but that of the war itself.

A melancholy interest will now attach to the ceremony of inauguration on the 6th of last March, and those who incline superstitiously to the notion of prognostics or coincidences will probably think with some emotion of the brief and even mournful speech in which the re-elected PRESIDENT characterized the occasion. The grave and despondent tone of his short address was so strongly contrasted with the usual oratory of his countrymen as to create remark at the time, and it seemed as if some insight into the future impressed him with misgivings unknown to others. Except, indeed, for such forecast or presentiment, there was nothing to suggest distrust. The dreadful storm by which the eve of the inauguration had been signalized, and which frightened the members of Congress from their seats in the dim gray of the dawn, had given way to fairer weather, and a streak of light in the sky enlivened the day. We read now, with a strange kind of sensation, of the popularity and security which the PRESIDENT enjoyed, and which enabled him to drive unprotected and in an open carriage through the streets of the capital. At the time, the fact seemed hardly worth recording, but we were reminded that four years before it had not been so, and that when in 1861 ABRAHAM LINCOLN first took office his appearance in public was thought not unattended with risk. With still deeper interest may we observe that on this last occasion, when all around the PRESIDENT seemed so hopeful, and yet he himself seemed so depressed, his life did, perhaps, hang by a thread. It appears not improbable that the crime just perpetrated was originally plotted for the day of inauguration. The mail of that time informed us that a man was actually arrested at Washington on suspicion of such a design, and it is now said that papers belonging to the assassin show that before the 4th of March the conspiracy had really been matured.

In all America there was, perhaps, not one man who less deserved to be the victim of this revolution than he who has just fallen. He did nothing to aggravate the quarrel; short of conceding the independence demanded by the South, he did everything to prevent or abbreviate it. He recognized it as his one great duty to preserve the Union, and, whatever opinions may be entertained in this country about the war and its policy, nobody can say that such a principle was otherwise than becoming in the PRESIDENT of the Republic. He was doubtless glad at last to see slavery perish, but his personal opinions on that subject were not permitted to influence the policy of the Government while there was a chance of escaping the extremities of strife. His homely kindness of feeling, his plain sense, and his instinctive aversion from violence combined to keep him in a course of clemency and to incline him to conciliation whenever it might be practicable. He was hardly a representative Republican so much as a representative American. He did not express the extreme opinions even of his own party. He did worship the Union, but next to that he put peace.

These are the feelings which have prompted our present manifestations, and if the Americans set as much store by our English opinions as they are said to do they may console themselves with the assurance that no incident in the history of a foreign State could have excited more universal or more genuine sensation. The addresses which they will receive from us are expressions of sincere and unaffected sympathy. In its political aspect the event is momentous enough, but of that at the moment we do not desire to take heed. We trust that the counsels of the Republic may be guided by a spirit like that of its late chief, but by our present proceedings we design only to put on record and communicate to Americans a feeling which can differ only in intensity from that of Americans themselves.

XIV

The Republic At Peace

With the defeat of the Confederate States of America, the government of the United States looked with confidence into the future. In the early nineteenth century, shoals of critical Europeans had come over to the United States and observed the gap between the national ambition and power. The idea of manifest destiny always had made sense to Americans, but the continuing doubts from Europe had been disquieting. The victorious end of the Civil War finished this commentary; Americans now could bask in the light of their accomplishments, unshaded by worry over slavery or by the theory which had persisted into the Civil War that a republic could not control large territories. In the next half-dozen years there was one diplomatic failure, when the administration of President Ulysses S. Grant proposed the annexation of Santo Domingo and saw the project ruined irretrievably by the wrath of Senator Charles Sumner. But there were glorious successes: French troops left Mexico, Seward annexed Alaska, and the British government shamefacedly paid the bill for its unneutrality during the late war.

40. Seward and the Emperor Maximilian

The continuing political confusion of Mexico after its independence from Spain invited European intervention, which occurred in 1861. Secretary Seward informed Minister Adams in London of the American attitude on March 3, 1862. Source: 37th Cong., 2d Sess., House Doc. No. 100, pp. 207–208. A check of this published version of Seward's circular against the original in the archives of the Department of State revealed only two slight changes of wording, both insignificant.

We observe indications of a growing opinion in Europe that the demonstrations which are being made by Spanish, French, and British forces against Mexico are likely to be attended with a revolution in that country which will bring in a monarchical government there, in which the crown will be assumed by some foreign prince.

This country is deeply concerned in the peace of nations, and aims to be loyal at the same time in all its relations, as well to the allies as to Mexico. The President has therefore instructed me to submit his views on the new aspect of affairs to the parties concerned. He has relied upon the assurances given to this government by the allies that they were seeking no political objects and only a redress of grievances. He does not doubt the sincerity of the allies, and his confidence in their good faith, if it could be shaken, would be reinspired by explanations apparently made in their behalf that the governments of Spain, France, and Great Britain are not intending to intervene and will not intervene to effect a change of the constitutional form of government now existing in Mexico, or to produce any political change there in opposition to the will of the Mexican people. Indeed, he understands the allies to be unanimous in declaring that the proposed revolution in Mexico is moved only by Mexican citizens now in Europe.

The President, however, deems it his duty to express to the allies, in all candor and frankness, the opinion that no monarchical government which could be founded in Mexico, in the presence of foreign navies and armies in the waters and upon the soil of Mexico, would have any prospect of security or permanency. Secondly, that the instability of such a monarchy there would be enhanced if the throne should be assigned to any person not of Mexican nativity. That under such circumstances the new government must speedily fall unless it could draw into its support European alliances, which, relating back to the present invasion, would, in fact, make it the beginning of a permanent policy of armed European monarchical intervention injurious and practically hostile to the most general system of government on the continent of America, and this would be the beginning rather than the ending of revolution in Mexico.

These views are grounded upon some knowledge of the political sentiments and habits of society in America.

In such a case it is not to be doubted that the permanent interests and sympathies of this country would be with the other American republics. It is not intended on this occasion to predict the course of events which might happen as a consequence of the proceeding contemplated, either on this continent or in Europe. It is sufficient to say that, in the President's opinion, the emancipation of this continent from European control has been the principal feature in its history during the last century. It is not probable that a revolution in a contrary direction would be successful in an immediately succeeding century, while population in America is so rapidly increasing, resources so rapidly developing, and society so steadily forming itself upon principles of democratic American government. Nor is it necessary to suggest to the allies the improbability that European nations could steadily agree upon a policy favorable to such a counter-revolution as one conducive to their own interests, or to suggest that, however studiously the allies may act to avoid lending the aid of their land and naval forces to domestic revolutions in Mexico, the result would nevertheless be traceable to the presence of those forces there, although for a different purpose, since it may be deemed certain that but for their presence there no such revolution could probably have been attempted or even conceived.

The Senate of the United States has not, indeed, given its official sanction to the precise measures which the President has proposed for lending our aid to the existing government in Mexico, with the approval of the allies, to relieve it from its present embarrassments. This, however, is only a question of domestic administration. It would be very erroneous to regard such a disagreement as indicating any serious difference of opinion in this government or among the American people in their cordial good wishes for the safety, welfare, and stability of the republican system of government in that country.

French troops in Mexico in 1864 propped up a throne for Archduke Maximilian of Austria, but the new emperor soon found himself with many ungrateful, rebellious subjects. Upon the end of the American Civil War, Secretary Seward on February 12, 1866, wrote to the French minister in Washington, the Comte de Montholon. Source: Foreign Relations of the United States: 1866, III (Washington, D.C., 1866), 819–820.

. . . The United States have not claimed, and they do not claim, to know what arrangements the Emperor may make for the adjustment of claims for indemnity and redress in Mexico. It would be, on our part, an act of intervention to take cognizance of them. We adhere to our position that the war in question has become a political war between France and the republic of Mexico, injurious and dangerous to the United States and to the republican cause, and we ask only that in that aspect and character it may be brought to an end. It would be illiberal on the part of the United States to suppose that, in desiring or pursuing preliminary arrangements, the Emperor contemplates the establishment in Mexico, before withdrawing his forces, of the very institutions which constitute the material ground of the exceptions taken against his intervention by the United States. It would be still more illiberal to suppose for a moment that he expects the United States to bind themselves indirectly to acquiesce in or support the obnoxious institutions.

. . . in the opinion of the President, France need not for a moment delay her promised withdrawal of military forces from Mexico, and her putting the principle of non-intervention into full and complete practice in regard to Mexico, through any apprehension that the United States will prove unfaithful to the principles and policy in that respect which, on their behalf, it has been my duty to maintain in this now very lengthened correspondence. The practice of this government, from its beginning, is a guarantee to all nations of the respect of the American people for the free sovereignty of the people in every other state. We received the instruction from Washington. We applied it sternly in our early intercourse even with France. The same principle and practice have been uniformly inculcated by all our statesmen, interpreted by all our jurists, maintained by all our Congresses, and acquiesced in without practical dissent on all occasions by the American people. It is in reality the chief element of foreign intercourse in our history. Looking simply toward the point to which our attention has been steadily confined, the relief of the Mexican embarrassments without disturbing our relations with France, we shall be gratified when the Emperor shall give to us, either through the channel of your esteemed correspondence or otherwise, definitive information of the time when French military operations may be expected to cease in Mexico. . . .

41. Alaska

Having settled Mexico, Seward suddenly found himself with an opportunity. It came at a time of domestic turmoil over the conduct of President Andrew Johnson. Source: Frederick W. Seward, Autobiography of William H. Seward, with a Memoir of His Life and Selections from His Letters (3 vols., New York, 1891), III, 346–350. 367–369. Seward's son Frederick was assistant secretary of state in 1867.

Chapter LII

While the Capitol was resounding with angry debate, the State Department was going on with an important measure, quietly and unnoticed. This was the negotiation which Seward had begun, for the annexation of Russian-America. As long before as September, 1860, he had said in his speech at St. Paul:

> Standing here, and looking far off into the North-west, I see the Russian, as he busily occupies himself in establishing seaports, and towns, and fortifications, on the verge of this continent, as the outposts of St. Petersburg; and I can say: "Go on, and build up your outposts all along the coast, up even to the Arctic ocean; they will yet become the outposts of my own country—monuments of the civilization of the United States in the North-west!"

During the war, he had found the Government laboring under great disadvantage for the lack of advanced naval outposts in the West Indies, and in the North Pacific. So at the close of hostilities, he commenced his endeavors to obtain such a foothold in each quarter.

Even as early as during the Oregon debate in 1846–7, the suggestion had been made, that by insisting on the boundary line of 54° 40′, and obtaining a cession from the Emperor Nicholas, the United States might own the whole Pacific coast, up to the Arctic circle. But the slave power, then dominant in the Federal councils, wanted Southern, not Northern extension. The project was scouted as impracticable, and the line of 54° 40′ was given up.

Renewing the subject now through Mr. Stoeckl, the Russian Minister, Seward found the Government of the Czar not unwilling to discuss it. Russia would in no case allow her American possessions to pass into the hands of any European power. But the United States always had been, and probably always would be, a friend. Russian-America was a remote province of the empire, not easily defensible, and not likely to be soon developed. Under American control it would develop more rapidly, and be more easily defended. To Russia, instead of a source of danger, it might become a safeguard. To the United States it would give a foothold for commercial and naval operations, accessible from the Pacific States. Seward and Gortschakoff were not long in arriving at an agreement, over a subject which, instead of embarrassing with conflicting interests, presented some mutual advantages.

After the graver question of national ownership, came the minor one of pecuniary consideration. The measure of the value of land to an individual owner is the amount of yearly income it can be made to yield him. But national domain gives prestige, power and safety to the State; and is not easily to be measured by dollars and cents. Hundreds of millions cannot purchase these, nor compensate for their loss.

It was necessary, however, to fix upon some definite sum, to put in the treaty—not so small as to belittle the transaction in the public eye—nor so large as to deprive it of its real character as an act of friendship on the part of Russia toward the United States.

Neither side was especially tenacious about the amount. The previous treaties for the acquisition by the United States of territories from France, Spain, and Mexico, though far from representing actual values, seemed to afford an index for valuation. The Russians thought $10,000,000 would be a reasonable amount. Seward proposed $5,000,000. Dividing the difference made it $7,500,000. Then, at Seward's suggestion, the half million was thrown off. But the territory was still subject to some privileges and franchises of the Russian Fur Company. Seward insisted that these should be extinguished by the Russian Government, before the transfer, and proposed to add $200,000 to the consideration money, on that account. This was accepted. At this valuation of $7,200,000, the bargain could be deemed satisfactory even from the standpoint of the individual fisherman, miner, or wood-cutter; for the timber, mines, furs, and fisheries would easily yield the annual interest on that sum.

Meanwhile the successful working of the Atlantic Cable had now rendered unnecessary any further work upon the inter-continental line via Behring's Straits. Replying to the intimation of this fact, from the Western Union Telegraph Company, Seward wrote:

> I would not have the Atlantic Cable become dumb again, if thereby I could immediately secure the success of the inter-continental Pacific telegraph enterprise, which was committed to your hands. Nevertheless, I confess to a profound disappointment in the suspension of the latter enterprise. I admit that the reasons which you have assigned for that suspension seem to be irresistible. It is impossible for private individuals, or corporate companies, to build telegraphs without capital; and it is equally impossible to procure capital for telegraphs that do not promise immediate, or at least speedy, revenues.

On the other hand, I abate no jot of my former estimates of the importance of the inter-continental Pacific telegraph. I do not believe that the United States and Russia have given their faith to each other, and to the world, for the prosecution of that great enterprise, in vain. The United States Government is enlightened and wise. The Emperor of Russia is liberal as well as sagacious.

Prince Gortschakoff is a pleasant, as well as a frank correspondent. I will with pleasure make your explanations known to him, and I will ask a conference upon the question. "What shall be done next?"

On Friday evening, March 29, Seward was playing whist in his parlor with some of his family, when the Russian Minister was announced.

"I have a dispatch, Mr. Seward, from my Government by cable. The Emperor gives his consent to the cession. To-morrow, if you like, I will come to the department, and we can enter upon the treaty."

Seward, with a smile of satisfaction at the news, pushed away the whist table, saying:

"Why wait till to-morrow, Mr. Stoeckl? Let us make the treaty to-night."

"But your department is closed. You have no clerks, and my secretaries are scattered about the town."

"Never mind that," responded Seward, "if you can muster your legation together before midnight, you will find me awaiting you at the department, which will be open and ready for business."

In less than two hours afterward light was streaming out of the windows of the Department of State, and apparently business was going on there as at mid-day. By four o'clock on Saturday morning the treaty was engrossed, signed, sealed, and ready for transmission by the President to the Senate. There was need of this haste, in order to have it acted upon before the end of the session, now near at hand.

Leutze, the artist, subsequently painted an historical picture representing the scene at the department. It gives with fidelity the lighted room, its furniture, and appointments. Seward, sitting by his writing-table, pen in hand, is listening to the Russian Minister, whose extended hand is just over the great globe at the Secretary's elbow. The gas-light streaming down on the globe illuminates the outline of the Russian province. The Chief Clerk, Mr. Chew, is coming in with the engrossed copy of the treaty for signature. In the background stand Mr. Hunter and Mr. Bodisco comparing the

French and English versions, while Mr. Sumner and the Assistant Secretary are sitting in conference.

To the Assistant Secretary had been assigned, as his share of the night's work, the duty of finding Mr. Sumner, the Chairman of the Senate Committee on Foreign Relations, to infcrm him of the negotiations in progress, and request his advocacy of the treaty in the Senate.

On the following morning, while the Senate was about considering its favorite theme of administrative delinquencies, the Sergeant-at-Arms announced, "A message from the President of the United States." Glances were significantly exchanged between Senators, with the muttered remark, "Another veto!" Great was the surprise in the Chamber when the Secretary ejaculated rather than read, "A treaty for the cession of Russian-America."

Nor was this surprise lessened when the Chairman of Foreign Relations, a leading opponent of the President, rose to move favorable action. His remarks showed easy familiarity with the subject, and that he was prepared to give reasons for the speedy approval of the treaty by the Senate.

In the cloak-room, after adjournment, the matter was talked over. Said one Senator, "I thought we were going to have another hack at Andy Johnson to-day, but it looks now as if we were going to vote for the biggest and most unheard-of thing the Administration has done yet." . . .

In regard to the Russian-American purchase, a private letter said:

The treaty does not get through the Senate yet, but will probably come up for discussion this week. Meanwhile, the discussion goes on actively outside.

The people who have been there describe the country as not unlike Scotland, Nova Scotia, and Norway.

The people who have not been there, describe it as full of ice and polar bears. To which opinion the Senate will incline remains to be seen.

The session will last a week or so longer.

The Senate considered the treaty in Executive session. Rumors of animated debate over it reached the public; but there was no authentic report of the proceedings. Finally on the 9th of April, announcement was made that the Senate had duly given "advice and consent" to its ratification. . . .

Chapter LVI

In the Senate Chamber the treaty with Russia had not met serious opposition. But the purchase of the new territory was not consummated without a storm of raillery in conversation and ridicule in the press. Russian-America was declared to be a "barren, worthless, God-forsaken region," whose only products were "icebergs and polar bears." The ground was "frozen six feet deep," and the "streams were glaciers." "Walrussia" was suggested as a fitting name for it, if it deserved to have any. Vegetation was "confined to mosses," and "no useful animals could live there." There might be some few "wretched fish," only fit for "wretched Esquimaux" to eat. But nothing could be raised or dug there. Seven millions of good money was going to be wasted in buying it. Many millions more would have to be spent in holding and defending it, for it was "remote, inhospitable and inaccessible." It was "Seward's folly." It was Johnson's "polar bear garden." It was an "egregious blunder," a "bad bargain," palmed off on a "silly Administration" by the "shrewd Russians," etc., etc., etc.

Most of these jeers and flings were from those who disliked the President's Southern policy, and condemned Seward for remaining in his Cabinet. It was curiously illogical to accuse him of "Southern proclivities," and yet object to his extending the Union northwards. Perhaps unwillingness to admit that any thing wise or right could be done by "Andy Johnson's Administration" was the real reason for the wrath visited upon the unoffending territory.

Sumner, though a leader of opposition to the Administration, took a more patriotic view. He warmly supported the treaty throughout, advocated the purchase, and expatiated upon its political and commercial advantages. He devoted days and nights to patient research into all that had been written or printed about Russian-America, and delivered a speech which was the most complete description of the territory and its resources, that had yet been published.

One evening, some Senators calling at Seward's house were expressing their surprise at the unfriendly criticisms. He amused himself, and them, by reading from old newspaper files, the unfavorable comments made upon Jefferson's purchase of the "desert waste" of Louisiana, and the treaty for the "noxious swamps" of "snake-infested Florida."

Ratifications having been exchanged, public proclamation of the treaty was made on the 20th of June. In August, commissioners were appointed by Russia and the United States, to complete the formal transfer. Although the $7,200,000 had not yet been appropriated by Congress, Russia, reposing entire confidence in the good faith of the United States, signified her readiness to make the delivery without waiting for the payment. Captain Pestchouroff, of the Russian Navy, and Major-General Rousseau, of the American Army, were selected as the commissioners. It was arranged that they should meet at San Francisco, and proceed together to New Archangel, or Sitka. Preparations were made to withdraw the Russian garrison, and replace it with American troops. Mr. Stoeckl wrote that the barracks there would hold about one hundred men, and added that there were also some advanced posts on the mainland, occupied by four or five men each. These were situated far to the north, and it would be difficult to turn them over before the next spring.

Embarking on the 27th of September, the expedition reached Victoria on the 4th of October. Pausing there to take in coal, they proceeded thence through the quiet and picturesque "inland passage," arriving at Sitka on the 11th.

General Rousseau's report to the Secretary of State described the ceremony:

The day was bright and beautiful. We fixed the hour of three and a-half o'clock for the transfer. General Jefferson C. Davis, commanding the troops, Captain McDougal of the *Jamestown*, Captain Bradford of the *Resaca*, and the officers of their respective commands, as, also, the Governor of the Territory, Prince Maksontoff, were notified, and invited to be present. The command of General Davis, about two hundred and fifty strong, marched up to the top of the eminence on which stands the Governor's house, where the transfer was to be made.

At the same time a company of Russian soldiers were marching to the ground, and took their place upon the left of the flag-staff, from which the Russian flag was then floating. Prince Maksontoff, and the Princess, together with many Russian and American citizens, and some Indians, were present.

It was arranged by Captain Pestchouroff, and myself, that in firing the salutes on the exchange of flags, the United States should lead off, in accordance with your instructions, and that there should be alternate guns from the American and Russian batteries, thus giving the flag of each nation a double national salute; the naval salute being thus answered in the moment it was given. The troops were brought to "present arms," the signal given to fire the salute, and the ceremony was begun by lowering the Russian flag. The United States flag (the one given us for that purpose, by your direction at Washington) then began its ascent, and again the salutes were fired as before, the Russian water battery leading off. The flag was so hoisted that, in the instant it reached its place, the report of the last gun of the *Ossipee* reverberated from the mountains around. The salutes completed, Captain Pestchouroff said: "General Rousseau, by authority from His Majesty, the Emperor of Russia, I transfer to the United States the Territory of Alaska." And, in as few words, I acknowledged the acceptance of the transfer, and the ceremony was at an end. Cheers were then spontaneously given by the citizens present.

This ceremony might be called a christening as well as a transfer. The Territory had previously been known as "Russian-America." During the progress of the treaty through the Senate, there were occasional discussions at the State Department and in the Cabinet, as to the name to be bestowed upon it by the United States. Several were suggested as appropriate, among them "Sitka," the name of its capital; "Yukon," that of its chief river; "Aliaska," or "Alaska," that of its great peninsula; "Oonalaska" and "Aleutia," derived from its chain of islands. Seward, with whom the final decision rested, preferred "Alaska" as being brief, euphonious, and suitable. The name was generally accepted with favor, and began to be used before the transfer was made.

It is a noteworthy coincidence that the same year which witnessed the extension of the United States to the Arctic Circle, was the year in which Great Britain organized the "Dominion of Canada," by uniting its colonies under one Government, with Ottawa for its capital. . . .

42. Naboth's vineyard

President Grant desired to annex Santo Domingo, and his military aide General Orville E. Babcock made an arrangement with the president of that republic, but Sumner on December 21, 1870, spoke in the Senate on the theme of "Naboth's vineyard" and the project collapsed. Source: The Works of Charles Sumner (15 vols., Boston, 1875–83), XIV, 122–124.

. . . Be taught by the experience of Spain, when in 1861 this power . . . undertook to play the part we are asked to play. Forts were built and troops were landed. By a document which I now hold in my hand it appears, that, when at last this power withdrew, she had expended forty millions of hard Spanish dollars and "sacrificed sixteen thousand of the flower of her army." From another source I learn that ten thousand Spanish soldiers were buried there. Are we ready to enter upon this bloody dance? Are we ready to take up this bloody lawsuit?

Vain to set forth, as the Message does, all manner of advantages, "commercially and materially." What are these, if Right and Humanity are sacrificed? What are these without that priceless blessing, Peace? I am not insensible to the commercial and material prosperity of my country. But there is something above these. It is the honor and good name of the Republic, now darkened by an act of wrong. If this territory, so much coveted by the President, were infinitely more valuable than it is, I hope the Senate would not be tempted to obtain it by trampling on the weak and humble. Admit all that the advocates of the present scheme assert with regard to the resources of this territory, and then imagine its lofty mountains bursting with the precious metals, its streams flowing with amber over silver sands, where every field is a Garden of the Hesperides, blooming with vegetable gold, and all this is not worth the price we are called to pay.

There is one other consideration, vast in importance and conclusive in character, to which I allude only. The island of San Domingo, situated in tropical waters, and occupied by another race, of another color, never can become a permanent possession of the United States. You may seize it by force of arms or by diplomacy, where a naval squadron does more than the minister; but the enforced jurisdiction cannot endure. Already by a higher statute is that island set apart to the colored race. It is theirs by right of possession, by their sweat and blood mingling with the soil, by tropical position, by its burning sun, and by unalterable laws of climate. Such is the ordinance of Nature, which I am not the first to recognize. San Domingo is the earliest of that independent group destined to occupy the Caribbean Sea, toward which our duty is plain as the Ten Commandments. Kindness, beneficence, assistance, aid, help, protection, all that is implied in good neighborhood,—these we must give, freely, bountifully; but their independence is as precious to them as is ours to us, and it is placed under the safeguard of natural laws which we cannot violate with impunity.

Long ago it was evident that the Great Republic might fitly extend the shelter of its protection to the governments formed in these tropical islands, dealing with them graciously, generously, and in a Christian spirit,—helping them in their weakness, encouraging them in their trials, and being to them always a friend; but we take counsel of our supposed interests rather than theirs, when we seek to remove them from the sphere in which they have been placed by Providence.

I conclude as I began. I protest against this legislation as another stage in a drama of blood. I protest against it in the name of Justice outraged by violence, in the name of Humanity insulted, in the name of the weak trodden down, in the name of Peace imperilled, and in the name of the African race, whose first effort at Independence is rudely assailed.

43. The Geneva arbitration

Sumner made a famous Senate speech on April 13, 1869. Source: ibid., XIII, 73–74, 77–78, 84–85, 90, 92–93.

. . . At last the Rebellion succumbed. British ships and British supplies had done their work, but they failed. And now the day of reckoning has come,—but with little apparent sense of what is due on the part of England. Without one soothing word for a friendly power deeply aggrieved, without a single regret for what Mr. Cobden, in the House of Commons, called "the cruel losses" inflicted upon us, or for what Mr. Bright called "aid and comfort to the foulest of all crimes," or for what a generous voice from Oxford University denounced as a "flagrant and maddening wrong," England simply proposes to submit the question of liability for individual losses to an anomalous tribunal where chance plays its part. This is all. Nothing is admitted, even on this question; no rule for the future is established; while nothing is said of the indignity to the nation, nor of the damages to the nation. . . .

Individual losses may be estimated with reasonable accuracy. Ships burnt or sunk with their cargoes may be counted, and their value determined; but this leaves without recognition the vaster damage to commerce driven from the ocean, and that other damage, immense and infinite, caused by the prolongation of the war, all of which may be called *national* in contradistinction to *individual*.

Our *national losses* have been frankly conceded by eminent Englishmen. I have already quoted Mr. Cobden, who did not hesitate to call them "cruel losses." During the same debate in which he let drop this testimony, he used other words, which show how justly he comprehended the case. "*You have been,*" said he, "*carrying on hostilities from these shores against the people of the United States,* and have been inflicting an amount of damage on that country greater than would be produced by many ordinary wars. It is estimated that the loss sustained by the capture and burning of American vessels has been about $15,000,000, or nearly £3,000,000 sterling. *But that is a small part of the injury which has been inflicted on the American marine.* We have rendered the rest of her vast mercantile property for the present valueless." Thus, by the testimony of Mr. Cobden, were those individual losses which are alone recognized by the pending treaty only "a small part of the injury inflicted." After confessing his fears with regard to "the heaping up of a *gigantic material grievance*" such as was then accumulating, he adds, in memorable words:—

> You have already done your worst towards the American mercantile marine. What with the high rate of insurance, what with these captures, and what with the rapid transfer of tonnage to British capitalists, you have virtually made valueless that vast property. Why, if you had gone and helped the Confederates by bombarding all the accessible seaport towns of America, a few lives might have been lost, which, as it is, have not been sacrificed; but you could hardly have done more injury in the way of destroying property than you have done by these few cruisers.

With that clearness of vision which he possessed in such rare degree, this statesman saw that England had "virtually made valueless a vast property," as much as if this power had "bombarded all the accessible seaport towns of America." . . .

This is what I have to say for the present on *national losses* through the destruction of commerce. These are large enough; but there is another chapter, where they are larger far: I refer, of course, to the national losses caused by the prolongation of the war, and traceable directly to England. Pardon me, if I confess the regret with which I touch this prodigious item; for I know well the depth of feeling which it is calculated to stir. But I cannot hesitate. It belongs to the case. No candid person, who studies this eventful period, can doubt that the Rebellion was originally encouraged by hope of support from England,—that it was strengthened at once by the concession of belligerent rights on the ocean,—that it was fed to the end by British supplies,—that it was encouraged by every well-stored British ship that was able to defy our blockade,—that it was quickened into frantic life with every report from the British pirates, flaming anew with every burning ship; nor can it be doubted that without British intervention the Rebellion would have soon succumbed under the well-directed efforts of the National Government. Not weeks or months, but years, were added in this way to our war, so full of costly sacrifice. The subsidies which in other times England contributed to Continental wars were less effective than the aid and comfort which she contributed to the Rebellion. It cannot be said too often that the *naval base* of the Rebellion was not in America, but in England. The blockade-runners and the pirate ships were all English. England was the fruitful parent, and these were the "hell-hounds," pictured by Milton in his description of Sin, which, "when they list, would creep into her womb and kennel there." Mr. Cobden boldly said in the House of Commons that England made war from her shores on the United States, with "an amount of damage to that country greater than would be produced by many ordinary wars." According to this testimony, the conduct of England was war; but it must not be forgotten that this war was carried on at our sole cost. The United States paid for a war waged by England upon the National Unity. . . .

With the lapse of time and with minuter consideration the case against England becomes more grave, not only from the questions of international responsibility which it involves, but from better comprehension of the damages, which are seen now in their true proportions. During the war, and for some time thereafter, it was impossible to state them. The mass of a mountain cannot be measured at its base; the observer must occupy a certain distance;

and this rule of perspective is justly applicable to damages which are vast beyond precedent. . . .

Shall these claims be liquidated and cancelled promptly, or allowed to slumber until called into activity by some future exigency? There are many among us, who, taking counsel of a sense of national wrong, would leave them to rest without settlement, so as to furnish a precedent for retaliation in kind, should England find herself at war. There are many in England, who, taking counsel of a perverse political bigotry, have spurned them absolutely; and there are others, who, invoking the point of honor, assert that England cannot entertain them without compromising her honor. Thus there is peril from both sides. It is not difficult to imagine one of our countrymen saying, with Shakespeare's Jew, "The villany you teach me I will execute, and it shall go hard but I will better the instruction"; nor is it difficult to imagine an Englishman firm in his conceit that no apology can be made and nothing paid. I cannot sympathize with either side. Be the claims more or less, they are honestly presented, with the conviction that they are just; and they should be considered candidly, so that they shall no longer lower, like a cloud ready to burst, upon two nations, which, according to their inclinations, can do each other such infinite injury or such infinite good. I know it is sometimes said that war between us must come sooner or later. I do not believe it. But if it must come, let it be later, and then I am sure it will never come. Meanwhile good men must unite to make it impossible.

Again I say, this debate is not of my seeking. It is not tempting; for it compels criticism of a foreign power with which I would have more than peace, more even than concord. But it cannot be avoided. The truth must be told,—not in anger, but in sadness. England has done to the United States an injury most difficult to measure. Considering when it was done and in what complicity, it is truly unaccountable. At a great epoch of history, not less momentous than that of the French Revolution or that of the Reformation, when Civilization was fighting a last battle with Slavery, England gave her name, her influence, her material resources to the wicked cause, and flung a sword into the scale with Slavery. Here was a portentous mistake. Strange that the land of Wilberforce, after spending millions for Emancipation, after proclaiming everywhere the truths of Liberty, and ascending to glorious primacy in the sublime movement for the Universal Abolition of Slavery, could do this thing! Like every departure from the rule of justice and good neighborhood, her conduct was pernicious in proportion to the scale of operations, affecting individuals, corporations, communities, and the nation itself. And yet down to this day there is no acknowledgment of this wrong,—not a single word. Such a generous expression would be the beginning of a just settlement, and the best assurance of that harmony between two great and kindred nations which all must desire.

The Treaty of Washington of May 8, 1871, was in part another instance of America's advantage from Europe's distress. The Franco-Prussian War approached almost visibly in the latter 1860's, and began in July 1870. In October the Russian government abrogated the Black Sea clauses of the Treaty of Paris of 1856, unilaterally revising one of the prime results of the Crimean War. This act alarmed the London ministry of William E. Gladstone. An Anglo-Russian war was possible, in which the Russians might construct commerce raiders in American shipyards. The Russian minister in the United States cannily confided to President Grant's secretary of state, Hamilton Fish, that now was the time to press the Alabama claims. Fish did so, and quickly obtained a treaty. Source: Statutes at Large, XVII, 863–866.

Article I

Whereas differences have arisen between the government of the United States and the government of her Britannic Majesty, and still exist, growing out of the acts committed by the several vessels which have given rise to the claims generically known as the "Alabama claims:"

And whereas her Britannic Majesty has authorized her high commissioners and plenipotentiaries to express, in a friendly spirit, the regret felt by her Majesty's government for the escape, under whatever circumstances, of the Alabama and other vessels from British ports, and for the depredations committed by those vessels:

Now, in order to remove and adjust all complaints and claims on the part of the United States, and to provide for the speedy settlement of such claims, which are not admitted by her Britannic Majesty's government, the high contracting parties agree that all the said claims, growing out of acts committed by the aforesaid vessels, and generically known as the "Alabama claims," shall be referred to a tribunal of arbitration to be composed of five arbitrators, to be appointed in the following manner, that is to say: One shall be named by the President of the United States; one shall be named by her Britannic Majesty; his Majesty the King of Italy shall be requested to name one; the President of the Swiss Confederation shall be requested to name one; and his Majesty the Emperor of Brazil shall be requested to name one. . . .

Article II

The arbitrators shall meet at Geneva, in Switzerland, at the earliest convenient day after they shall have been named, and shall proceed impartially and carefully to examine and decide all questions that shall be laid before them on the part of the governments of the United States and her Britannic Majesty respectively. All questions considered by the tribunal, including the final award, shall be decided by a majority of all the arbitrators.

Each of the high contracting parties shall also name one person to attend the tribunal as its agent to represent it generally in all matters connected with the arbitration. . . .

Article VI

In deciding the matters submitted to the arbitrators, they shall be governed by the following three rules, which are agreed upon by the high contracting parties as rules to be taken as applicable to the case, and by such principles of international law not inconsistent therewith as the arbitrators shall determine to have been applicable to the case.

Rules

A neutral government is bound—

First, to use due diligence to prevent the fitting out, arming, or equipping, within its jurisdiction, of any vessel which it has reasonable ground to believe is intended to cruise or to carry on war against a power with which it is at peace; and also to use like diligence to prevent the departure from its jurisdiction of any vessel intended to cruise or carry on war as above, such vessel having been specially adapted, in whole or in part, within such jurisdiction, to warlike use.

Secondly, not to permit or suffer either belligerent to make use of its ports or waters as the base of naval operations against the other, or for the purpose of the renewal or augmentation of military supplies or arms, or the recruitment of men.

Thirdly, to exercise due diligence in its own ports and waters, and, as to all persons within its jurisdiction, to prevent any violation of the foregoing obligations and duties.

Her Britannic Majesty has commanded her high commissioners and plenipotentiaries to declare that her Majesty's government cannot assent to the foregoing rules as a statement of principles of international law which were in force at the time when the claims mentioned in Article I arose, but that her Majesty's government, in order to evince its desire of strengthening the friendly relations between the two countries and of making satisfactory provision for the future, agrees that in deciding the questions between the two countries arising out of those claims, the arbitrators should assume that her Majesty's government had undertaken to act upon the principles set forth in these rules.

And the high contracting parties agree to observe these rules as between themselves in future, and to bring them to the knowledge of other maritime powers, and to invite them to accede to them.

Article VII

The decision of the tribunal shall, if possible, be made within three months from the close of the argument on both sides.

It shall be made in writing and dated, and shall be signed by the arbitrators who may assent to it.

The said tribunal shall first determine as to each vessel separately whether Great Britain has, by any act or omission, failed to fulfil any of the duties set forth in the foregoing three rules, or recognized by the principles of international law not inconsistent with such rules, and shall certify such fact as to each of the said vessels. In case the tribunal find that Great Britain has failed to fulfil any duty or duties as aforesaid, it may, if it think proper, proceed to award a sum in gross to be paid by Great Britain to the United States for all the claims referred to it; and in such case the gross sum so awarded shall be paid in coin by the government of Great Britain to the government of the United States, at Washington, within twelve months after the date of the award. . . .

The tribunal announced its decision on September 14, 1872. Source: Foreign Relations of the United States: 1872, Supplement, IV (Wash-

ington, D.C., 1872), 50–51, 53. The British arbitrator, Sir Alexander Cockburn, refused to sign the award.

. . . Whereas, having regard to the VIth and VIIth articles of the said treaty, the arbitrators are bound under the terms of the said VIth article, "in deciding the matters submitted to them, to be governed by the three rules therein specified and by such principles of international law, not inconsistent therewith, as the arbitrators shall determine to have been applicable to the case;"

And whereas the "due diligence" referred to in the first and third of the said rules ought to be exercised by neutral governments in exact proportion to the risks to which either of the belligerents may be exposed, from a failure to fulfil the obligations of neutrality on their part;

And whereas the circumstances out of which the facts constituting the subject-matter of the present controversy arose were of a nature to call for the exercise on the part of Her Britannic Majesty's government of all possible solicitude for the observance of the rights and the duties involved in the proclamation of neutrality issued by Her Majesty on the 13th day of May, 1861;

And whereas the effects of a violation of neutrality committed by means of the construction, equipment, and armament of a vessel are not done away with by any commission which the government of the belligerent power, benefited by the violation of neutrality, may afterwards have granted to that vessel; and the ultimate step, by which the offense is completed, cannot be admissible as a ground for the absolution of the offender, nor can the consummation of his fraud become the means of establishing his innocence;

And whereas the privilege of exterritoriality accorded to vessels of war has been admitted into the law of nations, not as an absolute right, but solely as a proceeding founded on the principle of courtesy and mutual deference between different nations, and therefore can never be appealed to for the protection of acts done in violation of neutrality; . . .

And whereas, with respect to the vessel called the Alabama, it clearly results from all the facts relative to the construction of the ship at first designated by the number "290" in the port of Liverpool, and its equipment and armament in the vicinity of Terceira through the agency of the vessels called the "Agrippina" and the "Bahama," dispatched from Great Britain to that end, that the

British government failed to use due diligence in the performance of its neutral obligations; and especially that it omitted, notwithstanding the warnings and official representations made by the diplomatic agents of the United States during the construction of the said number "290," to take in due time any effective measures of prevention, and that those orders which it did give at last, for the detention of the vessel, were issued so late that their execution was not practicable;

And whereas, after the escape of that vessel, the measures taken for its pursuit and arrest were so imperfect as to lead to no result, and therefore cannot be considered sufficient to release Great Britain from the responsibility already incurred;

And whereas, in despite of the violations of the neutrality of Great Britain committed by the "290," this same vessel, later known as the confederate cruiser Alabama, was on several occasions freely admitted into the ports of colonies of Great Britain, instead of being proceeded against as it ought to have been in any and every port within British jurisdiction in which it might have been found;

And whereas the government of Her Britannic Majesty cannot justify itself for a failure in due diligence on the plea of insufficiency of the legal means of action which it possessed:

Four of the arbitrators, for the reasons above assigned, and the fifth for reasons separately assigned by him,

Are of opinion—

That Great Britain has in this case failed, by omission, to fulfill the duties prescribed in the first and the third of the rules established by the VIth article of the treaty of Washington. . . .

The tribunal, making use of the authority conferred upon it by Article VII of the said treaty, by a majority of four voices to one, awards to the United States a sum of $15,500,000 in gold, as the indemnity to be paid by Great Britain to the United States, for the satisfaction of all the claims referred to the consideration of the tribunal, conformably to the provisions contained in Article VII of the aforesaid treaty. . . .

Note on Sources

The student of American foreign relations will find indispensable the scholarly annotations and perfect texts in Hunter Miller (ed.), *Treaties and Other International Acts of the United States of America* (8 vols., Washington, 1931–48). The late treaty expert of the Department of State was unable to carry his series beyond July 1863, but at least he covered the formative years and the era of continental expansion. Miller sought information for his annotations from all possible sources, and if his commentary hardly "reads like a novel," and indeed is often one long footnote, it is, again, essential reading. One must regret that the department has found it impossible to continue this series; for treaties after 1863 the student must turn to the *Statutes at Large*, to the badly edited volumes of William M. Malloy—*Treaties, Conventions, International Acts, Protocols, and Agreements between the United States of America and Other Powers: 1776–1909* (2 vols., Washington, 1910)—and in general a miscellany of sources.

For diplomatic correspondence the source with which to begin is Francis Wharton (ed.), *The Revolutionary Diplomatic Correspondence of the United States* (6 vols., Washington, 1889). As early as the 1820's Jared Sparks had brought together *The Diplomatic Correspondence of the American Revolution* (12 vols., Boston and New York, 1829–30), and he carelessly and sometimes too discreetly edited it but made it approximately available. Wharton corrected Sparks, pointing out the egregious errors of Sparks's edition. Wharton's edition provides texts of a reliability that deserve the description of definitive. This paragon of editors put the finishing touches to his great edition while he was dying of a throat malady, unable to converse, persevering with emendations and notes by painfully writing commentaries on slips of paper.

Wharton took the diplomatic record only to 1783, and documents of the Confederation appear in the unedited compilation, *The Diplomatic Correspondence of the United States of America, from the Signing of the Definitive Treaty of Peace, 10th September, 1783, to the Adoption of the Constitution, March 4, 1789* (7 vols., Washington, 1833–34). Walter Lowrie and Matthew St. Clair Clarke (eds.), *American State Papers: Foreign Relations* (6 vols., Washington, 1832–59), follows the diplomatic record from 1789 to 1828, and except for mistakes by printers is a reliable source, if unduly abbreviated. A gap then occurs until 1861 which the student can fill by resorting to special documentary publications by Congress, for the most part reliable although occasionally (as in Secretary of State William L. Marcy's part in the Ostend Manifesto) circumspect. For this material see the admirable guide by Adelaide R. Hasse, *Index to United States Documents Relating to Foreign Affairs: 1828–1861* (3 vols., Washington, 1914–21). Fortunately much of American diplomacy during this era dealt with Latin American affairs, and there are two excellent compilations by William R. Manning, *Diplomatic Correspondence of the United States Concerning the Independence of the Latin-American Nations* (3 vols., New York, 1925), and *Diplomatic Correspondence of the United States: Inter–American Affairs, 1831–1860* (12 vols., Washington, 1932–39).

The diplomatic record began to appear in an orderly way in 1862 (documents for the year 1861) in what indisputably is the finest series of diplomatic documents published by any government: *Foreign Relations of the United States.* For a while this series appeared as congressional documents, and also under the awkward title of *Papers Relating to the Foreign Relations of the United States.* It did not receive decent editorship until Tyler Dennett became historical adviser of the department in the 1920's. Some documents published before that time were hardly masterpieces of editorial art—for example, documents of William Jennings Bryan's policy toward China in 1915 were badly trimmed, without benefit of ellipsis points. But whatever the occasional faults the series has been basically accurate, certainly so since the time of Dennett's editorship. Annual volumes have appeared for every year except 1869, completing the American diplomatic record down to, at the present writing (1968), the year 1945—which year will require twelve volumes (including three volumes on wartime conferences), as compared to the initial single volume brought out in 1862.

Specially useful compilations are 57th Congress, 2d Session, House Executive Document No. 431, *State Papers and Correspondence Bearing upon the Purchase of the Territory of Louisiana* (Washington, 1903), and Carlton Savage's masterful collection occasioned by the neutrality debate of the 1930's, *Policy of the United States toward Maritime Commerce in War* (2 vols., Washington, 1934).

There are two principal diplomatic diaries for the era 1775–1872. Charles Francis Adams (ed.), *Memoirs of John Quincy Adams, Comprising Portions of His Diary from 1795 to 1848* (12 vols., Philadelphia, 1872–77) was an extraordinary documentary revelation, brought out little more than a generation after the death of its illustrious author. Printing about two thirds of the manuscript diary, this edition omitted only purely personal items. Both Samuel Flagg Bemis and Lyman H. Butterfield, biographer and editor respectively of "J.Q.A.," have testified that the nineteenth–century edition of the diary is trustworthy in editing and printing. Milo M. Quaife (ed.), *The Diary of James K. Polk* (4 vols., Chicago, 1910) is likewise an indispensable source, but represents the entire diary. As for lesser diaries, dealing in some part with diplomatic history, the diary of Charles Francis Adams is a prolix if interesting document, now available on microfilm preliminary to its editing at the Massachusetts Historical Society. C. F. Adams, according to his son, "took to diary writing early, and he took to it bad." Aida DiPace Donald and David Donald (eds.), *Diary of Charles Francis Adams* (2 vols., Cambridge, 1964) contains only entries for the 1820's, and with notes and index runs to nearly a thousand print pages. For the era of the Civil War a highly enjoyable diary is Sarah Agnes Wallace and Frances Elma Gillespie (eds.), *The Journal of Benjamin Moran: 1856–1865* (2 vols., Chicago, 1948–49).

Excellent editions of personal papers bearing on foreign relations now are available or soon will be. The George Washington (John C. Fitzpatrick, ed.), Andrew Jackson (John Spencer Bassett, ed.), and Abraham Lincoln papers (Roy P. Basler, ed.) appeared some years ago. American historians are hard at work on a variety of editorial projects affecting the foreign relations of the United States, under encouragement of the report of the National Historical

Publications Commission in 1957 and the availability of federal and private funds. The papers of John Adams, Benjamin Franklin, and Thomas Jefferson soon will be available for the diplomatic era, under the superb editorship of Lyman H. Butterfield, Leonard W. Labaree, and Julian P. Boyd. The James Madison papers edited by William T. Hutchinson and William M. E. Rachal have reached the 1780's. The Alexander Hamilton papers edited by Harold C. Syrett are advancing into the 1790's. The John Jay papers edited by Richard B. Morris soon will begin to appear. The papers of Henry Clay, edited by James M. Hopkins, have been published up to Clay's secretaryship of state.

Selected titles: revised June, 1967

harper ✦ torchbooks

HUMANITIES AND SOCIAL SCIENCES

American Studies: General

American Studies: Colonial

American Studies: From the Revolution to 1860

American Studies: The Civil War to 1900

† The New American Nation Series, edited by Henry Steele Commager and Richard B. Morris.
‡ American Persectives series, edited by Bernard Wishy and William E. Leuchtenburg.
* The Rise of Modern Europe series, edited by William L. Langer.
** History of Europe series, edited by J. H. Plumb.
¶ Researches in the Social, Cultural, and Behavioral Sciences, edited by Benjamin Nelson.
§ The Library of Religion and Culture, edited by Benjamin Nelson.
Σ Harper Modern Science Series, edited by James R. Newman.
° Not for sale in Canada.
△ Not for sale in the U. K.

1

3

Intellectual History & History of Ideas

Literature, Poetry, The Novel & Criticism

Myth, Symbol & Folklore

JOSEPH CAMPBELL, Editor: Pagan and Christian Mysteries. *Illus.* TB/2013

MIRCEA ELIADE: Cosmos and History: *The Myth of the Eternal Return* § △ TB/2050

MIRCEA ELIADE: Rites and Symbols of Initiation: *The Mysteries of Birth and Rebirth* § △ TB/1236

THEODOR H. GASTER: Thespis: *Ritual, Myth & Drama in the Ancient Near East* △ TB/1281

DORA & ERWIN PANOFSKY: Pandora's Box: *The Changing Aspects of a Mythical Symbol.* △ *Revised Edition. Illus.* TB/2021

HELLMUT WILHELM: Change: *Eight Lectures on the I Ching* △ TB/2019

Philosophy

G. E. M. ANSCOMBE: An Introduction to Wittgenstein's Tractatus. *Second edition, Revised* ○ △ TB/1210

HENRI BERGSON: Time and Free Will ○ △ TB/1021

H. J. BLACKHAM: Six Existentialist Thinkers ○ △ TB/1002

CRANE BRINTON: Nietzsche TB/1197

ERNST CASSIRER: The Individual and the Cosmos in Renaissance Philosophy △ TB/1097

FREDERICK COPLESTON: Medieval Philosophy ○ △ TB/376

F. M. CORNFORD: Principium Sapientiae: *A Study of the Origins of Greek Philosophical Thought* TB/1213

F. M. CORNFORD: From Religion to Philosophy § TB/20

WILFRID DESAN: The Tragic Finale: *An Essay on the Philosophy of Jean-Paul Sartre* △ TB/1030

A. P. D'ENTRÈVES: Natural Law △ TB/1223

MARVIN FARBER: The Aims of Phenomenology: *Husserl's Thought* TB/1291

MARVIN FARBER: Phenomenology and Existence: *Towards a Philosophy Within Nature* TB/1295

PAUL FRIEDLÄNDER: Plato: *An Introduction* △ TB/2017

J. GLENN GRAY: The Warriors: *Reflections on Men in Battle. Intro. by Hannah Arendt* TB/1294

W. K. C. GUTHRIE: The Greek Philosophers: *From Thales to Aristotle* ○ △ TB/1008

G. W. F. HEGEL: The Phenomenology of Mind ○ △ TB/1303

F. H. HEINEMANN: Existentialism and the Modern Predicament △ TB/28

EDMUND HUSSERL: Phenomenology and the Crisis of Philosophy TB/1170

IMMANUEL KANT: The Doctrine of Virtue, *being Part II of the Metaphysic of Morals* TB/110

IMMANUEL KANT: Groundwork of the Metaphysic of Morals. *Trans. & analyzed by H. J. Paton* TB/1159

IMMANUEL KANT: Lectures on Ethics § △ TB/105

IMMANUEL KANT: Religion Within the Limits of Reason Alone. § *Intro. by T. M. Greene & J. Silber* TB/67

QUENTIN LAUER: Phenomenology TB/1169

GABRIEL MARCEL: Being and Having △ TB/310

GEORGE A. MORGAN: What Nietzsche Means △ TB/1198

MICHAEL POLANYI: Personal Knowledge △ TB/1158

WILLARD VAN ORMAN QUINE: Elementary Logic: *Revised Edition* TB/577

WILLARD VAN ORMAN QUINE: From a Logical Point of View: *Logico-Philosophical Essays* TB/566

BERTRAND RUSSELL et al.: The Philosophy of Bertrand Russell Vol. I TB/1095; Vol. II TB/1096

L. S. STEBBING: A Modern Introduction to Logic △ TB/538

ALFRED NORTH WHITEHEAD: Process and Reality: *An Essay in Cosmology* △ TB/1033

PHILIP P. WIENER: Evolution and the Founders of Pragmatism. *Foreword by John Dewey* TB/1212

WILHELM WINDELBAND: A History of Philosophy
Vol. I: *Greek, Roman, Medieval* TB/38
Vol. II: *Renaissance, Enlightenment, Modern* TB/39

LUDWIG WITTGENSTEIN: The Blue and Brown Books ○ TB/1211

Political Science & Government

JEREMY BENTHAM: The Handbook of Political Fallacies. *Introduction by Crane Brinton* TB/1069

KENNETH E. BOULDING: Conflict and Defense TB/3024

CRANE BRINTON: English Political Thought in the Nineteenth Century TB/1071

ROBERT CONQUEST: Power and Policy in the USSR: *The Study of Soviet Dynastics* △ TB/1307

ROBERT DAHL & CHARLES E. LINDBLOM: Politics, Economics, and Welfare TB/3037

F. L. GANSHOF: Feudalism △ TB/1058

G. P. GOOCH: English Democratic Ideas in Seventeenth Century TB/1006

SIDNEY HOOK: Reason, Social Myths and Democracy △ TB/1237

DAN N. JACOBS & HANS BAERWALD, Eds.: Chinese Communism: *Selected Documents* TB/3031

HANS KOHN: Political Ideologies of the 20th Century TB/1277

KINGSLEY MARTIN: French Liberal Thought in the Eighteenth Century △ TB/1114

BARRINGTON MOORE, JR.: Soviet Politics—The Dilemma of Power ¶ TB/1222

BARRINGTON MOORE, JR.: Terror and Progress—USSR ¶ TB/1266

JOHN B. MORRALL: Political Thought in Medieval Times △ TB/1076

KARL R. POPPER: The Open Society and Its Enemies △
Vol. I: *The Spell of Plato* TB/1101
Vol. II: *The High Tide of Prophecy: Hegel, Marx, and the Aftermath* TB/1102

BENJAMIN I. SCHWARTZ: Chinese Communism and the Rise of Mao TB/1308

PETER WOLL, Ed.: Public Administration and Policy: *Selected Essays* TB/1284

Psychology

ALFRED ADLER: The Individual Psychology of Alfred Adler △ TB/1154

ARTHUR BURTON & ROBERT E. HARRIS, Eds.: Clinical Studies of Personality
Vol. I TB/3075; Vol. II TB/3076

HADLEY CANTRIL: The Invasion from Mars: *The Psychology of Panic* TB/1282

HERBERT FINGARETTE: The Self in Transformation ¶ TB/1177

SIGMUND FREUD: On Creativity and the Unconscious § △ TB/45

WILLIAM JAMES: Psychology: *Briefer Course* TB/1034

RICHARD M. JONES, Ed.: Contemporary Educational Psychology: *Selected Readings* TB/1292

C. G. JUNG: Symbols of Transformation △
Vol. I: TB/2009; Vol. II TB/2010

JOHN T. MC NEILL: A History of the Cure of Souls TB/126

KARL MENNINGER: Theory of Psychoanalytic Technique TB/1144

ERICH NEUMANN: Amor and Psyche △ TB/2012

ERICH NEUMANN: The Origins and History of Consciousness △ Vol. I *Illus.* TB/2007; Vol. II TB/2008

JEAN PIAGET, BÄRBEL INHELDER, & ALINA SZEMINSKA: The Child's Conception of Geometry ○ △ · TB/1146

JOHN H. SCHAAR: Escape from Authority: *The Perspectives of Erich Fromm* TB/1155

MUZAFER SHERIF: The Psychology of Social Norms TB/3072

Sociology

JACQUES BARZUN: Race: *A Study in Superstition* TB/1172

BERNARD BERELSON, Ed.: The Behavioral Sciences Today TB/1127

LEWIS A. COSER, Ed.: Political Sociology TB/1293

ALLISON DAVIS & JOHN DOLLARD: Children of Bondage ¶ TB/3049

ST. CLAIR DRAKE & HORACE R. CAYTON: Black Metropolis
Vol. I TB/1086; Vol. II TB/1087

ALVIN W. GOULDNER: Wildcat Strike ¶ TB/1176

8